D1300853

SPECIALTY RETAILERS— MARKETING TRIUMPHS AND BLUNDERS

SPECIALTY RETAILERS— MARKETING TRIUMPHS AND BLUNDERS

Ronald D. Michman
and Edward M. Mazze

Q

QUORUM BOOKS
Westport, Connecticut • London

Library of Congress Cataloging-in-Publication Data

Michman, Ronald D.
    Specialty retailers—marketing triumphs and blunders / Ronald D. Michman and Edward
M. Mazze.
        p. cm.
    Includes bibliographical references and index.
    ISBN 1–56720–342–6 (alk. paper)
    1. Retail trade—United States. 2. Specialty stores—United States. I. Mazze, Edward M.
II. Title.
HF5429.3.M52 2001
658.8'75—dc21   00–027655

British Library Cataloguing in Publication Data is available.

Library of Congress Catalog Card Number: 00–027655
ISBN: 1–56720–342–6

First published in 2001

Quorum Books, 88 Post Road West, Westport, CT 06881
An imprint of Greenwood Publishing Group, Inc.
www.quorumbooks.com

Printed in the United States of America

The paper used in this book complies with the
Permanent Paper Standard issued by the National
Information Standards Organization (Z39.48–1984).

10 9 8 7 6 5 4 3 2 1

To my daughter, Laura Michman Dessel.

To my family, Sharon, Candace, and Thomas Mazze.

Contents

Tables

Preface

This book is focused on the fundamentals necessary for sound management practices by specialty-store merchants. Retailers most likely to succeed are those who develop and implement their strategies in a comprehensive, systematic, and proactive manner. Specialty-store merchants who do not engage in these management practices are destined to encounter problems that will affect their survival in the marketplace. Profitable specialty-store merchants are risk-takers willing to innovate and closely identify their target market. Successful specialty-store merchants do not desire to be all things to all customers. Store image is of paramount consideration, as is the training of store personnel and the store's physical environment. The five key variables that have been identified for ensuring the success or lack of success of specialty-store merchants are: innovation, target-market segmentation, image development, physical store decor, and the effective use of human resources. Confronted by intense and new types of competition, specialty-store merchants face different types of challenges in the marketing environment. Today more than ever before, there will be a need to understand how these retailers will do business in the twenty-first century.

In considering the successes and failures of specialty-store merchants, the challenge is to discern whether or not retailers received high ratings by using all of the key variables or if success was determined by using some of the variables in a more effective manner than their competitors. Correspondingly, can failure or mistakes be attributed to the lack of use of all variables or to the ineffective use of some variables?

This book evolved from many years of observing the retail trade, teaching courses in retailing, consulting for major retail chains, and closely monitoring the literature in the public domain. Literature that reflects academic thought on the development of specialty-store retailing has been closely documented, but to avoid cumbersome references within the text, the source material in the public domain on which the framework and focus of this volume evolved is listed in the selected bibliography. Readers interested in pursuing specific types of retail organizations in more depth should refer to those listed works.

The new century is critical because of the anticipated impact of environmental and technological change on the structure of retail trade. Customer-friendly shopping malls, revitalized downtown cities, and the Internet will have altered the environment. Specialty stores are responding to these changes by developing distinctive images, targeting market segments, using information and technology in new ways, and employing physical and human resources with great proficiency and innovation.

Many accounts of retail failures have focused on the myopia of management executives. This work offers a much broader perspective by isolating five variables—innovation, target market segmentation, image, physical environmental resources, and human resources—that have contributed to retailing failures when not used correctly. Trends of Internet selling, niche retailing, and grass roots retailing are gradually changing the structure of retail specialty trade. To illustrate, Heilig-Meyers in furniture, Lowe's in home improvement, and Rex Stores in electronics have all been developed in small-town retailing. Each is making significant inroads in its specialties, and it must be remembered that Wal-Mart also developed through grass-roots retailing. Niche retailers such as Williams-Sonoma in furniture and Noodle Kidoodle in toys are reinventing the structure in their specialties. These trends at the beginning of the 21st century—Internet selling, niche retailing, and grass-roots retailing are intertwined with factors of innovation, market segmentation, image, and physical, environmental, and human resources. The gap between successful, failing, and merely surviving retail specialty organizations is widening each day.

This book is divided into ten chapters. The first chapter describes the development of specialty-store retailing. Subsequent chapters focus on drugstores, specialty clothing stores, furniture stores, shoe stores, home improvement stores, bookstores, electronics stores, toy stores, and automotive stores. Each chapter analyzes the inter- and intra-type environment and competition challenging that type of specialty-store retailing and discusses the five key variables identified above in contributing to either their success or their failure. Each chapter title reflects some dimension of market segmentation strategy. The fundamentals for sustaining competitive dominance are identified.

It is hoped that managers and students, by focusing in particular on these fundamentals, will understand why specialty-store retailers succeed or fail. This work provides a starting point for executives to obtain appropriate insights into this special category of retailers. It is also hoped that these insights will prevent mistakes and allow specialty-store retailers to take advantage of market opportunities.

Acknowledgments

This work is the product of a team of hardworking individuals who have assisted the authors by providing research, clerical, and administrative help. A great debt is owed to our research assistants Megan Barber Allende, Susan McCann, Jennifer Ganoung, and Jennifer Frank who helped collect the information for each of the chapters. Special recognition is extended to Kelly Glista, LaVonda Hayes, and Marie Garofano who typed many of the chapters. Special recognition must also be given to Kelly Glista who handled the administrative activities in preparing the manuscript for publication. Ron Michman would like to thank his daughter Laura for her input on chapters involving drugstores, shoe stores, specialty clothing stores, and toy stores. His grandchildren Marc Ross and Andy Robert presented a fresh reaction to toy stores, and his daughter Carol provided expertise on computer information technology. Ed Mazze would like to thank his wife Sharon, who has owned specialty retailing stores and has taught him about retail selling, and Herman and Alan Blumenthal who provided his education in the automotive market.

Any errors of omission or commission are the responsibility of the authors.

1

The Development of Specialty Store Retailing

Strategies to Combat Environmental Challenges

- Use technology
- Capitalize on new opportunities
- Use geographical market segmentation
- Use new distribution formats
- Cultivate narrow market segments
- Maintain a high level of customer service
- Make store easy to shop
- Improve chain management supply
- Recognize the importance of information

Specialty-Store Retailing Mistakes

- Weak private label brands
- The attempt to be all things to all customers
- Blurred store images
- Delayed recognition of Internet selling potential
- Inadequate personnel training
- Wrong merchandise assortment
- Improper use of technology and information systems

Strategies in a Changing Market

- Anticipate changing market segments
- Locate new stores in new markets
- Develop strong store images
- Establish an E-commerce effort
- Be customer friendly

The history of retail trade in the United States closely parallels the development of a country from wilderness to urban center. Early Indian trade marked the initial stages of the progression from the trading-post era to the general-merchandise store era and the rise of single-line specialty stores to today's large-scale retailers, including superstores, category killers, department, and chain stores. These changes came about because entrepreneurs were encountering opposition from traditional-thinking businesspeople and consumers looking for convenience and a wide variety of merchandise.

Among the explanations for the growth of the specialty store are:

- The general-type store lacked the space to accommodate the wide variety of goods in a particular line of products.
- Markets became large enough to be divided into submarkets.
- The specialty store acquired an in-depth knowledge of the product that was useful to and desired by the customer.

The general store was the dominant store in the United States in the early 1800s. The history of retail development seems to demonstrate an accordion pattern. Domination by general-line, widespread retailers alternates with domination by specialized, narrow-line merchants—thus the accordion impact.[1] The retail accordion theory maintains that retail store development and evolution can be explained by monitoring changes in the merchandise mix. The general store carried everything from food products to dry goods to clothing and was characterized by its nondepartmental nature and its lack of product specialization. In contrast, the earliest specialty stores in the United States were manufacturer-retailer operations in which the craftsman sold his merchandise in a shop. To illustrate, specialty stores in the middle 1850s offered bakery goods; books and stationery; boots and shoes; china, glass, and crockery ware; confectionery, drugs, dry goods, groceries, hardware, jewelry, liquor, lumber millinery, musical goods, and tobacco.[2] Furniture, furs, and toys were sold by specialty stores but were not considered important items in retail trade.

Specialty stores grew at a more rapid pace with advancements in production and technology and the development of urban centers. Specialty stores are generally located in neighborhoods, communities, or regional malls. This allowed specialty stores to attract a larger number of customers than a single individual store and also provided the consumer with a wide assortment of merchandise at a single location. Today, specialty stores are found in central business districts of large cities and along main streets of smaller cities, again reflecting the cluster strategy. The future for specialty stores appears promising, since trends in lifestyles, education, family income, and technology favor the growth of this retail sector. With new types of specialty stores selling computers and cellular telephones, and new services developing, new customers are entering the market every day.

Specialty-store strategy has focused on a particular market segment and customer. The merchant provides the services required by the store's customers, such as an experienced sales force, delivery, credit, personalized service, special order, and orders by mail, computer, or facsimile. The belief is that increased service will help to generate total customer satisfaction. Specialty stores can maintain a high promotional visibility by efficiently targeting their advertising and promotion budgets to carefully defined customer groups.

The glory days of department stores may be over. The past decade has witnessed such failures as Frederick & Nelson, Gimbels, Garfinkel's, Mays, and others because of competition, poor management, location in decaying urban centers, heavy debt, or slow recognition of changing consumer behavior.

Consumers who patronize specialty stores do not expect to benefit from all of the merchandise lines of a department store. Instead, the specialty-store shopper wants depth and breadth in a particular merchandise line. This strategy allows the specialty store to target selective market segments. Consumers frequently shop at specialty stores because of the expertise of sales personnel and the variety of choices within the merchandise or service classification. Moreover, the atmosphere of the specialty store can be an additional benefit. Specialty stores need to position themselves differently than their competitors and can accomplish this objective by determining their core competencies.

A consideration of the successes and failures of specialty stores shows that the stores that have survived are making constant adjustments to such variables as innovation, target market, and image as well as physical, environmental, and human resources and are taking advantage of information technology. Confronted by intense competition, these specialty stores operate in a marketing environment in which the manipulation of these variables is critical to success.

Innovation has been responsible for many new types of specialty stores, and new technology has also contributed to specialty stores gaining a wider market. For example, in an effort to quickly seize market share and promote name recognition, Bell Atlantic, AT&T, and Sprint PCS have opened retail stores to market their telecommunications products and services. Furthermore, new technology has allowed retailers to develop Websites so that customers do not need to leave their homes to shop. "E-commerce" is becoming the future of retailing. Companies such as *e*Bay offer the largest person-to-person auction Website, connecting almost 4 million buyers and sellers worldwide. The auction includes 3 million items such as collectibles, antiques, and other products sold through classified advertisements. Other companies such as Amazon.com help people find almost anything they want to buy online. Amazon.com started out selling books and now sells software, toys, and consumer electronics. It has a customer base of 8.4 million and is recognized by fifty-two percent of U.S. adults. The retailers that are going to be winners on the Internet are those with established names such as Gap Inc., Toys "R" Us, CVS, Home Depot, Circuit City, and Barnes & Noble. For online retailing to be successful, specialty retailers need to offer a full line of products in their category, have easy-to-use Websites, be able to get the products to their customers quickly, and have a seamless end-to-end e-fulfillment. Online customers are already becoming dissatisfied with their buying experiences because of confusing sites, delayed deliveries, store responses to inquiries, and billing errors.

The strategy of market segmentation and image has been used by specialty stores with considerable success. To illustrate, Lowe's, a home improvement chain, segments customers in small towns, satisfying their wants and needs. Lowe's has promoted an image as a one-stop home improvement center because of its policy of scrambled merchandising. The specific target market of Lowe's and other home improvement centers is the do-it yourself market that may need varying degrees of guidance.

Physical environmental resources have played an important part in the success of book superstores and specialty clothing stores. In fact, atmospherics has become a very successful strategy of the 1990s. Book superstores has provided a relaxed browsing environment that is conducive to customer enjoyment and satisfaction. Banana Republic has developed decor that reflects originality, creativity, and the personality of its location.

Bernard Marcus of Home Depot and Leslie Wexner of The Limited are legends in their respective retailing sectors. Both are people motivators. Both will rank with the late Sam Walton of Wal-Mart as effective users of human resources. Successful specialty-store organizations stress better training for employees, faster decision making, and quick action on new opportunities. A fear of a status quo mentality also permeates the organization. Specific goal achievement is a driving force.

Many of the failures of specialty store merchants have developed from their inability to both identify and respond to changing needs of consumers. In many instances specialty store retailers allowed their images to become blurred. Some merchants were unable to control costs and unfortunately increased prices. Other merchants expanded too quickly and lost control of their operations. Rather than a single reason for specialty store blunders, there have been a number of reasons.

MARKET STRUCTURE

In terms of sales volume, the home improvement chains are among the top specialty stores depicted in Table 1.1. Drug and toy stores are next. The leaders are Home Depot, CVS, and Toy "R" Us, respectively. Specialty-store retailers vary according to the type, selection, and quality of merchandise as well as their product-line pricing. The merchandise types include personal, such as shoes or clothing; home, such as furniture or fixtures; entertainment, such as toys or books; and electronics, such as stereo systems or computers.

Specialty stores also vary in the size, design, and location of stores. Store size ranges from small lifestyle shops to boutiques, to standard-size stores, to superstores, to category killers. Store designs range from boutiques, with an atmosphere of luxury, to warehouse formats. Most specialty stores cluster in shopping centers, specialty malls, or downtown centers. Large chains such as Eddie Bauer, Circuit City, and Staples are opening stores in small towns and rural areas and as a result are experiencing lower operating costs.

Consumers like the service of specialty stores. Salespeople are more knowledgeable, and their attention makes shopping faster when time is a concern for dual-income families and the career woman. Specialty stores have also earned high marks for ambience. For example, the Gap uses design, price, and style to attract customers. The matte-finish metal racks and rock music used at the Gap stores are aimed at a younger, more action-oriented shopper. Barnes & Noble and Borders bookstores have in-house espresso bars and comfortable chairs in which customers may relax and read books and magazines or listen to books on tape and CDs. FAO Schwarz, an upscale toy chain, is famous for its imaginative and functional store environments. Focal points include life-sized dollhouses, Lego submarines, Barbie Boutiques, and numerous animated characters and interactive displays.

Trends of Internet selling and niche retailing are changing the structure of retail specialty trade. For example, Amazon.com is selling not only books on the Internet but toys as well. The case for shopping online is strong since customers can avoid the malls and have immediate price information to make comparisons. Although a number of specialty retailers have established websites, Tiffany & Co. and others question the effectiveness of online retailing. Tiffany believes that customers purchasing items such as expensive jewelry are better served by in-store service. Shipping costs and merchandise returns are other concerns of these retailers. Niche retailers, such as Williams-Sonoma in kitchen cooking equipment and furniture and Noodle Kidoodle in educational toys, are reinventing the retail structure in their specialties. Grass-roots retailers, such as Heilig-Meyers in furniture, Lowe's in home improvement, and

Table 1.1
Top Specialty Store Chains

Store Chain	Type	Net Sales 1998	Number of Units 1998
	Drug		
Walgreens		$15.3 billion	2547[1]
RiteAid		$12.7 billion	3821
Eckerd (Thrift, Kerr, Fay's)[2]		$10.325 billion	2756
CVS (Revco)		$15.3 billion	4122
Long's Drug Stores		$3.27 billion	381
	Apparel		
Limited		$9.347 billion	5382[3]
Gap (Banana Republic, Old Navy)		$9.05 billion	2932[4]
Spiegel (Eddie Bauer)		$2.935 billion[5]	555[6]
Talbots		$1.142 billion[7]	638
Ann Taylor		$911.9 million	365[8]
	Furniture		
Heilig-Meyers		$2.413 billion	1253[9]
Pier 1 Imports		$1.139 billion	769
Ethan Allen		$679 million	310[10]
Bombay Company		$357 million	412
Levitz		$836.8 million	105[11]
Williams-Sonoma		$1.104 billion	298[12]

1. Walgreens also operates two mail service facilities.
2. Eckerd merged with J.C. Penney Company effective February 28, 1997; J.C. Penney also acquired certain Rite Aid and Revco stores, and purchased the Genovese Drugstore chain in 1998.
3. Includes 551 Limited, 702 Limited Express, 319 Limited too, 829 Victoria's Secret, 643 Lerner New York, 730 Lane Bryant, 532 Structure, 1 Henri Bendel, 14 Galyan's, and 1061 Bath and Body Works stores.
4. Number includes 2,074 Gap, GapKids, and baby Gap, 345 Banana Republic, and 513 Old Navy Stores.
5. Includes $1.710 billion from Eddie Bauer operations, $587 million from Spiegel catalogue, $345 million from Newport News Catalogue, and $293 million from Financial and other services.
6. Includes 507 Eddie Bauer retail stores and 48 Eddie Bauer outlets.

6

Store Chain	Type	Net Sales 1998	Number of Units 1998
	Shoe		
Nine West[13]		$1.917 billion	1499
Edison Brothers Stores[14]		$949.9 million	1605
Florsheim		$245 million	311[15]
Kinney			
Venator[16]		$3.753 billion	3625
Genesco[17]		$549.7 million	674
Footstar[18]		$1.829 billion	572
Payless ShoeSource		$2.62 billion	4570
	Home Improvement		
Home Depot		$30.2 billion	761[19]
Lowe's		$12.2 billion	484
Hechinger's		$3.449 billion	244[20]
Menard		$4.0 billion	135
Payless Cashways		$1.91 billion	154
Wickes		$910 million	101
	Books		
Borders (Waldenbooks, Books Etc.)		$2.6 billion	1167[21]
Barnes & Noble (B. Dalton)		$3.006 billion	1009[22]
Crown Books		$298 million	179
Amazon.com		$610 million	N/A[23]
Books-A-Million		$345 million	173[24]

7. Includes $973 million in retail store sales and $169 million in catalogue sales.
8. Includes 306 Ann Taylor, 46 Ann Taylor Loft, 13 Ann Taylor Factory stores.
9. Includes 813 Helig-Meyers, 97 Rhodes, 107 RoomStore, and 236 Mattress Discounters stores.
10. Includes 67 Ethan Allen-owned and 23 independently owned stores.

Table 1.1 (continued)
Top Specialty Store Chains

Store Chain	Type	Net Sales 1998	Number of Units 1998
	Electronics		
Tandy (Radio Shack, Computer City)		$4.789 billion	5140[25]
Circuit City		$10.8 billion	590
Best Buy		$10.08 billion	311
Rex Stores		$417 million	228
CompUSA[26]		$5.286 billion	162
	Toys		
Toys R Us		$11.17 billion	1481[27]
K-B Toys (Consolidated Stores)		$16.43 billion	1322[28]
Zany Brainy		$168.5 million	80
Noodle Kidoodle		$107.9 million	42
Imaginarium			>40
FAO Schwarz			41
Disney Stores			713
Warner Brothers Stores			180
	Automotive		
AutoZone		$3.2 billion	2657
Pep Boys		$1.99 billion	638
Western Auto/Parts America (Sears)[29]		$1.3 billion	1415[30]
Advance Auto		$848.1 million[31]	1700
NAPA (Genuine Parts)		$3.26 billion[32]	15,200[32]

11. Includes 58 warehouse-showrooms and 47 satellite stores.
12. Includes 163 Williams-Sonoma, 96 Pottery Barn, 33 Hold Everything, and 6 outlet stores.
13. Includes the following shoe brands: Amalfi, Bandolino, Calico, CK/Calvin Klein (under license), Easy Spirit, Enzo Angiolini, Evan Picone (under license), 9 & Co., Pappagallo, Pied a Terre, Selby, and Westies.
14. Data pertains to both the footwear and apparel division of Edison Brothers for fiscal year 1997 (total number of shoe stores is 449). Edison Brothers shoe brands include the following Bakers/Leeds, Precis, and Wild Pair.
15. Includes 218 company-operated specialty stores and 93 outlet stores (U.S. and international).

16. Includes Foot Locker, Lady Foot Locker, Kids Foot Locker, Champs Sports, Colorado and Eastbay. (Numbers refer to shoe division only.)
17. Includes Journeys, Jarman, General Shoe Warehouse, Johnston & Murphy, Nautica, and Dockers. (Numbers are for shoe division only.)
18. Includes Footaction, Meldisco, and Thom McCan. Footstar owns 572 Footaction stores and sells its Meldisco brand shoes through 2161 K-Marts, 327 Payless and Thrifty Drug Stores, and 20 Tesco department stores.
19. Includes 753 Home Depot(R) stores and eight EXPO Design Center(SM) stores.
20. Includes 133 Builders Square, 62 Hechinger, and 46 Home Quarters stores.
21. Includes 256 stores that operate under the Borders name, 885 mall-based Waldenbooks stores, and 26 Books, Etc. stores.
22. Includes 520 stores that operate under the Barnes & Noble Booksellers, Bookstop, and Bookstar trade names, and 489 stores that operate under the B. Dalton Booksellers, Doubleday Book Shops, and Scribner's Bookstore trade names.
23. Although Amazon.com is a purely Internet company and has no physical stores it is included here due to its strong competition in the market.
24. Includes 124 Books-A-Million superstores, 27 Bookland stores, and 22 traditional bookstores.
25. Includes 5,039 Radio Shack stores, and 101 Computer City stores. In August 1998, 100% of Computer City stock was sold to CompUSA Inc.
26. Information as of June 27, 1998.
27. Includes 704 Toys "R" Us, 212 Kids "R" Us and 113 Babies "R" Us Stores in the United States, as well as 452 Toys "R" Us Stores internationally.
28. Includes K-B Toys, K-B Toy Works, and K-B Toy Outlet stores.
29. Sears divested itself of Advance Auto in 1998 and sold it to Western Auto.
30. Includes 576 Parts America, 39 Company-owned Western Auto, and 800 locally owned Western Auto stores.
31. Net Sales for Genuine Parts Automotive Group only.
32. Includes 6,200 NPA Auto Parts and 9,000 NAPA AutoCare facilities.

Rex Stores in electronics, have all been developed in small-town retailing. All are making significant inroads in their specialties.

RETAILING AND THE MARKETING CONCEPT

The marketing concept is defined as the ability of a firm to mobilize all of its resources to satisfy the needs and wants of its customers at a profit. It becomes the operating philosophy of the organization. This philosophy permeates, integrates, and motivates all decisions made by the organization. When it is applied to retailing, customer satisfaction is paramount. However, there is a difference between retail organizations that just sell products to customers and those that conduct marketing research to determine what the consumer needs, and then sell the products customers want. Traditional drugstores, for example, limited their products and lost ground to mass retailing drug organizations with broadened product lines that included items such as greeting cards and household merchandise.

What is needed, then, is for retailers to become more consumer oriented. This requires more target-market customer research, certain types of market integration, and possibly organizational changes (twenty-four-hour-a-day operations). Even the retailer's sales support (such as delivery and credit) may require changes to satisfy customer requirements.

THE RETAILING MIX AND DIFFERENTIAL ADVANTAGE

Once a target market is selected, the retailer must design a strategy to serve it. Each specialty store merchant uses a particular retail mix to achieve the desired differential advantage. Change should be recognized as a driving factor for the retail organization. Innovation is viewed as a basis for retail action and is the foundation for retailing effort. The objective of differential advantage is to develop a set of unique features in a store's retailing mix that causes customers to patronize the store and not its competitors.

The retailing mix is divided into three areas: the goods and services mix, the communications mix, and the physical distribution mix. The goods and services mix includes the merchandise assortment, price lines, customer services, and store image. The components of the physical distribution mix are store location, inventory levels, and inventory controls. The communications mix includes advertising, displays, sales promotion, retail selling, use of the Internet and Web pages, mail and telephone sales, and publicity and public relations.

The store's merchandise assortment and store ambiance is a source of differentiation. For example, some bookstore chains provide reading clubs, book-signing events for authors, a place to read, and a coffee bar in contrast to Crown Bookstores, a discount bookstore that offers few amenities. Specialty bookstores stock an assortment of book titles in hardcover and paperback and on tape. At the other extreme, drugstores and supermarkets may carry only best-selling paperbacks and magazines. Department stores may stock a limited number of paperbacks and hardcover books. Waldenbooks concentrates on popular hard- and soft-cover titles of general interest but does not provide the shopping atmosphere of background music, coffee, or other encouragements to relaxation.

Price points are another component of the goods and services mix. Off-price retailers such as T. J. Maxx, Marshalls, and Syms offer branded merchandise at prices thirty to forty percent below what department stores charge. To reduce costs, off-price outlets are often found in freestanding locations along major highways where there are lower rental prices.

Specialty stores may offer high levels of customer service since their sales personnel are frequently more knowledgeable than those employed by department stores. This high level of customer service is true at Brooks Brothers, a well-known specialty clothing store. Home Depot, a home-improvement chain, is also known for its knowledgeable sales personnel who are available to advise on home decorating challenges. These stores invest substantial funds in hiring and training their salespeople. Many of the specialty stores located on Rodeo Drive in California, create an atmosphere of excitement through innovative displays and merchandising while at the same time employing salespeople who understand the importance of relationship marketing. There is a focus on customer satisfaction and the way the customer is treated. Customer satisfaction is having the customer feel very good inside the store making buying a pleasant experience.

The physical distribution mix, which includes store location, can also provide a differential advantage. A store located in a freestanding center or a mall offers parking for customers. In contrast, location, while providing many pluses, can also present a problem. For example, FAO Schwarz successfully operates stores of 30,000 to 40,000 square feet in New York, Boston, Chicago, and San Francisco, whereas smaller stores of 3,000 to 12,000 square feet in malls have drained profits. Similarly, stores located in downtown areas populated by office buildings may have little pedestrian traffic on weekends.

PATTERNS OF COMPETITIVE CHANGE

Retail institutions have undergone numerous changes and are still evolving in response to environmental trends. As institutions change, due to varying consumer demands, merchandise lines may either expand or contract. Consumers require a broad assortment of goods and services to maintain a household. Such products as furniture, floor coverings, stereo equipment, clothing, books, and other personal items are needed for work or pleasure.

To fulfill these requirements, each retailer maintains a certain assortment of goods. The consumer subsequently engages in a search to find retailers, that which maintain the desired product assortment. New types of retailers that sell computers or cellular telephones evolve in response to consumer wants. The merchandise assortment mix may be changed in order to satisfy customer demands—for example, drugstores selling toasters and summer furniture.

There is a self-perpetuating phenomenon associated with scrambled merchandising. Scrambled merchandising can spread quickly and develop competition among unrelated retailers. To illustrate, when supermarkets carry a full line of health and beauty aids, drugstores lose health and beauty aid sales. Consequently, drugstores respond by developing other merchandise lines such as greeting cards, periodicals, and pens. Gift stores counter by offering paper goods for parties, deli gift packs, and candy. Then the supermarket may respond by carrying toys, and drugstores may counter by offering cosmetics.

INNOVATION

Innovation is at the heart of competitive change. Innovative merchandising strategies and operational tactics are constantly developed to meet competitive threats. Innovation by merchants is frequently a determinant of profit or survival in retail trade and is often at the core of an evolving marketing system. There are risks involved, however, such as misreading customer interests and ending up with large inventories of unrealized profit. An example of innovation is Amazon.com, which pioneered the online bookselling industry in the 1990s. Amazon.com successfully dominated the market by utilizing the Internet and electronic commerce, a unique method of distribution for booksellers at the time, to maximize selection while minimizing inventory. Toys "R" Us in the past struggled against discounters like Wal-Mart and Target but today has stronger competition, an online retailer called eToys.

Innovation includes not only invention but also adjustment and adaptation. Toys "R" Us responded to the new competition by setting up its own online toy business. Innovation in retail trade involves an idea and its application to everyday business operations. New consumer purchasing patterns may serve as an impetus for the implementation of innovation as demonstrated by the proliferation of Internet Websites and online commerce in recent years.

Market opportunity is closely related to the innovative process. Market opportunity refers to potential demand for a particular service or product missing from the store's portfolio of products and service. Market opportunity interacts with the retailing mix inasmuch as it will determine the particular type of mix the retailer will offer. For example, customers at Radio Shack may now receive paging services, Internet access, and cellular phone service in addition to long-distance service from telecommunications providers such as Sprint.

Innovation by scrambled merchandising is a strategy for increasing sales of existing stores in which new products and services are sold that are unrelated to the store's merchandise assortment. For example, drugstores rent video cassettes and sell paperback novels, greeting cards, low-price watches, perfume, picture frames, grocery items, and toys. This practice frequently provides additional profits and helps to sell primary merchandise. It also increases inter-competition between drugstores, video rental stores, discount stores, jewelry shops, gift stores, supermarkets, and toy stores. Consequently, there is a contagious nature to scrambled merchandising, which has resulted in one-stop shopping to reduce the effects of seasonality and competition.

Limitations to scrambled merchandising include the lack of retailer expertise in purchasing, selling, and servicing items with which he or she is unfamiliar, the costs associated with a diversified merchandise mix, and the potential damage to the store's image if the added merchandise lines are received poorly by customers. The effective implementation of a scrambled merchandising policy includes several factors for consideration:

- Customer base and retail trade area. Since scrambled merchandising is an expansion strategy, a broad customer base and a large retail-trade area may be desirable.
- Customer characteristics, preferences, and shopping habits include frequency of patronage and a preference for one-stop shopping among other factors.
- Extent of competition in the retail trade area. What is the nature of scrambled merchandising policies among direct and indirect competitors?
- Store image. Would scrambled merchandising modify store image perception and would the result prove beneficial or negative?
- Resources available. Costs, size of investment in inventories, and stock turnover rates become more challenging and critical.

WHEEL OF RETAILING

The wheel of retailing is based upon the premise that price-sensitive consumers are not store loyal and that new institutions are able to implement lower operating costs than existing institutions. Retail innovators enter the market as low-status and low-margin institutions. These inconveniently located institutions save on rentals, offer few services, and are inexpensively furnished. Gradually, as these institutions mature, they offer many services, acquire more elaborate facilities, feature higher prices, and carry merchandise lines that convey higher status.[3] Moreover, as existing retailers move up the wheel, store image is upgraded and the target market broadened.[4] An emerging institution known as the "category killer" store appeals to consumers who are interested in low prices and a large selection of products.

The wheel-of-retailing explanation for the evolution and eventual demise of retailers has held true over the years. Moreover, the importance of some retailers for certain types of products has declined, and other types of retailers have become more important. Drugstores have become more important as sellers of toys in the past twenty years as independent toy stores have gone out of business and discount stores have gained prominence. Competition today is not between products but between business models such as the Internet, which will change the relationship between consumers and retailers. It was Main Street in the 1950s, shopping malls in the 1960s and 1970s, superstores in the 1980s and 1990s, and Internet in the 2000s.

RETAIL ACCORDION THEORY

The history of retail development seems to demonstrate an accordion pattern.[5] According to this theory, the merchandise mix expands and contracts much like an accordion in different time periods. Historically, the old general store led to the development of the department store, which led to the specialty store and now to the superstore. Domination by general-line, wide assortment retailers alternates with domination by specialized, narrow-line merchants, thus the accordion effect.

The most recent contraction of the retail accordion was the result of the tendency for specialty stores in the 1970s and 1980s to become more specialized by following a focus approach. In the 1990s, "the category killer" stores developed—such as Toys "R" Us in toys and Barnes & Noble in books. This type of store features a large selection in its product category with relatively low prices. This reflects a broad trend among almost all chains toward giant one-stop store units carrying an enormous variety of merchandise classifications, and with product lines in each classification, deep and sometimes broad.

NATURAL SELECTION THEORY

Dreesman was the first to apply Darwin's theory to the evolution of retailing organizations from the general store to the variety of retailing outlets seen today.[6] Through the use of biological analogies, Dreesman attempts to systemize the theory of evolution in retailing. His theory is

and Rite Aid have entered the market, and discounters such as Wal-Mart and supermarket chains have added pharmacy departments.

DIALECTIC PROCESS THEORY

The dialectic process views retailing as an evolutionary system in which different retail institutions adapt to each other, which results in new retail strategies. The central premise of the process is that, when challenged by a competitive advantage, the retail institution will try to negate the strengths of the competitor. For example, the drugstore sells many items sold by the supermarket. This will result in drugstores and supermarkets becoming more like one another and creating a competitive position of their own. The process is a "melting pot" theory of retail institutional change in which two substantially different forms of retailing merge into a new institution of retailing such as superstores. Dialectic theory applied to retailing is a development of Hegel's philosophy—the law of logical development, which stated that any idea by the very nature of things negates itself. Soon the original idea is combined with its negativism and called the antithesis. Eventually, the original idea and its negated form become indistinguishable and form a synthesis, which is then vulnerable to repeating the process. The dialectic process has been applied to the evolution of department stores, supermarkets, and service stations. The application to specialty-store retailing appears limited.

TARGET MARKET SEGMENTATION STRATEGIES AND IMAGE

Market segmentation is the process of dividing a market into smaller, more homogeneous submarkets of customers based on certain distinguishing characteristics such as geography and the demographic description of purchasers or potential buyers. Each segment has specific spending needs, shopping preferences, and attitudes.

Apparel specialty stores may select target markets based upon age, sex, income, social class, clothing sizes, or other characteristics. A store image refers to how a specific retailer is perceived by consumers and others. Lerner New York, owned by the Limited, has the image of serving women with budget constraints in an elegant environment.

An analysis of consumer behavior will determine those customer market segments that can best be served by the retailer. These segments are the target market. Information is then accumulated to determine how best to satisfy the most promising market segments. Market segmentation is useful in defining new markets. The process of market segmentation keeps the retailer alert to changes in market conditions, competitive actions, and environmental opportunities and threats. Promotional campaigns can be targeted to specific market segments. Retailer-market segmentation is important in developing a store's communication mix as well as selecting a location and price points.

PHYSICAL RESOURCES AND FACILITIES

Lerner changed its look by putting in marble floors, taking out the tile floors, and replacing its inexpensive-looking orange paint with a peaches and cream decor. The physical facilities of the retailer are important vehicles for developing a store image. The store's architectural design and the placement of signs, entrances, and display windows contribute to the store image. Other components of a store's image can be developed in part by the layout of departments and traffic aisles, the use of store displays, and the selection of store fixtures and equipment.

Retailers hope to influence the customer's mood by developing an atmosphere that induces buying. Waldenbooks, Inc., introduced a playground environment in its WaldenKids stores which sell books and educational toys and games. Children crawl into the store through a carpeted tunnel, and once inside they can watch a video monitor playing cartoon fairy tales. Children are also encouraged to play computer games and touch displayed toys.

SITE LOCATION: CRUCIAL RETAIL STRATEGY COMPONENT

Although retail stores are thought of as individual enterprises, retail stores tend to cluster together for the shopping convenience of customers. Good location is a combination of factors, including proximity to target market segments, appropriate facilities, and accessibility to suppliers. Location planning requires the retailer to select one of three basic types of locations: an unplanned center, a planned district, or an isolated location. Still others prefer a city neighborhood resided in by families with infants or by elderly individuals. Among the site locations are:

• The central business district, commonly referred to in many cities as "Main Street," is an unplanned shopping area where travel arteries converge. Public transportation is generally dispersed from the central business district where large department stores, banks, theaters, eating places, and numerous specialty stores are situated. Before World War II, this shopping area was the most important in retail trade. In recent times, however, the downtown area has suffered from traffic congestion, inconvenient shopping hours (compared to other shopping clusters), inadequate public transportation, antiquated stores, and slum areas. Attempts have been made with urban renewal programs to give new life to the downtown area and to alleviate traffic congestion. A number of central business districts, such as Tower City Center in Cleveland, Faneuil Hall in Boston, and Underground in Atlanta have revitalized the central business district situation. Walgreens and other specialty-store chains are opening new stores in the inner cities as the crime rates drop and the business infrastructure improves. America's inner cities seem to be the next retailing frontier.

- A string is an unplanned shopping area with a group of retail stores, frequently with similar or compatible product lines, located along a street or highway. A string may evolve from an isolated store whose success attracts competitors. Automobile dealers and furniture stores are examples of stores commonly locating in strings. Generally, a string has good visibility and a good automobile traffic count. On the other hand, there is no sharing of promotional and security costs.

- Regional shopping centers are large, planned shopping facilities designed to serve more than 100,000 people and usually include a major department store, banking facilities, and restaurants. These centers, with 40 to 100 stores, are generally smaller equivalents of downtown centers. Suburban clusters have grown because of the increase in the number of families owning one or more automobiles, and the failure of mass transportation to provide for the needs of shoppers. Generally, stores are larger and more modern than the downtown stores and have better parking facilities. Usually regional shopping centers have excellent parking facilities and allow for shared promotional and security costs. On the other hand, there can be traffic congestion during peak seasons and restrictive lease covenants.

- The isolated store is a freestanding retail outlet situated on either a highway or a street and without adjacent retailers. There is no competition and rental costs are relatively low. On the other hand, advertising costs may be high and operating costs cannot be shared, such as outside lighting security and maintenance of grounds. Walgreens, a drugstore chain, has found the isolated-store location ideal for its needs. Walgreens features one-stop or convenience shopping with a drive-through pharmacy. There is good road and traffic visibility and facilities have been adapted for a drug chain's needs. Eckerd, CVS, and Rite Aid have also established their new stores in freestanding locations. Sales volume increases, while costs remain relatively low, and stores are usually more profitable than in other site locations.

HUMAN RESOURCES

It is the effective use of personnel that makes a successful retail business. The behavior of personnel toward customers is frequently a reflection of the store's culture and work environment.

Wal-Mart has been successful in motivating employees. There is high esprit de corps, and principles of teamwork are integrated into performance standards. Much of the credit for employee motivation is due to Sam Walton, the founder of Wal-Mart. No other merchant in recent history has been able to duplicate his success as a people motivator.

Bernard Marcus, cofounder and former CEO of Home Depot, instilled the right culture in his company by developing a training program through which every store manager and assistant manager receives comprehensive and continuous training. Management considers its employees expertise in merchandising and home-improvement techniques essential to success.

Specialty-store retailers are confronted with special human resource challenges that can include inexperienced employees, long hours, and part-time workers. These variables make the hiring, staffing, and supervision of specialty-store employees a difficult task. Specialty-store merchants, especially those in such product categories as book, apparel, home-improvement, and electronic stores require well-trained, competent sales personnel who are knowledgeable about the products they sell.

The corporate cultures of high performing specialty retailers are dramatically different from other companies. Important priorities are teamwork, customer focus, and the encouragement of initiative and innovation. In contrast, the cultures of most specialty retailers appear to be minimizing risk, developing a sound budget, and respecting the chain of command.

The outstanding specialty retailers have a consensus of how to achieve company cultural priorities. For example, the management in companies like Gap and L.L. Bean agree on company mission and goals.

The top specialty retailers emphasize speed in decision making and swift action on new opportunities. These firms are concerned over complacency. The capability to move quickly and decisively will be an important characteristic of successful specialty retailers in the 21st century.

INTERNET RETAILING

There are more than 100 Web retailers, and online retailing is growing faster than previously expected. As more consumers shop the Internet, more retailers are establishing themselves in cyberspace, which in turn attracts more shoppers. The most successful firm selling on the Internet has been Amazon.com, the bookseller. A number of other specialty retailers such as the Gap, Toys "R" Us, and Brooks Brothers have established Web sites.

As the economy enters the 21st century, more than half the retail revenue generated online is from those retailers with Websites and traditional stores and catalogs. Specialty retailers such as Eddie Bauer have been among the pioneers. Books and clothing are currently the most commonly purchased online products. Other industries online include leisure travel, brokerage services, PC hardware, auto sales, drugstore products, furniture, music, shoes and hardware. As the innovating specialty retailers become successful, more merchants and industries will rush to join the surge in Internet retailing.

RETAILING TRIUMPHS

Customer satisfaction is an important variable in the customer-service framework. In order to serve the customer better, the Limited and Toys

"R" Us have established inventory-management systems and controls to reduce operating costs, speed deliveries, and avoid stock-outs. These systems have reduced the time span required to make decisions and effectively communicate information within and beyond the organization to suppliers. The Limited and Toys "R" Us have the ability to combine state-of-the-art information systems with excellent management to gain better knowledge of the markets they serve. These retailers can identify and capitalize on trends and improve profit through better buying, planning, and control decisions. At the Limited every garment in every store is tracked on a daily basis, and at Home Depot, thousands of items are tracked by the computer inventory management system from initial placement of the order to delivery to stores to customer check-out.

Victoria's Secret, a ladies lingerie specialty-store chain owned by the Limited has created a distinctive personality of an English lady, sensuous, feminine, and cloaked in mystery. Even the perfumes and soaps it sells are an enigma of romance. Victoria's Secret has created a successful mysticism that attracts even male shoppers.

Another retailing triumph has been the ability of Tiffany & Company, an upscale retailer of jewelry, tableware, and gift items, to successfully create and maintain a retail image. This 150-year-old specialty-store retailer satisfies customers with superior value and excellent customer service. Tiffany's is the embodiment of luxury and sophistication. A communications program using advertising and appropriate merchandise information booklets conveys the selectivity of its merchandise.

The development of private label or store brands has been a triumph for specialty stores. Specialty chains like Brooks Brothers, Gap, and Ann Taylor have developed their image and merchandising mix selling their own label.

RETAILING BLUNDERS

There are a number of reasons for retailing blunders. Even the most successful specialty store has made mistakes but manages to survive by making adjustments to such variables as innovation, image, target-market segmentation, physical environmental resources, and human resources.

A common reason for the mistakes of specialty retailers is complacency. Success encourages the perspective that the past will repeat itself. The retail environment is dynamic. For example, Laura Ashley, a British apparel and home furnishings company with outlets in the United States, was slow to update its traditional fabric patterns and designs. As a result, Laura Ashley has changed its traditional image as a purveyor of flowery women's fashions to a more classic line and decided to sell its manufacturing plants and concentrate on promoting its brands and managing its retail stores.

Another reason for the failure of retail organizations is overexpansion. Retailing blunders can be committed in the name of growth. For example, at one time, Herman's Sporting Goods tried to become a national chain but had to retrench when it found that it could not operate profitably on a national scale. Another illustration is Wickes, the fifth largest home-improvement center in sales volume, an organization that has suffered from poor acquisitions and too much expansion. Essentially, its diversification into the retail-furniture business proved to be Wickes' downfall. Wickes expanded in suburban markets where it competed unsuccessfully with Levitz Furniture and other warehouse-store furniture chains.

Another cause for retail blunders is the lack of a distinct retail-store image. To change or modify a retail image is a difficult process. A retail image is how customers and others perceive the retail store and its operations. A composite picture of the retailer is one of the most powerful tools in attracting customers. A tarnished or blurred image can spell disaster. Abercrombie and Fitch, founded in 1892, was considered one of the outstanding sporting goods stores in the United States. Its prestigious Madison Avenue location attracted such customers as Admiral Byrd, Amelia Earhart, Ernest Hemingway, and Theodore Roosevelt. However, with the days of furnishing complete safari clothing and equipment now over, Abercrombie & Fitch has had a difficult time redefining its image.

Levitz Furniture, the second largest home-furniture retailer, filed for bankruptcy protection in 1997, Levitz, established more than eighty years ago, pioneered the innovation of warehouse retailing in the early 1960s. Levitz targeted families who desired inexpensive furniture that they could take home with them. The company had tried to revise its image by targeting a more upscale consumer but failed. The change to emphasize style and quality did not succeed and many prospective customers turned to retailers such as Ethan Allen Interiors, which had successfully switched from carrying merchandise with a colonial style to merchandise that was more contemporary.

How Specialty Stores Try to Overcome Past Mistakes

- Do not attempt to be all things to all people
- Aim to cultivate only a precise segment of the market.
- Maintain a merchandise assortment that has both depth and breadth to satisfy target market.
- Maintain a high level of customer service above and beyond general merchandise stores.
- Focus promotion to appropriate customer segments. Develop high advertising visiblity.
- Develop greater location flexibility. Recognize that consumer convenience is paramount.

- Make shopping in the store fun.
- Create competitive advantage by the breadth of choice offered within each product category.
- Develop strong private label brands.

Whereas drugstores have increased variety through scrambled merchandising, Gap and Circuit City have gone in the direction of specialization. Specialty stores are succeeding because they have placed competitive pressure on department stores. Many specialty stores have also been able to better satisfy the lifestyles of individual market segments. Finally, specialty store chains have been able to use economies of scale to render competitive advantages over traditional department stores and other retailers.

MANAGING CHANGE

Change should be an obsession with retailers, whether it is merchandise planning, inventory control, or promotion. Several dramatic changes in retail operations have occurred and made a profound impact on retailing. The 1990s were marked by the equalization of power between large sellers, particularly large retailers and large manufacturers, and to a lesser extent, large wholesale organizations. Many large specialty retailers developed their own private brands in competition with manufacturer brands. On the other hand, some manufacturers such as Sherwin-Williams have established their own retail stores and are formidable competitors.

The emergence of off-price retailing, off-price shopping malls, unprecedented acquisitions, the expansion of home-improvement centers, in-home shopping by catalog or electronic commerce, and more effective promotion have contributed to the decline in market share of many types of retailers. All types of in-home shopping will grow in the future. The reasons most frequently cited include: less time for working women to shop; greater use of home computers; and the increased emphasis on the standardization and branding of products, thereby reducing purchasing risk.

Cost leadership and focus strategies adopted by many specialty-store retailers have caught mass merchandisers like Kmart in the middle. There has also been a development of boutiques, scrambled merchandising, and varied retailing styles that have contributed to the decline in market share of mass merchandisers. The growth of all-weather shopping malls has intensified retail competition, and many specialty retailers have located there.

The future for the specialty store is promising. Trends in lifestyles, urbanization, family income, education, and new product development favor the growth of specialty-store retailing. For example, the growth in VCR sales has led to the growth of entertainment stores such as Blockbuster. The introduction of home computers has led to the growth of computer stores. Specialty stores are designed to appeal to the ever changing needs of consumers.

2

Drugstores: Kings of Scrambled Merchandising

Strategies in a Mature Market

- Use of information technology to improve work flow
- New business formats: superstores, drive-through pharmacies, online drugstores
- Target-market segmentation: third-party payers, HMOs
- Scrambled merchandising
- Prescription price competition
- Convenient location and a clean store
- Acquisition programs to build dominant market position
- Category management
- Fast service and delivery
- Selective medical testing
- Emergence of mega drug chains
- Building of private brand equity

Drugstore Mistakes

- Status-quo mentality
- Poor locations
- Inadequate information systems
- Delay in changing store layouts
- Poor monitoring of consumer shopping patterns
- Absence of personalized customer service
- Failure to invest in technology
- Poor understanding of marketing and merchandising

The drugstore specialty-retail market is characterized by the disappearance of independent stores and the growth of chains such as Walgreens, CVS, and Rite Aid. In 1998, there were more than 30,000 pharmacies operated by traditional chain pharmacy companies, supermarkets, and mass merchandisers. There were about 20,000 independent pharmacies. The 21st century will witness a further decline of the independents as drugstore chains, full-line discount stores, supermarkets with pharmacy departments, hospital pharmacies, and mail-order and online pharmacy services increase their market share to shift the balance of power in their dealings with managed care. Drugstore chains are investing in technology and becoming more adept at marketing and merchandising. The chain drugstore dispenses more than 60 percent of the more than 2.8 billion retail prescriptions dispensed each year, more than four million each day. The average American uses seven prescriptions per year and those over sixty-five consume seventeen per year. The chain pharmacies have annual sales of prescription drugs, over-the-counter medications, and health and beauty aids of over $125 billion a year.

Managed-care alliances are considered a prize by drugstore chains since consumers purchase other products when filling their prescriptions. Independents are unable to realize this benefit without the economies of scale necessary to gain leverage with drug manufacturers and managed-care organizations. While the drugstore chains are responding to the drastic changes in the wake of the managed health-care revolution by acquiring small chains, independent drugstores do not provide third-party prescription services. Pharmacies often account for over 50 percent of a store's total volume, with low paying third-party prescription plans representing more than 75 percent of the department's revenue. In many cases, third-party contracts do not provide a profit acceptable to the drugstore owner.

Similarly, independents have a difficult time competing with chains in the areas of pricing and promotion for over-the-counter drugs, toiletries, cosmetics and fragrance, and general merchandise. Although they are linking together in cooperative purchasing groups, independents are unable to match the specialized management and central buying of drugstore chains. The buying power of drugstore chains reflects the ability to make purchases in greater quantities and, consequently, to obtain lower costs. Drugstore chains also have the resources to provide better promotional support and can promise suppliers significant sales volume.

These advantages provide chains with the opportunity to experiment with new products and selling methods that cannot be matched by independents. Walgreens, CVS, and Rite Aid have the resources to develop and promote their own store brands, which are sold below the prices of national brands. Size is important to success and survival in the drugstore industry.

Although unable to compete with drugstore chains in a number of ways, independent drugstores do enjoy support because of personalized service. They often reflect the owner's personality, are comfortable environments in which to shop, and may offer special services. For example, many independent drugstores provide delivery to customers who are unable to come to the store and will also advise customers on over-the-counter drugs. Some independents even sell exclusive lines of cosmetics and greeting cards.

Historically, a pharmacist was high in prestige, status, and respect. The neighborhood pharmacy dates back to 1825 when Elias Durand opened a shop in Philadelphia at the corner of Sixth and Chestnut streets that specialized in medical supplies and the sale of sparkling water. Initially, it was a place where local scientists and physicians met to discuss their work and eventually it became a social hub where everyone met to discuss local issues and exchange gossip. The drugstore featured mirrors, wooden display cases, and an apparatus for vending carbonated water.[1] After World War II, drugstores learned that cosmetics, nylon stockings, and convenience groceries derived more profits than soda fountain sales, and by the 1950s, the independent drugstore and the soda fountain had begun to disappear. With the passing of the soda fountain and the decline of the independent drugstore, the prestige and status of the pharmacist also declined.

Independent drugstores continue to lose market share to the large chains due to an over-dependence on the owner-pharmacist. Continuity of management is generally not present upon retirement, death, or illness of this owner-pharmacist. Since the owner is involved in daily operations, long hours are a necessity as are the headaches involved in competing with the large chains. Many owner-pharmacists have neither the time nor background necessary to sell the wide range of goods unrelated to prescription drugs available in drug stores today.

Today, with scrambled merchandising, the distinctions have blurred as retailers expand their offerings to generate store traffic and satisfy customers' needs for one-stop shopping. For example, a drugstore may stock a mix of such dissimilar goods as garden items, cosmetics, personal care products, some groceries, hardware, photo supplies, and small appliances in addition to prescription and over-the-counter drugs. Customers also want to shop close to their homes and workplaces for drug store related merchandise.

More than ever before, drugstore owners need to be aware of changing consumer shopping behavior where convenience has become more important to customers. There is not much that drugstores sell that cannot be purchased elsewhere. Therefore, Walgreens, Eckerd, CVS, and Drug Emporium subscribe to a program developed by Information Resources Inc. that allows them to track sales on health and beauty aids, detergents, and food. New opportunities are presented as manufacturers target space in drugstore chains not available in supermarkets for such products as cosmetics, shampoo, foot care, and premium hair conditioners. The development in checkout-scanning technology has allowed information gathering for drugstore chains to include ways to monitor customers purchases continually and adjust the product mix, analyze stores sales, monitor the impact of new sales strategies, and control inventory replenishment. The Internet is also an important source of revenue, and Walgreens is currently exploring its use in the sale of products, including online prescription refills. This allows shoppers who have the Rx number from the prescription label to reorder online and pick up the medicine at the local Walgreens store. At www.Eckard.com, online shoppers can arrange to fill or refill a prescription through the Eckerd Pharmacy Mail Service. CVS and Rite Aid allow on-line users to ask pharmacists for advice, which is later sent to the user via e-mail.

A consideration of the successes and failures of drugstores shows that mistakes have been made, but these organizations have survived by making constant adjustments of such variables as innovation, target market and image, physical environmental resources, and human resources. Many of the leading chains such as Rite Aid and CVS have accelerated their acquisition programs in order to service the growing number of health maintenance organizations. Favorable population demographics and trends in managed care remain positive for future growth of the drugstore industry. A downside to this strategy has been the overexpansion of Rite Aid, which has created a debt problem causing the chain to divest some recently acquired holdings.

Innovation in the drugstore trade has developed through the merchandising mix with scrambled merchandising, the carrying of merchandise unrelated to the store's primary mission, and the sale of products over the Internet. Target market and image have varied, and multiple targets have been selected such as the elderly and women from the ages of twenty to fifty-five. There has not been a single drugstore chain that has been more successful than others in target market selection. Store image has been more enhanced through time than other factors and therefore, Eckerd and Walgreens, which were founded almost a hundred years ago, have a decisive edge. Walgreens would seem to have developed freestanding stores and drive-through pharmacies earlier than the other chains and thus has employed physical resources well. None of the drugstore chains stand out as does Home Depot with the training and selection of human resources. Drug chains such as Walgreens, CVS, and Rite Aid all deserve credit for adaptability by promoting relationships with HMO's and third-party payers. However, JC Penney, with the acquisition of Eckerd, may become a formidable competitor in the future. Customer satisfaction has been increased by using a Merck-Medeo system that can advise customers about possible drug interactions even if medications were prescribed by several doctors and were filled at different pharmacies.

STRUCTURE

Chain-drug organizations are changing their store formats to adapt to a new competitive environment and attract customers. In an effort to give their store units an image of individuality, drugstore operators are experimenting with new store formats. Osco Drug, a division of Albertson's, operates conventional drugstores of 8,500 to 15,000 square feet. Generally, the pharmacy is located in the rear of the store and over-the-counter drugs and durable medical equipment are situated near the pharmacy to support the store's image as a health-care provider. Recently, Osco Drug introduced new units called Vision which include waiting and consulting areas at the pharmacy. Walgreens typically operates stores similar to Osco Drug; however, the company is implementing express stores of 2,000 to 4,000 square feet. These units provide an express drive-through for prescription purchases and refills. Express drugstores feature a pharmacy and include such over-the-counter drugs as aspirin and cough syrup, and other items with typically high turnover.

Rite Aid is opening both bantam drugstores of 4,000 to 7,000 square feet and large outlets of 10,000 square feet. The bantam drugstore generally provides less general and seasonal merchandise than a conventional drugstore, while the larger stores allow for the expansion of the merchandise mix to include cosmetics and fragrance departments.

Although Longs Drugs Stores is known for its super drugstores, it too is experimenting with express stores. Super drugstores, which are about 30,000 square feet, are a cross between the conventional and deep discount drugstores. Cosmetic and household products departments are presented as stand-alone units. The emphasis of these departments is a stores-within-a-store format.

Drug Emporium operates nearly 140 units under the names; Drug Emporium, the F & M Super Drug Store, "Big D," and 100 franchise units. It is a major competitor in the deep-discount trade. Deep-discount drugstores typically range from 20,000 to 30,000 square feet. The company targets middle-to-upper-income women aged twenty-five to fifty-four. Most units provide full-service pharmacies and discount-priced merchandise including health and beauty aids, cosmetics, and greeting cards.

Table 2.1 does not reveal Internet selling efforts. Although the major drug chains sell through mail order, these chains have been slow to take advantage of Internet selling potential. The two best-known online drugstores are Drugstore.com and Planet RX. Planet RX is licensed to sell drugs in all fifty states, while Drugstores.com is only licensed to sell in

Table 2.1
Major Drug Chains

	Net Sales 1998	Number of Units 1998
Walgreens	$15.3 billion	2547
CVS (Revco)	$15.3 billion	4122
Rite Aid	$12.7 billion	3821
Albertson's (Osco, Sav-On)	$16.0 billion	893[1]
Eckerd	$ 6.1 billion	1873
Long's Drug Stores	$3.27 billion	381
Drug Emporium	$840 million	193[2]
Genovese Drug Stores[3]	$769 million[4]	141

1. Includes 866 combination food-drug stores, 86 conventional supermarkets and 31 warehouse stores.
2. Includes 141 company owned stores operated under the Drug Emporium, F&M Super
   Drug Stores, and Vix Drug Stores names, as well as 52 franchise stores.
3. Acquired by JC Penney November 22, 1998 (became part of Eckerd chain).
4. Sales for year ended January 30, 1998; fiscal year 1998 sales information is unavailable.

forty-four. When shipping charges are added, it probably would be less
expensive to make purchases through a neighborhood chain pharmacy.
However, if convenience and avoiding long lines at drugstore chains are
prized, the extra shipping charge might be worthwhile to some consumers. In 1999, Rite Aid purchased a twenty-five percent interest in Drug-
store.com, Inc. Drugstore.com started to sell products in February 1999
and is one of the largest online drugstores in terms of traffic. Also in
1999, CVS purchased an online pharmacy, Soma.com. Rite Aid will sell
only prescription drugs and nutritional products through Drugstore.com.
Consumers will be able to either receive products mailed to them or pick
up their purchase the same day at the nearest Rite Aid store. Drugstore
chains are scrambling to catch up with Internet competitors. With particularly fierce competition, pharmacy chains undersell their own online
stores. Walgreens and CVS offer free mail delivery and discounts to online purchasers. Internet prescription sales provide a small market share
since elderly households often lack access to the Internet. Also, consumers
prefer to purchase medications such as antibiotics or painkillers directly
at the store.

PRODUCT MIX

Items sold in drugstores are referred to as convenience products, with
the exception of surgical product lines. Usually convenience products
have a high replacement rate and a low gross margin. Convenience products are readily available and accessible to consumers and require, as in
the case of aspirin, widespread distribution. Consumers take very little
time when purchasing convenience items and normally buy these items

close to home. For this reason, items such as candy and soft drinks are placed near the register and are purchased as customers leave the drugstore. A substantial promotional budget is necessary to gain a high turnover with convenience items. Manufacturers promoting such items as pain relievers, cough medicine, toothpaste, first aid products, and other such merchandise lines support drugstores with cooperative advertising allowances. However, it is also necessary that drugstores add to this promotional budget and take responsibility for promoting their own private-label brands.

Rite Aid, CVS, and Walgreens have all developed store and private-label brands as important merchandising strategies. In the past, consumers often considered private labels as inferior merchandise. Now, many consumers accept private-label brands as equal to the quality of national brands.

By achieving brand loyalty for their own products, Rite Aid, CVS, and Walgreens have gained significant power over wholesalers and manufacturers. Store brands allow drugstore chains to switch suppliers when necessary without an impact on their customer loyalty. Store brands also allow for long-term relationships that can be advantageous in price, delivery, and other terms that benefit drugstore chains, suppliers, and consumers. Some economies of scale may result since many activities are eliminated, simplified, or shared such as financing, billing, and merchandise labeling. Thrifty PayLess has introduced a full-scale private brand that incorporates bath, body, skin, and color cosmetics. CVS launched the Down to Earth brand that includes milk baths, hand and body lotions and gels, and Eckerd Drug has extended its Paul Milan brand name from skin-softening bath additives into complete bath care. Some drugstore chains also contain a photo-finishing business, fax machines, and mail center as traffic builders.

Although Walgreens, according to Table 2.1 does not have the most outlets, it has the highest sales volume. JC Penney controls Thrift Drug and, with its acquisitions of Eckerd and Genovese, is now a leader in the industry. Other mergers include CVS with Revco, Arbor and Fay's; Rite Aid with Thrifty PayLess and K&B. In addition to franchising many of its units, Medicine Shoppe differentiates itself from the more conventional drugstore chains with its large mix of medical and surgical supplies. Albertson's acquired American Stores in 1998 and with it about 750 free-standing drugstores under the Sav-on-Drugs or Osco Drug names. This acquisition makes Albertson's the sixth-ranked pharmacy chain in the United States since American Stores has over 1,700 pharmacy operations. Albertson's opened its first store in 1939 and has been known primarily as a supermarket chain with pharmacy operations. This venture pits Albertson's directly in a competitive fight with the drug store chains. Rite Aid's rapid expansion has posed problems for the chain. For example,

Thrifty PayLess, which was the largest drugstore chain on the West Coast, had relatively small pharmacies and used heavy promotion to sell everything from low-priced shoes to gun ammunition. Consequently, the merchandise mix needed adjustment, and many of the store units were unprofitable.

POWER IN THE DRUG CHAIN INDUSTRY

Retail drug chains draw on their size to gain the cooperation of manufacturers and wholesalers. Scrambled merchandising allows retailers to sell thousands of products without dependency on particular manufacturers. This strategy allows Rite Aid, CVS, and others to become power retailers. Another strategy is to be priced oriented and cost effective to appeal to price-sensitive customers. Drug chains are also convenience oriented to attract customers interested in nearby locations and long store hours.

Many environmental factors will influence the power relationships between retail drug chains and manufacturers. A buyer's market has led to the rise of retail giant firms developing their own national brands. Rite Aid, CVS, and Walgreens all have extensively promoted their store brands in competition with national brands. Power in the retail drugstore industry can serve as a basis for conflict or as a foundation for harmonious relationships that generate cooperation among industry members.

Rite Aid has been accused of using coercive power to pressure suppliers to make concessions that were not authorized. Coercive power is the perceived capability to punish, in this instance, suppliers. The fear would be that the giant retailer might decide not to stock the manufacturer's product, give the product a poor shelf position in relation to competitors, reduce purchasing quantities, or negotiate pricing and promotional terms unfavorable to the manufacturer. In this case, Rite Aid made vague claims of unsaleable merchandise and accordingly deducted money due the manufacturer without authorization. Dial, Bic, and Mars corporations claim that unauthorized deductions were made by Rite Aid. The contention has been made that drugstore chains and other large retailers in other sectors have attempted to improve their finances by pressuring suppliers for more concessions and that this is an escalating practice. CVS and Eckerd have also been cited for taking large deductions for "damaged" goods.

Rite Aid has denied the allegations but has furnished reportedly scant documentation for obtaining credit for damaged goods. Since retail drug chains maintain multiple sources of supply, they can avoid the coercive power of any single supplier. Moreover, by developing a strong private-brand program the drug chains can not only avoid the coercive power of national producers but are in a position to demonstrate their own power.

WALGREENS: USE OF PRODUCTIVITY

Walgreens was founded in 1901 with the purpose of providing customer convenience, and that mission has remained important to this day. On January 31, 1998, Walgreens operated 2,547 drugstores in thirty-four states and Puerto Rico. They serve more than 2.4 million customers daily and annually average $5.5 million sales per store.

Time is precious to the American family today because of dual-income earners, single-parent homes, and changing work patterns. Although many families are more affluent, this greater wealth results in less free time because the alternatives competing for their time have expanded accordingly. Walgreens's strategy reflects an integral focus on saving customers time. How fast customers are able to get into the store, how fast customers are served in the drive-through pharmacy, and how fast customers can find what they desire to purchase are all elements of Walgreens' strategy. This means convenient locations, drive-through pharmacies, touch-tone prescription refills, and even one-hour photo labs. At Walgreens the customer is considered the most important asset, and the stores' staffs are encouraged and rewarded for recommending ways to improve the customer's experience.

Walgreens attempt in the 1960s to diversify failed. Supermarkets and fast-food chains among other businesses were acquired but were divested during the 1980s. Management and financial resources were stretched, and Walgreens was unable to transfer its competencies in drugstore operations to other businesses.

Two critical strategies in building Walgreens have been its selection of store locations and its ability to attract, develop, and retain employees. Walgreens was innovative in pioneering the freestanding retail outlet, which is usually located on either a highway or a busy street. The isolated or freestanding store is found in the inner city to provide convenience for customers. The freestanding store does not have adjacent retailers to share traffic, but it does offer several advantages such as relatively low rental costs and a lack of competition. Since larger space may be attained, the freestanding format is beneficial for a drugstore involved in one-stop or convenience shopping. When the store is located on a highway, better road and traffic visibility is possible, and easy parking is available.

Although Walgreens provides convenience for customers by establishing freestanding stores, there are limitations to this format. Frequently, a store must be constructed rather than rented, and operating costs such as outside lighting, security, and maintenance of grounds cannot be shared.

Moreover, promotion costs can be high. Walgreens also operates in business district and shopping center sites. Emphasis today is on remodeling stores to overcome the age of the average Walgreens outlet.

Walgreens has directed its promotional resources to attract a heavy user market segment. Markets can be divided into light, medium, and heavy-user groups. Heavy users are frequently a small percentage of the market but are responsible for a high percentage of total consumption. Heavy users may often have common demographics, psychographics, and media habits.

There are problems related to targeting the heavy-user segment. It is a mistake to view heavy users as either product-loyal or store loyal. Stores that sell convenience products such as drugstores usually do not generate strong consumer loyalty. High volume purchasers may easily shift their loyalty if a competitor opens a store in close proximity or may be price sensitive if discounters locate nearby. Heavy users may purchase many items elsewhere but because of location and other variables shop in conveniently located drugstores. Moreover, heavy users do not necessarily make purchases for the same reasons and further segmentation based on consumer needs may be required.

Walgreens wants to achieve higher productivity as a form of competitive strategy. The new prototype stores are 14,000 square feet and contain pharmacy waiting areas, consultation windows, fragrance bars, food departments, and clerk-served one-hour photo finishing departments. Walgreens is an industry leader in its use of information technology and has spent more than $100 million developing proprietary software. Intercom Plus is Walgreens' advanced pharmacy system. It provides tax/insurance records and patient profiles and allows the pharmacy to better manage its workflow and increase productivity and volume. It allows customers to enter prescription refill information from touch-tone telephones and helps pharmacists determine the best time to fill prescriptions. Walgreens also has its own proprietary inventory system, which allows store managers to tailor merchandise mix to local situations. This constitutes a differential advantage in the drugstore industry.

Walgreens is a major private brand with more than 1,000 products having its name. The chain advertises its brands in both print and television media using the tagline "The Brand America Trusts." The private-brand products contain a 100 percent guaranteed satisfaction seal and in some cases a comparative statement to national brands. Walgreens also uses compare and save signs to get customers to buy their products. The objective is to shift customers from nationally branded products to the more lucrative Walgreens store brands.

Another competitive advantage is the chain's pharmacy mail-service subsidiary, Walgreens' Healthcare Plus. A major entry in managed-care pharmacy, Walgreens' Healthcare Plus is able to fill more than 15,000 prescriptions per day. Walgreens managed-care division, in cooperation with health-managed-care organizations, has generated record growth sales, and profits. Thus, Walgreens has been able to outperform the competition by providing quality services to managed-care organizations.

Walgreens has gone beyond the retailing mix by participating in community programs. For example, in Chicago it sponsored tutoring programs for fourth through sixth graders. After several fires in Memphis, Walgreens stores distributed free-fire prevention literature and applications for free smoke detectors.

RITE AID: CHALLENGES FROM GROWTH

The first Rite Aid store was opened in 1962 in Scranton, Pennsylvania, as the Thrift Discount Center. The company has grown rapidly, mainly through acquisitions, and was officially named the Rite Aid Corporation in 1968. Over the years, Rite Aid has acquired small chains including Daw Drugs, Warner Drugs, Read's, Fay's, Gray Drug-Drug Fair, People's Drug-Line, Perry Drug Stores, Inc., Thrifty PayLess, K&B, Inc. and Hargo, Inc. By 1997 Rite Aid had extended into more than thirty states and owned about 3,623 units, and by 1998 it had more than 3,800 stores. Rapid expansion, the need to integrate information systems, adjustment of the product mix, and store remodeling has negatively affected profitability.

Rite Aid was prevented from merging with Revco Drug Stores in 1996 by the Federal Trade Commission because the two chains operated in the same markets. For example, in Ohio, Rite Aid would double its market share, while its closest competitor, Kroger, would trail by approximately 25 percent of market share. Industry experts do not believe that the FTC decision against Rite Aid precludes further consolidation in the retail-drugstore industry. Rite Aid was able to merge with Oregon-based Thrifty PayLess. Thrifty PayLess had more than 1,000 stores and allowed Rite Aid to gain a major presence in the western states.

Rite Aid approaches drugstore marketing differently than Walgreens and CVS. While Walgreens and CVS have developed their own pharmacy mail-order services, Rite Aid has entered into a joint venture to provide mail-order pharmacy services to select managed care customers with SmithKline Beecham's Diversified Pharmaceutical Services. In contrast to Walgreens' and CVS's commitment to the senior citizen market segment, Rite Aid targets young working women with their own money to spend and women twenty-five to fifty-four years old with families. The company has expressed long-range objectives of category management in the vitamin, photo, and greeting card categories. However, cosmetics is the store's fastest-growing product category today. Rite Aid may charge more for some products than its competitors but its stores are well located and carry what the customer wants. Rite Aid also uses newspaper inserts and coupons to attract thrifty housewives.

Until 1982, Rite Aid did not have comprehensive information system that included matching sales with inventory. Customers were checked out with electronic cash registers. Sales and department totals were the only data gathered. Store personnel would manually record sales information and mail this data to the Harrisburg, Pennsylvania, corporate headquarters. It was not until the early 1990s that Rite Aid installed a store-based point-of-sale system. This system records customer names and credit card information to target customer groups for selected direct mailings. The system allows the manager of the store to view data at the product level to identify the best-selling mix of merchandise and the effectiveness of promotions.

Today, PCs have been placed in all store units to electronically link the individual stores with headquarters. Planning is easier since performance is quickly monitored, and reporting is now relatively paperless compared to the past. The computerization of the pharmacy department has made Rite Aid more competitive with Walgreens and others. Patient profiles can be maintained, and there is improved processing of third-party prescription claims.

Rite Aid has had difficulty integrating its information system with its recent drugstore-chain acquisitions. An alliance was made with McKesson, a drug distributor, to use its information system. Whether or not these changes in computerization will help Rite Aid to compete favorably with Walgreens and JC Penney (Eckerd and Thrift) is uncertain. In 1999, Rite Aid introduced a prescription and vitamin Website with GNC, a chain of health food stores. Also in 1999, Rite Aid was confronted with accounting problems and increasing debt, and sold some of its stores.

Rite Aid plans to focus on building its convenience food and cosmetic departments as well as its private label program, which includes more than 1,200 products. Rite Aid's prototype store includes easy access, parking for at least fifty cars, a full service and drive-through pharmacy, one-hour photo finishing, express mail service (which includes fax services, photocopying, packaging, and shipping), convenience foods (including frozen goods and dairy products), and a complete cosmetic department. Competition from convenience food stores such as 7-Eleven, discount stores, and supermarkets will be formidable. In addition, national brand cosmetics such as Revlon have a better image than drugstore cosmetics. Discounters such as Wal-Mart could prevent growth in drugstore-cosmetic departments by continuing to provide such name-brand cosmetics at lower prices.

CVS: AN AGGRESSIVE TRANSFORMATION

CVS was founded in 1963 in Lowell, Massachusetts, under the name "Consumer Value Store," and grew through acquisitions. Unlike Rite Aid and Walgreens, CVS was under a huge organization umbrella—the Melville Corporation, best known for its Thom McAn and Stride Rite shoes and Marshall's clothing chain. In 1996, Melville's corporate name was changed to CVS so that it could concentrate on drugstores. Melville divested itself of its other businesses. With the acquisition of Revco in 1997 (which the FTC permitted because the two companies were not in the same markets), and Arbor Drugs in 1998, CVS became the largest drugstore chain in the United States, operating more than 4,100 stores in twenty-four states with major market share in the Northeast, Mid-Atlantic, Midwest, and Southeast. The acquisitions of Revco and Arbor Drugs permitted CVS to reduce expenses for advertising, production, and warehousing, and to negotiate lower insurance and credit card processing fees. Because of its acquisitions, CVS has a slight lead over Walgreens in pharmaceutical sales.

CVS has developed a category management approach to product categories such as greeting cards, film and photo finishing, beauty and cosmetics, convenience foods, private-label items, and seasonal items so that existing customers will purchase more per visit. For example, with Kodak and Hallmark, CVS created a store within a store concept to sell these services and products. A category management approach affords CVS the ability to tailor its merchandise selection market by market based on demographics. The object is to monitor a product group as a whole, thus strategically fitting the individual brands together rather than brands competing against one another. The category manager is responsible for the profitability of the entire category product line and has the authority to make quick decisions. The scope of the category manager's responsibilities includes the evaluation of the product mix of new and existing products within the category and consideration of the impact of line additions and deletions on the profitability of other lines in the category.

CVS currently fills more than 4.3 million prescriptions per week. CVS's client-server based centralized RV2000 system allows pharmacists to manage their prescription-filling responsibilities more effectively, giving them more time to spend with customers. The system provides pharmacy data that can be used by CVS and its managed care customers by making the processing of a third-party claim 40 percent faster. An interactive Voice Response System enables customers to place refill orders by telephone by keying in the prescription number and the preferred pick-up time. This system handles more than 100,000 refills a day.

The target markets of CVS are families with young children, seniors, and young professionals with disposable income. CVS wants to promote an image of convenience, caring, value, and world-class service. CVS's corporate advertising campaign uses the theme, "care that touches everyone, one at a time." Convenience food departments have been added in many stores in an attempt to reinforce the image that CVS is a highly convenient place to shop. Private store labels are an integral part of CVS strategy. CVS carries more than 1,200 private-label items, which account for over 1 percent of sales. In contrast to Walgreens, which stocks hibachis and stereos, CVS concentrates on selling quick-sell items such as one-hour photo, greeting cards, health and beauty aids, and pharmaceutical items.

In the past, CVS has avoided urban areas; however, new stores have now opened in such urban areas as Philadelphia, New York, and Baltimore. A cluster strategy approach is used. For example, in Brookline, Massachusetts, CVS has established multiple outlets within a few city blocks. This places pressure on independent drugstores who are offered buyout proposals. CVS is involved in moving its stores from strip malls to freestanding locations, which has increased sales as much as 25 percent. However, only about 15 percent of CVS's store base consist of freestanding stores and drive-through pharmacies compared to approximately 50 percent of Walgreens stores. Through research, CVS has developed a store layout prototype that customers prefer: low-profile gondolas and an in-store environment that is neat, clean, and comfortable. Also, CVS operates more than 200 twenty-four-hour stores for the convenience of its customers in selected markets.

The factors that could affect CVS's ability to grow in the future include changes in market conditions in the markets they serve, competition from other drug store chains and alternative distribution channels such as supermarkets, membership clubs, mail-order companies, E-commerce, and third-party plans. They will also be faced with the effort of health maintenance organizations, managed care organizations, pharmacy benefit management companies, and other third-party payers to reduce the number of prescriptions issued each year.

ECKERD CORPORATION

In early 1997, JC Penney acquired Eckerd Corporation. The Eckerd chain, founded in 1898, was primarily located in the Sunbelt states. In 1999, the Eckerd chain consisted of 1,800 stores in the eastern and sunbelt states. In its forty-five-year history, the Eckerd drugstore chain had built a strong market position in areas where demographic characteristics were favorable to drugstore growth, with its stores being concentrated in ten of the twelve metropolitan statistical areas with the largest percentage growth in population from 1980 to 1990. JC Penney also operates Thrift Drug, Fay's, and Genovese drugstores. This acquisition made it the fourth-largest chain after CVS, Rite Aid, and Walgreens.

JC Penney decided at the time of the acquisition that all of its drug operations would be converted to the Eckerd name, bringing the name into eleven new states. The belief was that a name that had been around for 100 yeas would convey an image of trust in the minds of consumers and research revealed that the Eckerd name had strong consumer acceptance. Demographically, the Eckerd customer is also the JC Penney customer.

Eckerd's reputation and its strategic store locations complement JC Penney's expertise in merchandising. Since Eckerd's acquisition, emphasis has been placed on the construction of Eckerd Express-Photo, its one-hour photo finishing minilabs, and the upgrading of existing beauty departments. Thrift's small beauty departments are being renovated to resemble the upscale format of Eckerd stores with their prestige fragrances under glass and a vast assortment of pegged cosmetics in the front of the store.

In addition to its dominant presence in the beauty industry, Eckerd also has a proven commitment to store brands, which are competitively priced but provide a higher margin than similar national brand products. A result of this strategy is that Eckerd is more motivated than most drug chains to push the quality aspects of its store brands. In the 1980s there was a distinct gap in the level of quality between store and manufacturer brands, but the 1990s found that gap narrowed. Encroachment by drugstore chains' private-label brands should be taken seriously. The private-label strategy is now gaining leverage to national brand suppliers on the basis of quality as well as price.

Eckerd believes that customer service and convenience are critical to its success. Thus, the company places emphasis on service and convenience through pharmacy support services, store location and design, merchandising programs, and operating hours geared to local customer needs. The primary focus of Eckerd is the sale of prescription and over-the-counter drugs. In 1999, 75 percent of the total prescription sales came from managed care plans. Eckerd believes that it has become a managed care provider of choice because of its market coverage, service capabilities, and strong retail mail-order business. Mail service prescriptions accounted for 44 percent of total prescription sales. Pharmacists are promoted in Eckerd's advertising campaign as health-care professionals who build relationships with their customers. JC Penney sees opportunities to grow Eckerd's business in non-drugstore lines through the "front of store" merchandise that represents 45 percent of revenues and 55 percent of operating profit in such product categories as photo finishing, home accessories, bath-and-body products, and apparel merchandise.

Unfortunately, 300 of the units acquired from Thrift Drug, Fays, Genovese, and Eckerd either under-performed or were in need of renovation. With the latest trend to construct drive-through pharmacies, a decision was made to close under-performing store units. This restructuring can be viewed positively in the long term, since competition from CVS, Walgreens, Wal-Mart, and Internet firms have made the drugstore sector a battleground.

OTHER CHAINS

American Stores (Albertson's), under the names of Osco Drug and Sav-On-Drugs, operate more than fifty freestanding drugstores and 250 combination stores with groceries in more than twenty states. The freestanding drug store is about 16,500 square feet with about 30,000 products. The sites provide convenient access, parking, and a drive-up pharmacy window whenever possible. American Stores also operates Acme Markets, Jewel Food Stores, Lucky Stores, and Jewel Osco. American Stores is the parent of American Drug and was among the first in the chain drug industry to begin implementing scanning technology in 1983. This technology was helpful in aligning product line, store layout, and marketing efforts to local customer demand.

Drug Emporium is a national chain of 138 company-owned stores using the name of Drug Emporium, F&M Drug Stores, and "Big D." There are also ninety franchised and licensed Drug Emporium store locations. All stores specialize in discount-priced merchandise—including health and beauty-aids, cosmetics, and greeting cards—and operate full-service pharmacies. The typical store has 25,000 square feet and offers a selection of private-label products and national brands. In 1997, an electronic auto-replenishment ordering system became operational connecting all company-owned pharmacies with the Emporium's primary suppliers. The benefits of this system include improving pharmacy in-stock level while reducing inventory, raising generic dispensary performance, improving contract compliance, reducing costs for daily ordering, and freeing pharmacists to work with customers.

There has been a movement for supermarkets to add pharmacies, medical supplies, and testing facilities to their offerings. For example, Wegmar's Supermarkets, Inc., provides diabetes disease-management centers in two of its stores in Syracuse, New York. The centers, equipped with classrooms and blood testing labs, are managed by doctors from area hospitals. Safeway stores in Washington, D.C., offer prenatal and other maternity care. Other supermarket chains provide flu shots and health screenings. Many supermarkets are open on a twenty-four-hour basis and thus can provide health care in a relatively safe environment. Although supermarkets are considered only a minor competitor of drugstores for health-care services today, this could change in the future.

There is little doubt that the trend of drive-through pharmacies will benefit drug chains in their battle with key supermarket chains containing pharmacies, such as Safeway, Kroger, and Albertson's. Mass merchandisers such as Kmart, Wal-Mart, Target Stores, and deep discounters such as Drug Emporium will also feel the impact of this new type of store format. Nevertheless, an important limitation of the drive-through pharmacy is that customers will not purchase the higher-price convenience products found in the store as the traffic is reduced.

There are other factors that might have an impact on Albertsons' drug operations in the future. These include an increase in low-profit managed-care prescription. Walgreens, Rite Aid, CVS, and Eckerd all appear to have stronger affiliations with managed-care providers. A second factor is the declining reimbursement rates of Medicaid prescriptions. A third is the replacement of high margin generic drugs with newly branded products. These reasons for the decline of pharmacy profit margins are indigenous to the drugstore industry but will probably affect Osco Drug and Sav-on-Drugs more than the larger chains that have stronger third-party payer affiliations. Although Albertsons gains strength in pharmacy operations with its acquisition of American Stores, much more in financial resources will be needed in the competitive struggle with drugstore chains.

MEDICINE SHOPPE INTERNATIONAL: A MAJOR FRANCHISER

Medicine Shoppe was founded in 1970 as a franchise operation with approximately 1,100 independent owners. Cardinal Health, Inc., its parent company, is the second largest wholesaler in the United States. Cardinal Health has a strategic alliance with Kmart and administers approximately 1,600 Kmart pharmacies nationwide. As a franchiser, Medicine Shoppe recruits independent pharmacies for an initial investment of $2,000 and in return will invest $48,000 in the conversion of the store to include leasehold improvements, furniture and fixtures, new signage, and training of the storeowner. The Medicine Shoppe private-label brand of over-the-counter products is sold in the stores.

Medicine Shoppe is a specialty chain of neighborhood pharmacies that have the ability to dispense counseling and health information. Health screenings are an integral strategy in establishing and maintaining the Medicine Shoppe store image. For example, with CIGNA Health Care in Kansas City, Medicine Shoppe is engaged in a pilot study to manage the care of patients with peptic ulcers and congestive heart failure. There has also been a nationwide program for baby health care with foot examinations by podiatrists. A program established for the elderly provides diabetes care packs filled with product samples and promotional items.

Retail outlets are typically 1,000 square feet or smaller, with space for related merchandise. Medicine Shoppe does not carry cosmetics. Prescriptions generate more than 90 percent of its volume. Medicine

Shoppe's narrow focus permits greater efficiency and provides a high level of service. Customers who wait more than fifteen minutes for a prescription to be filled are given a $2 credit. The chain selects sites situated in small strip malls and freestanding locations in established neighborhoods, particularly those populated by senior citizens. Not surprisingly, Medicine Shoppe supports the Senior Olympics.

Medicine Shoppe, like many other drug chains, cooperates with third-party payers. A managed-care network called InterNet was established to contract for third-party business. The InterNet marketing program allows for a competitive basis with drug chains for third-party contracts.

MAIL-ORDER AND ONLINE PHARMACIES

The increase in mail-order pharmacy sales has been made at the expense of independent drugstores. In the 1990s mail-order pharmacy sales increased more rapidly than any other segment of the retail pharmacy market. As the population grows older, more and more people are taking maintenance medications and this lends itself to mail order. The market for mail order is especially attractive for people who live in an area with limited selection and high prices or have transportation or mobility problems. It is possible for mail-order pharmacy firms to provide cost savings, an effective delivery of maintenance drugs, and the opportunity for health plans to consolidate their purchase of maintenance drugs and for the pharmacist to have more time to deal with prescriptions.

Consequently, a number of manufacturers, retailers, and others have started mail-order and online pharmacies to increase sales. One of the largest mail-order pharmacy firms is the American Association of Retired Persons. National manufacturers, such as Merck, have witnessed a growing increase in sales to mail-order pharmacies and have developed mail-order facilities. Merck owns Medco Containment Services, which dominates the mail-order pharmacy industry because it manages prescription drug benefits for 51 million members. Walgreens instituted its mail-order business in 1985 to be more attractive to third-party plans and HMOs. Other chains that have incorporated mail-order operations over the years include Eckerd, American Stores (via Rx America), Rite Aid, and CVS. Competitors such as Wal-Mart are fighting back not only by matching low prices but also by filling prescriptions in a few hours and starting their own mail-order services.

In 1999, Drugstore.com was launched, allowing customers to select from 16,000 health and beauty products on the market. Amazon.com is a 40 percent owner of this company. It is estimated that the online health and beauty market will be $6.3 billion by 2003. This online store focuses on customers who at regular intervals order maintenance medications for everything from high blood pressure to high cholesterol. Visitors to the Website will be able to fill up an electronic "shopping cart" with other purchases, then pay by credit card and await delivery via one of the main package services. Online pharmacies such as Planet RX are allowing pharmaceutical companies to advertise products and information on healthy living on its Website.

ETHICAL PROBLEMS

Advances in computer technology have presented ethical problems in the loss of customer confidentiality and privacy. These new methods of gathering patient information about health problems yield a promising opportunity for marketers. For example, *Reader's Digest* gathered health information through a survey with a sweepstakes offer of attractive prizes. Such opportunities also present dangers. A legal suit filed against CVS charged that its use of prescription data violated rights to patient confidentiality and privacy. CVS has denied the charges, and it is uncertain whether or not any other drug chain, HMO, or third-party payer has revealed health data to drug manufacturers.

One facet of the ethical problem is that direct-mailing lists are available to other sources. One example is health magazines that solicit information through health questionnaires. Another example is a list of asthma sufferers gathered by Grey Healthcare Group, Inc., a unit of Grey Advertising, which gathered a list of asthma sufferers when television viewers were invited to call a toll-free number to learn more about asthma. Although the health information was revealed willingly by respondents, it is not certain if they had full knowledge about the potential use of this information. CVS, on the other hand, used a direct-mail house to send out booklets to people with chronic diseases such as diabetes.

The drug safety system is subject to errors. Dispensing errors such as incorrect drugs or improper dosages are partly attributable to increasing workloads of pharmacists. Some drugstore chains schedule pharmacists to work twelve-hour shifts rather than have two pharmacists overlap. Moreover, there is the rate of prescriptions to be filled per hour per day. When the workload is increased, prescription errors also increase.

Another facet of the problem is that pharmacists are seeking and gaining the authority to counsel patients and modify prescriptions. Pharmacists claim that patients need monitoring more often than physicians can provide it. Twenty-one states have given pharmacists the authority to initiate or modify drug treatment as long as the physician agrees. Eckerd Drug is directing its pharmacists towards counseling. Most states have laws regarding counseling, pharmacy licensing, and electronic transmission of prescription data; presently there are no laws regulating Internet pharmacy practices. Some online pharmacies have been targeted by regulators for selling drugs without adequate prescriptions.

REVCO BLUNDERS

Revco was one of the largest drugstore chains in the United States with 2,000 store units in 1988. Yet, despite years of success, the company approached bankruptcy. Revco made a decision to become private, and this involved a leveraged buyout. Revco generated a huge debt in an effort to buy back the company's stock.

Resources were severely strained by the large interest payments. Cost slashing on employee training and inventory led to frequent stock-outs and disgruntled customers. To illustrate, stores would stock only one toaster or one microwave. As a result Revco lost its merchandise focus as one stopgap measure after another was employed. Finally in 1997, CVS acquired the chain.

REXALL BLUNDERS

Louis K. Liggett established the first nationally successful wholesaler-voluntary chain in 1903. Liggett was at first a wholesaler but later entered manufacturing. The most successful features that attracted independent retailers in the Rexall voluntary chain were the private-label Rexall brand and national advertising support. In the past, Rexall granted many other benefits to independent drugstores, such as gaining a national image with a relatively small investment and economies of scale in group purchasing. Moreover, the popularity and recognition of Rexall was much like McDonald's.

The wholesaler-voluntary chain organization failed by 1977 because Rexall was limited in the amount of control that could be exercised over independent retail outlets. Consumers wanted to patronize stores with modern decors and facilities. The days of the soda and lunch fountains were over; the Rexall organization was not able to influence the members of the voluntary chain in broadening their merchandise assortment. The overall image of the Rexall chain was tarnished. Customer loyalty declined at a rapid rate. As a result, royalty fees were affected by poorly performing individual stores.

WEBB'S CITY BLUNDERS

Webb's City was founded in 1925 by "Doc" Webb and during its time period was known as "The World's Most Unusual Drugstore." The heart of Webb's City was its drugstore, but it was a giant complex of more than seventy stores in a seven-block area. Included were a beauty shop; supermarket; clothing, hardware, and furniture stores and even gasoline stations. For some years everything was sold for cash and only prescription items were delivered free of charge.

James Earl "Doc" Webb was the P. T. Barnum of specialty-store retailing. Markups were so low and promotional expenses so high that when expansion was necessary cash was not available. One of Webb's innovations was the express checkout line for customers with ten or fewer items. Another innovation was a free check-cashing service, but losses from bad checks were high.

The success of Webb's City was based largely on its location in St. Petersburg, Florida. The area was populated by a larger than average number of elderly citizens who desired to patronize an interesting complex to spend their pension money. Prices were extraordinarily low, and "Doc" Webb put on an entertaining show. It was not unusual for circus acrobats to perform at the store. Retailing was fun for "Doc" Webb, which translated into fun for the shopper as well.

Eventually, many customers charged items and wanted delivery. Cash flow became a constant problem. The days of high promotional costs not supported by profits were coming to a close, and the store began to falter in 1974. Store operational costs were mounting, and control over expenditures was needed. "Doc" Webb was a showman and could not adapt to competitive forces. Webb's City closed its doors in 1979.

SUCCESS DOES NOT GUARANTEE CONTINUED SUCCESS

Walgreens, CVS, and Rite Aid made mistakes but were able to survive because they maintained a respectable batting average. The independent drugstore, on the other hand, grew complacent with success and developed a status quo mentality. Once the independent drugstore was the social hub of society and the pharmacist a highly respected member of the social structure. Today the independent drugstore is becoming an endangered species.

The independent drugstore was slow to realize advantages of scrambled merchandising. The cherished old soda fountain occupied store space that could have been more productive. Store modernization was placed on the back burner. This lack of adaptive strategies and the complacency with success was to make the weaknesses of the independent drugstore glaring.

The independents' lack of cost focus placed them at a disadvantage in competing with large chains stores. The financial productivity of each foot of store selling space was not a primary concern. Moreover, for cost and other reasons, the independents were unable to profit from the use of technology for day-to-day management. In contrast, Walgreens, CVS, and Rite Aid are all profiting from modern technology, a cost focus, and the development of new business formats.

MANAGING CHANGE

Retail drugstore institutions live in world of change. Three of the largest retail drug chains, CVS, Rite Aid, and JC Penney (Eckerd and Thrift), have grown through acquisitions, resulting in the decline of regional chains and independents. The aging of the population bodes well for the growth of pharmacy sales. Americans over sixty use fifteen prescriptions per year. The discovery of new drugs has also made a major impact on sales. Pharmacies operated by Wal-Mart, Kmart, and supermarket chains have radically changed the character of competition in the drug trade along with pressure from HMOs and third-party payers to decrease prescription profit margins.

The variables of innovation, store image, market segmentation strategies, and the use of physical and human resources have changed and will continue to change even more as competitive patterns evolve. Consumer satisfaction becomes an important target as drugstores change their merchandise mix to include greeting cards, photography supplies, paper products, ATMs, phone cards, and food departments. Store image has been modified to express one-stop shopping to save customers time. Market segmentation strategies have been especially effective, with Walgreens targeting the elderly market and Eckerd targeting women. The establishment of drive-through pharmacies has been an effective utilization of physical resources by Walgreens and others. Medicine Shoppe has successfully used franchises to develop its operation. There are three factors that will have an impact on drugstores in the future. First is an increase in low-profit managed-care prescriptions. Walgreens, Rite Aid, CVS, and Eckerd have strong affiliations with managed-care providers. Second is the declining reimbursement rates of Medicaid prescriptions, and third is the replacement of high margin generic drugs with newer branded products.

Moreover, the drugstore industry must respond to such forces as slow market growth, private branding, and higher costs. Drug chains are confronted with increased competition as convenience-food-store chains establish in-store pharmacies. Market share has eroded as discount stores and supermarkets compete with drugstores. Price, location, store atmosphere, and service are the key ways for drugstore retailers to differentiate themselves in order to gain a competitive advantage.

3

Specialty Clothing Stores: Masters of Market Segmentation

Customer-Driven Strategies

- Development of precise customer segments
- Image development with physical store attributes and fixtures
- Development of quality store-label merchandise
- Appeals to cross-shopping behavior
- State-of-the-art information systems
- High level customer service
- Strategic positioning strategies
- Attention to style, color, and fashion
- Use of new store formats
- Talented work force

Specialty Clothing Store Mistakes

- Use of market-driven rather than customer-driven strategies
- Delay in grasping changes in consumer demographics
- Slow realization of "dress down" consumer habits
- Slow realization of Internet selling potential
- Not recognizing target market shifts
- Too-rapid expansion
- Unappealing merchandise

Specialty clothing stores have been able to apply the concepts of market segmentation to changing customer preferences and attitudes. This is important since the average per capita expenditure on clothing in America is $700, and there is much competition for this expenditure. Consumers enhance their self-image by purchasing clothing as symbols and tend to shop in stores that have atmosphere, status, sales and service personnel—and that makes them feel comfortable.

Specialty clothing stores run the gamut in target marketing from consumers purchasing Gucci or Anne Klein branded items to those who make purchases of private brands in Kmart. Many retailers have developed their stores as brand names to take advantage of market segmentation and to broaden their product mix. For example, Gap, Banana Republic, Ann Taylor, and others have entered the health and beauty aids market with their own brand-name products. These retailers draw shoppers who know and trust their brands and are therefore able to extend their product lines with little or no advertising expenditures.

Store image is a composite attitude that consumers in a particular market segment have about a retail store. The personality of the store is the combination of perceptions, emotions, and attitudes of consumers toward the store's various characteristics. Market position is the sum of images that consumers have about a retail store. These impressions are based on merchandise assortment, ambience, personal communications, and internal and external nonpersonal communications. These factors are combined to develop a favorable store image to attract the consumer. Specialty clothing stores have identified target customer groups and are masters of market segmentation.

By using market segmentation, the stores can adopt a micro-merchandising strategy to take advantage of controlling their inventory while satisfying the immediate needs of their target market. Specialty chains keep inventory for an average of six to seven weeks. Micro-merchandising, which involves analyzing stock-keeping units, helps retailers maximize product performance. The retailers can focus on their customers' purchasing traits on a store-by-store basis. Through the use of technology, the retailer can measure the rate of sales to determine replenishment of merchandise.

Clothing stores can be adversely affected by seasonality or a decline in the popularity of a particular fashion. The fashion cycle in recent years is growing shorter in both women's and men's clothing. There is a trend toward a casual look and "dressing down" which means less money spent on apparel.

Five key ingredients are important for success or failure among specialty clothing stores: innovation, target market segmentation, image development, physical store decor, and human resources—which if implemented appropriately should lead to consumer satisfaction.

Location is a given. Retailers such as Gap and the Limited are returning to downtown areas for their store chains, recognizing that a neighborhood store is better at meeting customer needs than stores in large malls. Yet these retailers recognize problems such as parking shortages and less customer traffic in the evenings and on weekends.

Innovation in specialty clothing store retailing developed when the Limited redefined how its stores should operate. Gap targeted consumers who desired conservative and basic apparel of high quality. Lane Bryant targeted large-size women. Leslie Wexner, founder of the Limited, has been both a visionary and a people motivator. Wexner has been credited with a great ability to motivate top level managers to implement changes in strategies and policies with enthusiasm. The Limited changed the physical environment of Lerner's by putting in marble floors, taking out the tile floors, and using a peaches and cream decor. Banana Republic's decor reflects originality, creativity, and the personality of its location. Banana Republic presents tailored sportswear for men and women seeking upscale European styling. Its prices are moderate compared with designer stores but still attractive to upscale customers. Its products can be compared to Barney's New York and Bergdorf Goodman. Finally, L.L. Bean has been successful in developing an image for customer satisfaction in the post-purchase phase.

LIFESTYLE MARKET SEGMENTATION

Market segmentation and lifestyle analysis are two important concepts that, when used properly, can maximize store profitability. Lifestyle analysis is composed of consumers' activities, interests, and opinions. Activities are classified as sports, work, entertainment, and hobbies. Interests include job, home, family, fashion, and food. Opinions are classified as to social issues, politics, education, business, and the future. Demographic factors, such as age, occupation, geography, and stage in the family life cycle, are also used with activities, interests, and opinions for identifying market segments.

Linked together in the retailer strategic decision process are positioning strategies, retail market segmentation strategies, and the identification of customer patronage motives. The retailer must identify a specific consumer segment and learn as much as possible about those buyers' behavior. Positioning involves defining the store type to merchandise lines, precisely how the store will complete, and how to communicate so that consumers understand the unique value offered. Positioning establishes a high level of consumer loyalty and differentiates a retailer from its competitors. For example, the Limited offers clothes for fashion-conscious women from ages twenty to forty while the Limited Express offers trendy clothing for women fifteen to twenty-five years of age and Lerner's sells budget apparel for young women. The Limited and Victoria's Secret are known for fashion, innovation, and image.

Identifying the target market often necessitates changes in the retailing mix—that is, the way a firm uses its merchandise assortment, prices, services, and promotional efforts to cultivate particular customers. Retailers need to adjust goods and services, communications, and physical distribution to the needs of the market they want to serve. When the baby boom ended, Lane Bryant, a ladies specialty store, reassessed its goods and services mix and eliminated maternity departments from new stores. Lane Bryant then decided to target women who needed large-size clothing. It took the Limited nearly two years to open its first 100 Bath & Body Works stores after the concept had been tested and refined, its potential proven, and the market opportunity recognized.

Another aspect of retail market segmentation and lifestyle analysis is consumer patronage motives. The most important patronage motives are price, merchandise selection, purchasing convenience, store services, merchandise quality, customer treatment by store personnel, and store reputation and status. Consumers patronize retail stores because of their proximity, in-store shopping convenience, the wide selection of merchandise, and the particular branded merchandise they carry.

The retail store choice decision can be one of high involvement or low involvement. For example, a man's or lady's suit to be worn for a job interview may have a high relevance because of its price, complex features, large differences between alternatives, and the high perceived risk of making a wrong decision. In contrast, the purchase of a T-shirt might be regarded as a low involvement decision. There is not much risk if one brand is purchased rather than another.

According to Reynolds, Darden, and Martin in a classic article, the store-loyal consumer is a potential profitable market segment toward which retailers may desire to focus their efforts; consumer loyalty is a dominant construct for examining repeat purchasing behavior; and lifestyle characteristics are a useful basis for describing store loyal behavior.[1] Consumers engage in a decision process approach for store choice as well as for product and brand choices. These decisions may be of a complex or a routine nature. Demographic and life characteristics as well as other purchase characteristics, such as perceptions of store attributes, lead to general opinions and activities related to shopping and search behavior.

Every function performed by the retailer has some impact on the customer. In this competitive environment retailers must focus their efforts on strengthening their strategic position. Manufacturers and wholesalers can help by providing product augmentations to the specialty retailers' carefully defined groups of consumers. Although the Limited's Victoria's Secret market has successfully penetrated its target market, mistakes can be made. In an effort to broaden this market, Cacique was launched in

1988, and it has duplicated the Victoria's Secret market. Each market segment should be measurable, and this means that the market potential should be of significant size. Although a market existed, it was not that large or distinct enough from the market already served by Victoria's Secret for Cacique to be successful. Meanwhile, Gap Body has emerged as a direct competitor of Victoria's Secret.

MARKET STRUCTURE

Since clothing specialty stores carry a narrow but deep assortment of merchandise and target selective segments, these stores are able to maintain better selections and sales expertise than their competitors, which are frequently department stores. This allows specialty clothing stores to control inventory management and exercise a certain amount of flexibility. Some clothing stores have elaborate fixtures and upscale merchandise for affluent customers, while others have a discount orientation for price-sensitive consumers. Sales per average selling square in these specialty stores can average anywhere from $169 in a Lerner New York store to $684 in Bath & Body Works. Service is especially noteworthy in such chains as Talbots, Gap, and Eddie Bauer. Exceptional service has also developed a customer base in the Ann Taylor chain and contributed largely to its reversal of financial difficulties.

A new type of specialty store known as the category killer is gaining strength. A category killer is very large in square feet of shopping area. There is an enormous selection of merchandise at all price points. The Limited and Gap are examples of specialty clothing chains that are opening new category killer stores to complement existing ones.

Table 3.1 lists the major clothing store chains. Despite a contraction of some chains, the total number of stores has increased. For example, the Limited's Intimate Brands will close the entire Cacique lingerie chain, and employees will be absorbed into Victoria's Secret and Bath and Body Works chains. In contrast, Gap's Old Navy and Ann Taylor chains expect to add stores.

The big change in clothing store chains has been online stores. Shopping over the Internet is growing, with more than 100 visual shopping malls, each of which contains a large number of stores. A big winner has been Gap, with standard styles appropriate to online shopping and Eddie Bauer with staples like turtlenecks and slacks. Eddie Bauer offers a virtual dressing room where consumers can put together outfits and change colors on different items with a click of a mouse.

Chain apparel stores are able to have more stock-turns than independents or department stores. Operating services can be standardized to decreased costs. Centralized purchasing of fashion goods in volume performed by specialists generates better purchasing terms and therefore

Table 3.1

Selected Specialty Apparel Organizations

Limited Umbrella	Net Sales 1998	Number of Units 1998
Limited Stores	$757 million	551
Limited Express	$1.356 billion	702
Limited Too	$377 million	319
Victoria's Secret	$1.829 billion	829
Lerner New York	$940 million	643
Lane Bryant	$933 million	730
Structure	$610 million	532
Henri Bendel	$40 million	1
Galyan's Trading Company	$220 million	14
Bath & Body Works	$1.272 billion	1061
Abercrombie & Fitch[1]	$156 million	
Other	$857 million	
Total	*$9.347 billion*	*5,382*
Gap Umbrella		
The Gap		1109
Gap Kids		640
Banana Republic		292
Old Navy		407
Total	*$9.05 billion*	*2448*
Off Price		
Loehmanns	$443.3 million	69
Marshalls (TJX Companies, Inc.)	$3.455 billion	475
TJ Maxx (TJX Companies, Inc.)	$3.741 billion	604

52

Independents		
Charming Shoppes	$1.035 billion	1135[2]
Fashion Bug (Charming Shoppes)	Info. Not Available	1090
Ann Taylor	$911.9 million	365
Talbots	$1.142 billion	638
Corporate Affiliation		
Plums (Dayton Hudson)[3]	$3.2 billion	63
McKids (Sears)[4]	$23.14 billion	845
Pinstripes Petites (Sears)	$23.14 billion	845
Brooks Brothers (Marks & Spencer)	$27.55 million[5]	191
Eddie Bauer (Spiegel)	$1.710 billion	555
Direct Retailing		
Spiegel	$587[6]	N/A
L.L. Bean		

1. Abercrombie & Fitch was split off effective May 19, 1998, via a tax-free exchange offer.
2. Includes 1,090 Fashion Bug and 45 Fashion Bug Plus Stores.
3. Total clothing sales in Dayton Hudson department stores.
4. Total number of and net sales for Full-Line Sears stores.
5. Converted from British pounds at exchange rate of 1.64, as noted in Marks & Spencer Annual Report 1998.
6. Net sales of Spiegel catalogue alone.

achieves reduced costs. These stores have greater sales per square foot than independents and target precise market segments better than Kmart or traditional department stores. Fashion Bug, a chain with about 2,000 stores, has grown by cultivating its target customers, generally women in the workforce with a family income of $30,000 to $40,000 and whose husbands are most likely blue-collar workers. The newer stores are located in small towns and emerging suburbs. Fashion Bug maintains low prices by stocking private-label merchandise, which accounts for about 75 percent of sales. Fashion Bug stores compete by carrying a wide assortment of blazers, dresses, skirts, sweaters, and jumpsuits. Talbot's, with more than 600 stores and twenty-five catalogs, sells classic apparel, shoes, and accessories for women, boys, and girls. Its private label collection includes sportswear, career separates, casual wear, and special occasion classics. The company also sells infant and children's clothing through its catalog, which has an annual circulation of 52 million worldwide, and in Talbot's Kids and Babies retail stores.

The specialty apparel market is fragmented into various consumer segments based upon demographics, shopping patterns, fashion preferences, and lifestyle changes. There was, in the 1980s and 1990s, an increased number of women in the labor force. The men's apparel market began to grow in the 1990s. The Limited's Structure led the way. Private labels have increased in popularity. Sales of apparel through catalogs have been lucrative in the past for Sears, Roebuck and Montgomery Ward. Today retailers like L.L. Bean and Spiegel are the leaders in this type of retailing. This market segment is better educated with a higher income.

CONSUMER BEHAVIOR AND CROSS SHOPPING

A new consumer behavior phenomenon has developed that has had a profound impact on specialty store and department store retailing: cross shopping. Cross shopping means a blouse purchase at Gap and a pair of jeans purchased at Kmart. The new consumer is better educated and has developed clearer buying objectives that facilitate cross shopping. Higher educational levels coupled with higher incomes allow consumers to spend more time assessing the quality of products before buying. This accounts, in part, for the popularity of off-price retailers such as Loehmann's and Marshalls. Cross-shopping behavior accounts for the purchase of a virtually look-alike turtleneck sweater at Wal-Mart instead of at Banana Republic. Gap, with its Old Navy division, is the first specialty apparel retailer to make a concentrated attempt to solve the cross-shopping challenge by taking market share away from the mass merchants and discounters like Wal-Mart, Target, Sears, and JC Penney. A caveat would be that Old Navy would also take away sales from The Gap.

Consumers want to purchase store-label fashion merchandise. This was not always the case, as in previous years consumers had expressed preference for manufacturers' national brands. Mass merchants like JC Penney have reduced their inventories of designer labels such as Ralph Lauren and have placed their own labels on their clothing. The reason is that many designer-labeled products are now available at much lower prices in stores such as Target, thus encouraging cross-shopping behavior. Specialty stores are in competition with national manufacturer brands. Since many mass merchants and discounters carry designer label brands, cross-shopping behavior has been accentuated.

The bulk of the population is middle aged and growing older. As consumers grow older, they have more self-confidence, they do less impulse shopping and are less fashion oriented. This diminished fashion orientation is reflected, in part, with "dress down" work-days in industry. The result has been a growing polarization that favors the low-margin, mass-volume retailers on one end and high-price, haute-service boutiques offering one-of-a-kind or unusual items on the other. Unless addressed, cross shopping, or polarization, spells difficulties for Gap, the Limited, Benetton, Ann Taylor, and other merchants in the middle.

Specialty clothing stores are the fastest growing sector in retailing. Mass merchandiser Sears opened McKids and Pinstriper Petites, and Dayton-Hudson opened Plums to compete with specialty retailers. Consumers want name brands in deeper assortments. Specialty apparel stores such as Gap offer more personalized service in a small-store environment. In an effort to further segment the market, Gap opened Gap Kids and Baby Gap and the Limited opened Limited Express and Limited Too.

FASHION AND CONSUMER BEHAVIOR

Various ideas about the diffusion of fashions have been advanced. At one time there was some evidence that fashion trickled down from higher to lower status levels, but the advent of rap music and clothing associated with this movement has caused a reversal in part of this theory as some clothing styles trickle up. Social status should be considered, for fashion leadership in the past has been associated with people who have high status. Reference groups such as celebrities and business executives are also influencing variables. For new clothing items to become fads or fashionable, they must be adopted by some group with acknowledged respectability.

Many fashions have come from Rome or Paris; and in the United States, New York and Los Angeles have become fashion centers. This is especially true in regard to lifestyles, sports clothing, and apparel for recreational and leisure activities. The lag between urban and rural areas has been closing with the development of communications and transportation technology.

As specialty apparel retailers plan their strategy, factors such as the fashion cycle stages, market appropriateness, lifestyle implications, and competitive positions must be considered. The risk associated with selling fashion apparel comes from the uncertainty of the consumers' degree of acceptance and the duration of this acceptance of the fashion. An important force driving the consumer is the continual search for newness. The fashion cycle—introduction, accelerated development, and decline—provides guidance for retailers when planning strategy.

THE LIMITED: UNDERSTANDING THE CUSTOMER

The Limited reaches its markets through Victoria's Secret, Bath & Body Works (the intimate brands group), Limited stores, Limited Express, Limited Too, Lerner New York, Lane Bryant, and Structure with a total of more than 5,300 stores and 28 million square feet of selling space. The company is a $9 billion specialty retailer that sells women's, men's, and children's apparel; lingerie, personal care products, and sporting goods through retail stores and two catalogs. In 1998, the Limited announced the closing of Cacique and Henri Bendel (with the exception of only one store) and the establishment of Abercrombie & Fitch as an independent public company.

The Limited, a women's ready-to-wear store chain, started in 1963 in Columbus, Ohio. The store name denoted its limited assortment of merchandise of women's sportswear, which it carried only in its first two years of operation. A reason for the success of the Limited has been its emphasis on fashion, which is coordinated and presented as a total look, beginning at the windows and encompassing the entire store. Displays vary with the season and are changed weekly in each store. In the 1980s, the Limited acquired the 800-store Lerner chain, which sells lower-priced women's clothing; the 200-store Lane Bryant chain, which specializes in clothes for large women; Victoria's Secret, a chain of 545 lingerie shops; and the Henri Bendel upscale clothing store in New York City. The Limited's objective is to build leadership brands.

The Limited's problems were the result of poor implementation of upscale market segmentation strategies. Cacique was presented as a high-quality lingerie store for elegant, sophisticated women over age twenty-five. However, it was difficult to differentiate Cacique from Victoria's Secret, and the Limited made the wise decision to close Cacique, allowing the company to concentrate its resources on the brand that has the greatest potential for return. Another example is Henri Bendel selling fashion apparel, cosmetics, accessories, and gifts for today's modern women over age thirty-five with a high income. Henri Bendel, an upscale specialty store, had only six outlets and did not fit with the company's mall-based shops.

Among the Limited's successes have been Victoria's Secret and Bath & Body Works. Victoria's Secret, a retailer of women's intimate and fashion apparel, concentrates its resources on a market segment that has a good potential for return and a loyalty to brands. Victoria's Secret dominates the lingerie category with new product introductions each year supported by television advertising. This position is then reinforced by a catalog, Internet selling, and an active direct marketing program. Victoria's Secret has penetrated a middle-market segment for elegant intimate apparel, foundations, and products for personal care and gifts. Bath & Body Works also segments that middle female market concerned with a courtly, polished, sophisticated appearance. Its products have penetrated the gift market, and the store's service-oriented strategy has facilitated this growth.

The Limited is in the process of reinventing and reorganizing its women's apparel divisions, namely Limited Express, Lane Bryant, and Lerner New York. Lane Bryant has a presence in many malls, and it is doubtful that there will be growth for this division in the future. The original Limited stores offered women's sportswear such as blouses with Peter Pan collars, madras shorts, and Shetland sweaters. Customers of the Limited are typically young women on the forward edge of fashion, spending a higher percentage of their disposable income on clothing. These customers shop for a total fashion image and are influenced by social forces, especially reference groups like professional organizations.

Limited Too has emerged as the leader in its category. Close to its customers, it has expanded by launching a preteen catalog. Abercrombie & Fitch has a defined target market and remains true to it. Founded in 1892 to outfit safari hunters such as Teddy Roosevelt, Abercrombie & Fitch was an upscale menswear chain when the Limited bought the name in 1988. The Limited introduced a new format: casual, classic American clothes that would appeal to customers of all ages. Abercrombie & Fitch was the first of the Limited's apparel division to create its own design team. Abercrombie & Fitch has a catalog/magazine to promote and sell its products. Abercrombie sells most of its products at full price and resists sales except four times a year for clearance to react to changing consumer tastes.

The Limited is concerned with the deployment of human resources and motivates its sales associates and the sales management team. The company has a department whose major function is to develop contests each season for the store's personnel to obtain maximum sales. The company has also been able to integrate competence and results into a performance management system for managers. A number of top executives have been lured away from competing specialty chains, and it would appear the Limited has attracted the human resources to effect change. In fact, the company has an active change agenda that includes creating a new governance model, leveraging the core capabilities of its brands, investing in core processes and business disciplines , and vertically integrating business disciplines to support the strategic business units and the internationalization of the business. To implement this agenda, the company invests in developing successful leaders, and manager's performance is evaluated on the strategic business unit's objectives. The Limited's employees are among the highest paid in retailing, and expectations for performance by both managers and sales associates are high.

Leslie Wexner founded the Limited on a philosophy that a specialty store should focus on a narrower, more limited assortment of merchandise than was traditional up to that time. This concept helped redefine specialty retailing. Leslie Wexner is perhaps one of the most visionary merchants in retail trade in the 20th century. He was one of the first merchants to recognize that larger stores would have higher productivity than traditional size stores. Wexner has the ability to identify the potential of a niche market and either to develop a new retail format or take a failing enterprise and reverse its fortunes. When first acquired, Lerner's, Lane Bryant, Victoria's Secret, and Abercrombie & Fitch were failing institutions and needed revitalization. Wexner is also not afraid to close under-performing stores. Since 1995 he has closed 213 stores. His philosophy is that fashion changes and we have to recognize what works.

The Limited is not without problems. The Limited Express lost its focus and thought of its customers in generalized terms somewhere between eighteen and forty years of age. The fashions floundered, and the clothing got boring. Lerner New York changed the chain's target from young women to those in their late thirties and forties, an age group that few apparel retailers had pursued. The chain developed a new look that included a strong merchandising tie-in with the excitement of the New York fashion industry while retaining its traditional budget price points. With more than 600 stores, averaging 7,700 square feet, Lerner New York is the Limited's biggest store.

Lerner has been a victim of consumer cross-shopping behavior as some of its customers' shop at Wal-Mart and Kmart and are able to make purchases at lower prices. The Limited must solve its internal problems of divisions cannibalizing each other's sales, such as the Limited and Express, while taking advantage of market niches that had not existed before, as in the case of Victoria's Secret or Bath & Body Works. Other competitors such as Talbots, Ann Taylor, and Eddie Bauer also present threats. The Limited's strength is in developing new innovative ideas. The Limited has initiated test-marketing lipstick and eye pencils in some Bath & Body Works stores and is developing a line of Victoria's Secret cosmetics. The Limited has had merchandising problems as a result of its sourcing and distribution system that stressed speed of delivery. As a result, quality began to slip, and there were pricing problems such as merchandise being discounted the day it was put in the store.

GAP: LIFESTYLE MARKET SEGMENTATION

Gap, an $9-billion-dollar company with 2,448 stores, is a specialty retailer selling apparel under five trade names: Gap, Banana Republic, Old Navy, Gap Kids, and Baby Gap. Gap's name is compared with great brands like Coca-Cola and Disney because of its market acceptance. Gap is an international chain. Banana Republic is at the high end of the company's price and fashion spectrum while Gap is in the middle and Old Navy at the lower end. There has always been a danger that a blurred image in the minds of consumers would develop between the offerings of Gap and Old Navy. Although the physical facilities are different, the merchandise offerings could present a serious problem if not carefully monitored.

There are similarities between Gap and the Limited in that they both have their own branded products, but there are also differences. Gap sells a simple, practical, conservative product in contrast to the Limited, which stresses fashion. Gap is a master of the basics and carries merchandising items in large assortments of sizes and colors, necessitating a significant inventory prior to peak selling seasons. Gap does not sell anything that is not available elsewhere. Gap needs to place orders in advance and is vulnerable to demand and pricing shifts. In contrast, the Limited is on the cutting edge of each fashion that is offered.

Banana Republic is one of the success stories of the 1990s. Banana Republic was acquired in 1983 and was originally a two-store chain with a small catalog business. The company became known for the multi-pocketed photojournalist's vest and the traveler's raincoat.

Gap opened its first store in San Francisco in 1969. The store sold Levi's jeans and discounted record albums. Gap Kids was added in 1986, and Old Navy emerged in 1994. Old Navy stores are located in strip and power centers and are stocked with large selections of stylish value-priced apparel, accessories, and shoes. Old Navy competes primarily with Sears and Target. Old Navy stores are decorated with exposed pipes and raw concrete floors. The stores have listening booths and old grocery-store refrigerator cases stocked with shrink-wrapped clothing. In addition to apparel, the store carries personal-care items, home goods, paper products, candy, and packaged foods.

Donald Fisher, founder of Gap, revolutionized retailing in terms of merchandising concepts and product development. Gap's objective is to become a global brand. The Gap brand is synonymous with casual sportswear and is identified with khaki pants, denim jeans, woven denim shirts, and the one-pocket T-shirt. Speed and convenience are the key ingredients for the success of the Gap store, in addition to its location, the quantity of merchandise displayed per square foot, customer service, and brand image. Salespeople at Gap have relatively little training compared to other retail chains; they are paid less and get no sales commission because shoppers looking for speed and convenience do not want this type of service. Gap has created the sale of ordinary clothes to a powerful status. The results are higher price points and more sales per store.

Gap and its divisions are masters of lifestyle market segmentation. Banana Republic's lifestyle approach promotes versatile apparel that enables its customers to live simply and comfortably. Old Navy makes shopping exciting and fun; high quality, value-priced clothing is offered for the entire family. The physical environment is designed to evoke a classic, timeworn motif as floor-to-ceiling shelving units display products in vertical color ranges or in coordinated groupings. Steel racks on wheels serve as freestanding floor fixtures. A bazaar-like atmosphere and many references to the past make shopping a memorable experience. Old Navy is discount shopping that appeals to people who can afford better-known merchandise.

Gap is an innovator as Banana Republic experiments with opening single-sex units as well as moving into areas such as footwear and home products. Gap stores have been making a greater effort to develop brand differentiation and customer loyalty with brand development in many merchandise areas. Success has come from narrowing merchandise assortment to present a sharp and distinct viewpoint. Gap has reacted to demographic growth markets by opening Gap Kids and Baby Gap shops. The Internet has been another strategy used by Gap to attract shoppers who desire the basics in apparel. Since 1997, Gap has had one of the most detailed Websites among apparel retailers. The online store offers more than 100 styles of men's and women's Gap clothing and accessories and updates its merchandise offerings every month. Gap is locating some of its new stores on main street in cities that once would have been considered too small. The objective is to attract those consumers who desire the ambience and convenience of a shopping experience that reminds them of a small town or an old-fashioned city neighborhood. In June 1998, Gap-To-Go opened in New York City on the theory that buying clothing should be as easy as going to a fast food franchise. Gap-To-Go lists twenty-one basic Gap items for which you can fax in your order and have the merchandise delivered to your home or office by the end of the day. In addition, Gap was among the first specialty-clothing stores to sell merchandise online in late 1997. It has been estimated that 1999 Gap sales resulting from online retailing will range anywhere from $50 million to $100 million. Although this is a small amount of its annual sales, future income potential is great.

The success story behind Gap stores is a chain immersed in a culture where all activities are aimed at bringing the customer in. Corporate culture has become an effective marketing tool for Gap. Gap designs its own clothes and has made its store label a major competitor of manufacturers brands. Gap's challenge is to be able to compete with the Limited. Gap uses advertising and marketing to promote its products and build its image, spending more than $300 million a year on advertising.

BROOKS BROTHERS: WALKING A TIGHTROPE

Brooks Brothers was founded in 1818 and has the distinction of being one of America's oldest clothing stores. Theodore Roosevelt, Ulysses S. Grant, and Woodrow Wilson wore Brooks Brothers suits when taking their oaths of office. Authors such as Ernest Hemingway, F. Scott Fitzgerald, and Somerset Maugham depicted characters in their novels who wore Brooks Brothers suits. Male movie stars who have patronized Brooks Brothers include Fred Astaire, Burt Lancaster, and Gary Cooper. Female movie stars such as Elizabeth Tayor, Katharine Hepburn, and Audrey Hepburn have purchased dressing gowns, slacks, and sweaters among other items at Brooks Brothers.

Brooks Brothers has vertically integrated and manufactures many of its own suits and shirts. The conservatism that has characterized apparel made by Brooks Brothers is one of the factors that has made the firm a legend. Personal service is outstanding. It is not uncommon for generations of a family to patronize Brooks Brothers and deal with the same salesperson. Customers feared that this conservatism and personal service would end when the firm was purchased by Julius Garfinckel & Company of Washington, D.C., in 1946. The firm's culture continued but many changes were resisted by loyal customers. The tradition for the most part continued but production efficiencies and other measures were instituted to allow Brooks Brothers to compete effectively against the downtown department stores and the suburban shopping centers. In 1988, Marks and Spencer, a firm based in Great Britain, purchased Brooks Brothers.

The perception that Brooks Brothers sells only three-button "sack suits" with a center-vested jacket and foxy fit needs to change for the store to survive. Brooks Brothers now offers more two-button versions, suits with a tapered fit, and suits cut for athletic men with broader upper bodies. The installation of escalators in its flagship store on Madison Avenue in New York jarred many customers. These older customers liked things the way they were remembered in the past. However, the store still remains its signature wood-and-brass look. The challenge confronting Brooks Brothers is how to attract new customers, including women and younger adults, without losing loyal customers. The flagship store has lost customers to stores that offer more variety in clothing lines such as Paul Stuart of New York.

Marks and Spencer want to change the image of Brooks Brothers to enlarge the market. The store's profits have increased and new stores have opened. After years of selling its famous button-down oxford shirts it added purple gingham shirts and turquoise striped ties to the product line. Once the average age of the customer was fifty-five and now it is close to forty. Therefore, the merchandise has to appeal to a younger, more impulsive consumer. The salespeople are more receptive to the twenty-something customers. Aloofness has changed to a smile and a welcome. Employee-training programs are used to prepare a new customer-friendly salesperson. Female salespeople have been hired to attract female customers shopping for themselves and the men in their families.

Physical facilities have been refurbished to reflect better lighting and more open store fronts. Store layout and clothing displays have also been changed to group shirts and accessories together. More merchandise has been added in the stores to increase selection and present a one-stop shopping experience for its customers.

Brooks Brothers in the late 1990s concentrated on improving its product lines, customer service, and availability of merchandise. It had missed out on the trend for apparel to be worn on casual days or dress-down days. A transformation took place as khaki pants, casual shirts, and selection of brightly colored shirts and ties made the merchandise more appealing to fashionable male shoppers. Brooks Brothers has expanded and now has stores throughout the United States. Years ago Brooks Brothers was located downtown but now enclosed upscale shopping malls include its stores. Brooks Brothers is doing a balancing act with a brand franchise that has strong meaning to the professional person and upscale customer.

OFF-PRICE APPAREL RETAILERS: REACHING PRICE-CONSCIOUS SHOPPERS

Off-price apparel retailers such as T.J. Maxx, Marshalls, Syms, Filene's Basement, Burlington Coat Factory, and Loehmann's price their merchandise lower than their competitors in order to attract price-sensitive consumers. These prices-conscious shoppers want to purchase well-known brands of apparel but refuse to pay the high prices charged by department and specialty stores. Since the off-price retailers are frequently 30 to 40 percent below competitor's prices, store or private label brands would seem to serve as protection. Off-price retail outlets are typically located in freestanding sites along major suburban roads where rental costs are lower than mall-based department and specialty stores. Costs are also reduced by infrequent promotions compared to competitors.

Off-price retailers purchase closeouts and canceled orders in addition to regular seasonal merchandise. Off-price chains are less demanding than department stores in terms of advertising allowances, often do not advertise specific brands, do not return merchandise, and pay suppliers promptly.

In 1995, the TJX Companies, operator of off-price retailer T.J. Maxx, acquired Marshalls, previously owned by Melville Corporation, which was founded in 1923. Together T.J. Maxx and Marshalls account for more than half of the off-price industry. This gives TJX tremendous buying power and widens the pricing gap between TJX and department and specialty stores. Moreover, operating expenses such as payroll, benefits and advertising are also lowered. Together T.J. Maxx and Marshalls have more than 1,000 retail units. Marshalls was a 496-store chain when it was acquired. T.J. Maxx is the largest off-price apparel retailer in the United States offering brand-name family apparel, giftware, domestics, women's shoes, accessories, and fine jewelry at prices 20 to 60 percent below department store regular prices. The average T.J. Maxx store size is 29,000 square feet compared to Marshalls, which is 32,000 square feet. Marshalls, in addition to brand-name family apparel, giftware, domestics, and accessories, offers shoes for the entire family and a broader assortment of menswear. The TJX Companies, Inc., also owns Women's Apparel Ltd., which operates seventy-six off-price family apparel stores in Canada, and Home Goods, a chain of twenty-three off-price home fashion stores.

Marshalls carries men's suits and footwear but T.J. Maxx does not. While Marshalls sells costume jewelry, T.J. Maxx sells fine jewelry. In recent years T. J. Maxx has targeted lingerie, juniors and menswear as growth areas. Marshalls has learned the hard way that off-price retailers do not sell goods of lower quality at low prices. Marshalls has undergone a number of strategic changes including more aggressive markdowns, faster flow of fresh merchandise, better inventories and the elimination of point of sale events. This change has reestablished Marshalls' image of quality brand names, better layout of stores, and more attractive merchandise displays.

The off-price apparel chain is aimed at the low-income market segment with household incomes under $30,000. Sales are continuing to increase but at a much slower rate than in previous years. The decrease in sales growth has been due to overexpansion, competition from other retailers, and saturation of the market niche.

Other off-price retailers are owned and operated by independents or are divisions of major retail corporations. Although many off-price retailers are owned by small independents, most large off-price retailers are controlled by large retail chains. Examples include Loehmann's operated by Associated Dry Goods, owner of Lord & Taylor, and Designer Depot, controlled by Kmart. Factory outlets are also off-price retailers; they are owned by manufacturers and carry the manufacturer's surplus, discontinued, or irregular goods. Examples are Burlington Coat Factory Warehouse and the factory outlets of Levi Strauss and London Fog. These outlets are located in factory outlet malls. Gucci, Anne Klein, and Charles Jourdan have located in factory outlet malls offering merchandise at discounts of 40 to 60 percent off department store prices. Since consumers continually look for value, these factory outlets and off-price retailers are formidable competitors to traditional specialty apparel retailers, department stores, and discounters such as Kmart. Merchandising and expense control are the key factors in the success of off-price retailers. Many off-price retailers use state-of the-art technology for inventory management and distribution, store operations, and corporate administration.

DIRECT RETAILING: CHANGING LIFESTYLE VALUES

Many of the leading firms in the direct retailing of apparel are well-known retailers or manufacturers that have used direct retailing strategies to supplement their conventional strategies. They include Banana Republic, Victoria's Secret, JC Penney, Bloomingdale's, L.L. Bean, and Spiegel. Spiegel is the second largest catalog retailer in the United States after JC Penney. The company markets apparel, home furnishings, and other merchandise via its catalog and by computer. The company introduced a CD-ROM catalog in 1996, displaying more than 3,000 items. The CD-ROM catalog is the largest display of a single catalog retailer's merchandise in that format. Catalog sales are growing faster, compared with retailing as a whole. The average American receives about two catalogs a week. The real competition is coming from store retailers such as Abercrombie & Fitch that appeal to the high school and college market. Other retailers such as Banana Republic are adept at targeting well-defined customer market segments. Lands' End, a traditional direct retailer, may be among the first casualties. Spiegel is in difficulty, and L.L. Bean is trying to enlarge its target market as the competition accelerates.

Consumers who purchase apparel by mail are generally more style conscious and convenience oriented. The affluent customer has been the traditional target market for direct retailers, and this type of customer is also a target for electronic shopping. However, the increase in the affluent market segment—particularly among dual-income married couples—will most likely mean a continued increase in direct retailing sales volume from both catalogs and electronic shopping. The rise in affluence may decrease price sensitivity for consumers who are willing to make purchases from direct retailers. As affluent consumers feel more time constraints, they are more likely to want better quality goods and services.

The heart of the market for the two mail-order giants before the turn of the century, Montgomery Ward and Sears, Roebuck, was rural America. Farm families eagerly awaited the arrival of the catalog. A money-back guarantee was offered if the customer was not satisfied, and these mail-order giants became the most trusted names in retailing. The Sears catalog was to surpass Ward's and the Sears name was better known than the manufacturer's brands advertised in the catalog.

With urbanization, the importance of the rural market diminished. Although the catalog could reach all parts of the country, operating a mail-order business was especially difficult in periods of rising prices. Moreover, with the advent of the automobile, rural customers could make purchases from a variety of nearby stores. Another factor working against mail order was the growth of chain store retailers, some of which pursued a cost leadership strategy and achieved economies of scale through volume purchasing and could offer products at lower prices. Also, customers desired to see and try on merchandise before buying. Sears is no longer in the catalog business, and Ward has established specialty catalogs.

As the 21st century emerges there are a number of favorable conditions that are present to bring back the catalog:

• Consumers are more concerned with self-identity through the purchase of goods and therefore desire a broader product assortment than most retail stores can display.

• A higher proportion of dual-income families have less time to shop.

• There is a greater demand for specialty products and services that are not available to many consumers locally.

• More consumers have home computers to facilitate in-home shopping.

L.L. BEAN: PROFITING FROM NEW LIFE-STYLE TRENDS

Freeport, Maine, is the home of L.L. Bean, a firm specializing in the sale of sporting goods to hunting and fishing enthusiasts. The backbone of the L.L. Bean business has been the sale of its own boots and shoes. Originally, Bean designed a hunting shoe in 1913, and by the early 1920s sales passed the $100,000 a year mark. By 1937 sales reached $1 million .

Customer satisfaction is fundamental to L.L. Bean. The company refunds the purchase price on merchandise sold if the customer is not totally satisfied. The L.L. Bean organization values word-of-mouth referrals. L.L. Bean personally tests every item sold either in the retail store or catalog. More than 2 million people a year visit Freeport, Maine, a small village of 6,000 people, to make purchases at the store.

L.L. Bean's target market includes outdoor enthusiasts and the educated "preppie" type. During the 1960s, the recreation boom focused upon family camping and backpacking. Many young adults sought to return to nature and indulge in outdoor activities. Soon these customers wanted to wear their outdoor apparel and footwear for everyday purposes.

The lifestyle trend of voluntary simplicity contributed to L.L. Bean's growth. This lifestyle developed in the 1960s and 1970s and became more widely accepted in the 1980s. Consumers who adopt this lifestyle seek material simplicity, strive for self-actualization, and adopt an ecological ethic. Voluntary simplicity is marked by a new balance between inner and outer development and growth. It is a throwback to frugality and puritanical self-reliance. Outdoor activities such as camping, rafting, and fishing reflect a part of this lifestyle. Ecological awareness becomes paramount and so does the interconnection between people and natural resources. This new consciousness is concerned with the reduction of environmental pollution and is receptive to new products, such as bottled water, that preserve and maintain the natural environment.

Consumers desired value in their purchases. Customers wanted lighter weight, longer wear, extra comfort, more safety, and higher product performance. L.L. Bean responded to these new demand patterns. The store offers free clinics in hunter safety, fly fishing, game cooking, winter camping, whitewater canoeing, and other outdoor activities. Since 1995 sales have trailed off and therefore a new strategy has been developed. The Freeport Studio line targets the female executive who desires a casual look, offering dresses, skirts, and jewelry. Bean will need to be careful not to alienate its traditional customers. But competition has increased from Macy's and Banana Republic and others as they join the crowded catalog market. In addition six to eight L.L. Bean stores will be opened from Baltimore to Boston.

SPIEGEL: A NEW QUESTION MARK

Joseph Spiegel founded Spiegel in 1865 as a quality retail furniture store in downtown Chicago. By the early 1900s, Spiegel began issuing catalogs to appeal to the large number of lower-income immigrants who settled in Chicago. Spiegel pioneered the concept of the no-money-down credit plan. Sales were strong until the 1970s when Spiegel began to lose market share to Sears and Ward's, which were better known and where customers could return the merchandise to the store. At the time, Spiegel targeted low-income consumers who were situated in small rural communities in the South and Midwest.

As a result of declining sales and market share, Spiegel changed its marketing strategies and selected a different target market. The new target market was the upscale consumer, particularly the female, engaged in the workforce or in activities outside the home, who was fashion, quality, and brand conscious. Spiegel aimed to target a younger, better-educated customer employed in a managerial or professional position, with a higher income than other catalog users. Competition was primarily from L.L. Bean and Neiman-Marcus. Spiegel's repositioning meant replacing its merchandise assortment with high-fashion home furnishings and apparel. Spiegel has also gone after precise segments of the target market. For example, Spiegel received a 1991 Gold Award from the American Catalog Awards for placing a plus-sized woman on the catalog cover. Spiegel specializes in satisfying the apparel needs of working women. Women are targeted according to lifestyle analysis: Starting Out, Career Growth, Family Growth, Starting Out II, Mid-life Crisis, Aging Well, and Mature.

After missing the biggest fashion movement of the 1990s, the career casual revolution, Spiegel is reinventing itself. Once its target market was in the mid-twenties and now it is in the mid-forties. Spiegel has introduced a MasterCard that will not only provide rebates to cardholders but will also contribute funds to the National Alliance of Breast Cancer Organizations.

Spiegel's catalog business has declined sharply. Spiegel has reduced the number of items in its catalog by half, to 1,000. About half of the merchandise is apparel, and the remainder, home furnishings and kitchenware. The catalog also includes more merchandise with European labels. Whether Spiegel can successfully reinvent itself as a leading direct retailer remains a question. The industry is expanding but its differential advantage is unclear and competitors such as Victoria's Secret, Gap, and Banana Republic have become market leaders. Substantial investment is needed to regain market share in the face of such competition.

Spiegel established Eddie Bauer, which has strong brand recognition with more than 500 stores in North America and 3.4 million active catalog customers. The mission was to develop Eddie Bauer worldwide as the leading brand of casual lifestyle products. Its strategic motto is "one customer, one brand, one voice." To achieve this objective, major market superstores have been opened in high-traffic locations. Eddie Bauer has carved out a distinct niche in the mid-to-upper segment of the market, offering apparel and home furnishings for the casual lifestyle. Catalogs and electronic shopping are also available. Eddie Bauer is expanding and also has established catalog and retail operations overseas through joint ventures in Japan, Germany, and the United Kingdom. Eddie Bauer surpassed $1 billion in net retail sales excluding outlet store sales in 1997.

As customers' needs have changed, Eddie Bauer has updated its merchandise while shifting its focus to establishing Eddie Bauer worldwide as a leading brand of casual lifestyle products. To keep its employees motivated, Eddie Bauer has instituted a wide range of employee programs including on-site mammography and emergency child-care services. Its Balance Day gives employees one free day annually to make a "call in well" absence, while its Customized Work Environment Program provides opportunities to engage in job sharing, a compressed workweek, and telecommuting.

Newport News, another division of the Spiegel Group, competes with discounters and Sears. Newport News is a specialty catalog business that offers fashionable apparel and home decor at moderate prices for women who value style, comfort, versatility, and quality. The catalog is aimed at a niche market with a sharply focused product following its "Easy Style" positioning which emphasizes a casual way of life. The catalog has also capitalized on growth opportunities in its home furnishings business and increased offerings of extended sizes. The division's success has been built on market programs that build customer loyalty such as the Newport News Discount Club, an improved merchandise planning cycle, cost control, and reduced expenditures.

The Spiegel catalog is now aimed at the female in her mid-forties who is career oriented. Catalogs have been developed for other customer segments. These smaller books will be published every five to six weeks compared with the catalog, which is about 500 pages and is published twice a year. However, much of the merchandising offered still reflects efforts to be all things to all people. Eddie Bauer is perceived by many consumers to reflect California, west-coast outdoor styles. This image may not be received well in other parts of the country. Newport News offers value at low prices and competes with discounters and department stores.

THE LIMITED'S PROBLEM CHILDREN: LANE BRYANT, LERNER'S, ABERCROMBIE & FITCH

Lane Bryant can be traced back to 1904 when its specialty was designing maternity clothes. A mail-order business was started in 1910. Lane Bryant's maternity business grew and the company's sales passed $1 million for the first time in 1917. Lane Bryant also began to sell plus-size clothing. Initially half sizes were developed to eliminate excessive alterations for the average woman. Lane Bryant gradually added extra sizes in foundation garments, suits, blouses, sweaters, skirts, shoes, hosiery, coats, gloves, sportswear, and bathing suits. In the mid-1920s, Lane Bryant turned its attention to satisfying the needs of tall women and plus-size girls. By 1923 Lane Bryant had stores in Manhattan, Brooklyn,

Chicago, and Detroit. By 1955 stores were established in Pittsburgh, Cleveland, Miami Beach, Minneapolis, Beverly Hills, Milwaukee, and Houston. There are now more than 700 stores in the chain.

Double-knit polyester pants leggings and black tunics represented the fashion apparel of Lane Bryant from the 1970s through the 1980s. The Limited's 1982 acquisition of the chain brought about some change in merchandise offerings. Plus-size women's clothing became a hot retail category. Lane Bryant is now focusing on stylish plus-size fashion for women, departing from the plain basics it usually sells. The new merchandising direction includes sheer, slinky knits, pinstripes, fashion-forward evening wear, and designer sportswear. The average retail price for Lane Bryant's fashion is less than $100. Jackets retail for $80 while pants and skirts retail for $49. Blouses are $39 and dresses are $79. Their stores average about 4,900 square feet with new stores having interiors using tones of sage green, off-white, and khaki which is more refined than the black and gold decor of existing stores. JC Penney also entered the field and has been successful with a specialty plus-size catalog. Bullock's, a Los Angeles-based department store chain, launched a separate specialty chain for plus-size women known as Bullock's Woman. It is estimated the plus-size market will continue to grow as the baby boomers mature. Moreover, special services need to be emphasized in fitting and sizing this market.

Lerner's was founded in 1918 and purchased by the Limited in 1985. Lerner's, at that time, was a budget-priced store with a grim decor that was serving the lower-income working women. A sweeping renovation effort was made to create elegant shops that still offer low prices. merchandise lines such as hats, socks, and sleepwear have been withdrawn in favor of offering more expensive sportswear. The objective was not to remind customers of budget restraints. Once primarily directed at juniors, Lerner's is directed toward the more fashion-conscious, budget-minded women.

Lerner's now has more than 600 stores. Although Lerner's is more upbeat, the chain continues to perform below potential. Lerner's has a low share in a high-growth market of women in their thirties and forties. For example, discounters such as Kmart and Wal-Mart seem to be serving the budget-conscious customer better.

NEW DIRECTION FOR ABERCROMBIE & FITCH

Abercrombie & Fitch, founded in 1892, was once considered one of the outstanding sporting goods stores in the United States and became known as a supplier of rugged, high quality outdoor gear who placed a premium on complete customer satisfaction with each item sold. Its prestigious Madison Avenue, New York, location attracted customers from all over the world. In 1977 the nine-unit Abercrombie & Fitch chain filed for bankruptcy protection. The Limited bought the chain in 1988. By 1997, Abercrombie had quickly become one of the Limited's fastest-growing divisions. With more than 135 stores, Abercrombie has proved to be a case study in reinventing an established brand. This included defining a target market and remaining true to it in all aspects of the business while engaging in slow, structured growth. On its store walls, Abercrombie has great black-and-white photographs of young adults in various degrees of undress from their Abercrombie shorts, tanks, boxers, and chinos. They are having fun, usually in large groups. The average store size is 7,900 square feet. Menswear plays a key role at Abercrombie, accounting for 55 percent of the mix despite a new emphasis on women's wear. In 1998, personal care, fragrance and hair-care products, shoes, luggage, and intimate apparel were introduced. At a time when niche merchandising has gained in popularity, Abercrombie & Fitch has been unable to establish an identity.

Abercrombie & Fitch competes directly with the Banana Republic, which is operated by the Gap Stores. Banana Republic offers the same safari clothing. The Banana Republic is also planning to emphasize women's fashions that are current but not trendy. Abercrombie & Fitch can be looked at as a poor imitation of Banana Republic. Abercrombie & Fitch also competes with L.L. Bean and Eddie Bauer; however, apparel sold by L.L. Bean and Eddie Bauer includes larger and better selections than Abercrombie & Fitch.

In the 1990s, the Limited began to rebuild Abercrombie & Fitch by repositioning the store as a more fashion-oriented casual apparel business. One of the most important reasons for the chain's turnaround has been branding. The target market has been redefined for a youthful lifestyle of thirty-something men and women. An established brand has been reinvented and Abercrombie, now a casual apparel chain, has quickly become one of the Limited's fastest growing divisions. Abercrombie created its own design team so that its brands would have a clear and vivid personality. Sales are resisted and products are sold at full price except for seasonal clearance sales. The youthful image of the apparel is promoted by the sales staff. The sales staff is carefully selected and well trained. Focus is on the generation-plus customer group. No detail has escaped management in its attempts to create a new identity for the operation. A possible drawback is that generation-plus customers will grow older as will their tastes.

Abercrombie & Fitch, at the beginning of the 21st century, has adjusted its target market to include teens and young adults and establish itself as a popular specialty store serving a youthful market. This performance has been consistent and led the Limited, Inc. to spin off this specialty retailer in 1998. Meanwhile, after building an enthusiastic following on shirt tails, baseball caps, and frequently racy catalogues, competition from the J. Crew Group and Banana Republic is slowing growth.

ANN TAYLOR: A NICHE STRATEGY

Ann Taylor Stores, once considered the store for urban career women in their thirties and forties is going through difficult times. The Ann Taylor chain became a fixture in malls in the 1980s. But by the 1990s, Ann Taylor product line did not fit in with the career woman's new relaxed style. A loyal customer base has played a critical role in reestablishing financial performance but its status is still a question mark.

Ann Taylor has more than 300 stores. In 1998, Ann Taylor introduced its Loft store concept in outlet malls and strip centers selling primarily the Loft label, developed exclusively for the stores. The Loft is aimed toward women who cannot afford the clothing prices of the original Ann Taylor stores. The average size of the store is 10,000 square feet. The Loft label was put on merchandise ranging from casual to tailored apparel. It is positioned to compete with department stores such as JC Penney. Recently, Ann Taylor has closely integrated design planning, merchandising, and sourcing for all of its operations.

Ann Taylor compounded its problems by a number of marketing missteps. First, it bought inferior products and sold them at a high markup. Second, a costly expansion program drained company resources. Customers noticed the higher prices and inferior goods and deserted in droves. At the same time, those customers who stayed were loyal and continue to return to the store. Subsequently, prices were reduced, existing stores were redecorated, and new management arrived as many former executives departed. To regain consumer confidence heavy promotion will be needed.

Ann Taylor had difficulty in establishing a fashion identity. Sales of clothing, shoes, and accessories have faltered as customers shun fashions targeted for younger women. Competition from other apparel specialty stores worsened the situation. Ann Taylor had carried so many different clothing manufacturers that a major problem was getting fashion-right styles for its customers. Ann Taylor is trying to carve out a niche making its clothes more fashionable than those at Talbot'', where the classic styles can be a little dowdy. Ann Taylor is less trendy than Limited Inc.'s women's chains. In big-ticket categories like business suits and evening wear, Ann Taylor tends to charge less than Saks, Inc., and Nordstroms, Inc. Ann Taylor has blurred its image and confused customers. In reestablishing itself, Ann Taylor label is a sign of belonging in the business world, just as Brooks Brothers is for men. Although the turnaround in fortune is considered remarkable in the fickle fashion world, Ann Taylor's target market is limited for the most part to female executives in their thirties and forties wearing relatively small sizes. These executives are pressed for time and therefore demand a large selection. This means a large inventory that incurs higher costs.

MANAGING CHANGE

The decision by Wexner of the Limited to set the model for specialty retailing was indeed a controversial decision. This allowed the Limited to offer a very narrow merchandise assortment with both breadth and depth to a selective target market. In turn each division of the Limited such as Lane Bryant and Lerner's offered a narrow merchandise assortment with both breadth and depth to a specific target market. Lane Bryant and Lerner's were both drifting and had to renew their search for purpose. Such fundamental questions as what is our business, who is the consumer, what should our business be are often the most difficult for a company to answer. The Limited decided to phase Lane Bryant out of the maternity business and serve large-size women. Lerner's, which once served a lower socioeconomic class, was redesigned to target a more upscale customer.

The Limited's Henri Bendel has gone through a number of transformations. Its merchandise is considered boring and unexciting. The image of Henri Bendel became blurred. Managing change requires the answers to such questions as what products are sold in the outlet and what must be done to sell through this outlet? Henri Bendel would seem to be outside the Limited's objectives.

Brooks Brothers sold originally to men but with the increasing numbers of women in executive positions, they defined a target market limited to male and female executives. These executives are pressed for time and therefore demand a large selection; this means a large inventory that could be risky.

An organization's mission and objectives need adjustment over time. Gap has found that its safari image in its Banana Republic division and its theme park appeals have faded from popularity, and the Banana Republic is now trying to reflect the personality of its locations. For example, a Banana Republic store has been designed to reflect a converted dairy barn in Pittsburgh, a vintage storefront in Vermont, and a barn in Salt Lake City. Banana Republic stores are imaginative and emphasize casual clothes rather than a safari fashion image.

The Limited is confronted with the challenge of fashion change. A theme of the 1980s was the belief in endless upward mobility. Fashion items once sold as enhancements to personal style are repositioned to emphasize their practical value. Cross-shopping behavior now allows the purchase of apparel items at discounters such as Kmart, Wal-Mart, and Target. Gap has profited from this trend, and the Limited has lost ground.

Moreover, the casual look has become popular and even offices on Wall Street allow employees to arrive at work in informal wear such as jeans. The fashion trend would seem to be "dressing down" and the Limited must modify their strategies accordingly. A question remains whether the Limited can profit from the past mistakes made by other organizations and adjust to future trends in the marketplace.

4

Furniture Stores: Targeting a Fragmented Market

Customer-Driven Strategies

- Product differentiation
- Excellent use of niche strategy
- Innovation in servicing customer needs
- Knowledgeable sales personnel
- Image development
- Use of geographical market segmentation

Marketing Mistakes

- Slow delivery service
- Poor product quality control
- Indistinct brand images
- Lack of proactive strategies
- Inability to target consumer needs

The retail home furnishings industry is a highly competitive and fragmented market. Retail furniture stores deal with complex consumer purchasing habits. Economic pressures encourage manufacturers to produce
furniture based upon economies of scale and supply retailers with standardized products. However, there are sizable submarkets that demand
customization. Furniture styles such as Colonial, Italian, Provincial,
French Provincial, Modern, and Contemporary encourage the targeting
of fragmented markets.

Product differentiation is a strategy that has encouraged further frag-
mentation of the market. For example, Century Furniture, a manufacturer, provides more than three thousand different frames for sofas and
upholstered chairs. There are also thousands of combinations of fabrics,
skirts, pillows, springs, and fringes. Unlike market segmentation, which
focuses on consumer differences, product differentiation strategy focuses
on developing and promoting differences among products that compete
with one another within market segments or in the mass market. As a
result, the retailer is confronted with endless delivery delays that are
passed on to the consumer. Thus, retailers demand faster delivery for
their customers, and conflict can develop between manufacturers and
retailers. Most furniture has been manufactured in or around the Carolinas, and this is an important supplier source for retailers. But this common supply source intensifies the desire to satisfy individual customers
and makes product differentiation even more important.

Full-line retail furniture stores provide customers with a variety of
styles ranging from modern to colonial to French and Italian Provincial.
A variety of furniture frames and fabrics has caused a situation of escalating costs and delayed deliveries to customers. Shopping for furniture
causes endless difficulties for customers in an age of instant gratification.
Consumers, in the hope of obtaining better service and bogged down in
a maze of confusing choices, shifted their demand patterns away from
the full-line store toward the small (5,000 to 6,000 square feet) specialty
retailer. These retailers market individual furniture categories such as
waterbeds and motion or upholstered furniture. Crate & Barrel, Restoration Hardware Inc., and the Pottery Barn unit of Williams-Sonoma
stresses a limited selection of styles, fabrics, and colors. It is uncertain if
these approaches will change traditional selling practices in the furniture
industry which emphasizes price and a wide product selection.

The furniture industry is a highly competitive and fragmented market.
Competition varies significantly according to geographic areas and consists of national and regional specialty furniture retailers, general merchandisers, and local independent, specialty furniture retailers.
Wholesale clubs also compete in certain limited categories. The largest
100 furniture retailers account for no more than 40 percent of sales while
the remainder is comprised mostly of independents. Ethan Allen and

La-Z-Boy have vertically integrated, but the remainder of the furniture retailers make their purchases primarily from the Carolinas, Michigan, and overseas.

In a highly fragmented market, furniture retailers endeavor to gain a competitive advantage. A differential advantage can be achieved by following market segmentation strategies, pursuing a distinctive selling approach, developing special manufacturing expertise, providing a distinctive product offering, or using geographic location factors. Determining a differential advantage is a major management challenge. Ethan Allen is a retailer that appears to have discovered successful competitive advantage strategies.

Ethan Allen has gained a competitive advantage by specializing in American traditional furniture. A strong competitive position has been established by targeting the medium to high quality sector of the consumer market. A selective distribution strategy was developed around independently owned and company owned "Ethan Allen Showcase Galleries." Strong consumer and product acceptance have allowed Ethan Allen to achieve higher profit margins than are typical in the industry. A promotional program emphasizes the scope of its product offerings and decorating services. Dealers are provided with a decorating guide and site selection assistance and are offered frequent seminars. Ethan Allen has developed a total program to gain an impressive position in the furniture industry. Great detail has been emphasized in satisfying customer needs, developing product design, establishing manufacturing efficiencies, and implementing distribution approaches. Responses to opportunities and competitive threats include developing new products and eliminating products that do not satisfy customer needs. Ethan Allen's strategy illustrates the importance of achieving a differential advantage.

Another strategy to target a fragmented market is the use of effective service. According to Michael Porter, potential purchasers try to find suppliers that offer them the greatest added value.[1] Furniture retailers have long feared that superior customer service means hiring additional employees, but the conventional wisdom is not necessarily true. IKEA, the world's largest furniture retailer, has found that superior customer service does not mean being overwhelmed by salespeople. IKEA meets customers with catalogs, tape measures, pens, and notepaper. The shortage of salespeople affords customers the opportunity to shop in freedom and to take notes. IKEA also offers services to parents while they shop such as the supervision of toddlers, infant-changing rooms, and attendants who warm baby bottles. Snack bars sell Swedish specialties at low prices.

The strength of IKEA is its ability to shift a variety of cost burdens to the customer that might be found desirable or perceived as an added value. For example, customers are encouraged to deliver the merchandise themselves or arrange for delivery. Should the customer be unable to take delivery, there would be an extra charge. There is also an extra charge if customers do not assemble the merchandise. The customer is usually eager to perform these services because of low prices, ease of assembly, and superior styling. The privilege of foregoing services and thereby lowering the cost of the purchased furniture is greeted enthusiastically by IKEA customers.

Five key ingredients seem to be important for either success or failure in the retail furniture industry: innovation, market segmentation, image, physical environmental resources, and human resources. A high degree of innovation should be useful as an effective strategy in a fragmented industry, but while there are some expectations in the retail furniture industry, for the most part many consumers approach furniture shopping with a sort of dull dread. Furniture retailers seem to lack imagination. Retailers can decrease the risk of product dissatisfaction by carefully inspecting the furniture before it leaves the warehouse. This strategy would constitute a competitive advantage in an industry noted for a record of product defects. This strategy would increase consumer quality perceptions of both the product and the retail store. Retailers could make necessary adjustments centrally, thereby saving travel time and decreasing costs. IKEA and Ethan Allen are noted for their innovations, but these are exceptions in the retail furniture industry. Market segmentation has been used by Heilig-Meyers in targeting consumers in Small Town U.S.A. There has been a real contribution to the retail furniture industry as niche retailers further segment a fragmented market. Niches in the retail furniture industry are pockets of demand that possess a unique willingness to pay premium prices for certain product attributes such as a high quality, rapid delivery, or customized designs. These niches are defensible, at least temporarily, for competitors who cannot offer the valued attributes demanded by consumers. Williams-Sonoma and IKEA are successful niche retailers in the furniture industry. Williams-Sonoma has effectively penetrated the kitchen market while IKEA has offered Swedish lifestyle furniture that is ready-to-assemble and less costly to ship. Ethan Allen is doing an outstanding job of training sales associates and other personnel. The corporate culture of Pier 1 Imports reflects a dedication to the training and hiring of effective personnel.

MARKET STRUCTURE

Table 4.1 demonstrates a lack of presence of large corporate chains. Heilig-Meyers is the largest retail furniture organization with over 1,200 units. Pier 1 Imports is the second largest with more than 700 retail stores and the Bombay Company is third with more than 400 units. Ethan Allen is a vertically integrated operation encompassing manufacturing plants

Table 4.1
An Overview of the Retail Furniture Industry

	Number of Units 1998	
Heilig-Meyers	1253	
Heilig-Meyers		*813*
Rhodes		*97*
RoomStore		*107*
Mattress Discounters		*236*
Pier 1 Imports	769	
Ethan Allen	310	
Bombay Company	412	
Levitz	105	
Satellite Stores		*47*
Warehouse Showrooms		*58*
Williams-Sonoma	298	
Williams-Sonoma		*163*
Pottery Barn		*96*
Hold Everything		*33*
Outlet Stores		*6*
La-Z-Boy	> 20,000 Distributors	
Proprietary Dealers	*43%*	
Major Dealers (ex., Montgomery Ward)	*16%*	
General Dealers	*41%*	
In-Store La-Z-Boy Furniture Galleries		*275*
Independently Owned La-Z-Boy Furniture Galleries		*200*
Kincaid In-Store Galleries		*195*
Hammary Living Center Galleries		*500*
Sam Moore		*Not Available*
Sears Homelife	128[1]	
Haverty's Furniture	100	
IKEA	140 (15 US)	

1. Includes 100 freestanding stores and 28 located within Sears full-line stores.

as well as ownership or franchise of more than 300 retail outlets. A vertical marketing system is a tightly coordinated distribution system designed to achieve operating efficiencies. Control is maintained by ownership and contract with the franchised systems. Ethan Allen is the oldest furniture retailer. The company was established in the early 1930s, and approximately 80 percent of its stores are owned by independent retailers. Many of these independent retailers have been family operations for two or even three generations and constitute a strong dealer network.

The Heilig-Meyers Company is divided into four divisions. The Heilig-Meyers Furniture stores are typically situated in small towns with populations of less than 50,000. The Roomstore division offers home furnishings in complete room packages that are coordinated by professional interior decorators. Rhodes was acquired in 1996 and expanded the firm's target market. Rhodes stores are typically situated in mid-sized metropolitan markets and specialize in selling furniture and bedding. The fourth division is Mattress Discounters, which is the largest specialty retailer of bedding in the United States. These stores are typically located in high traffic sites near regional malls in metropolitan areas.

Ethan Allen and Haverty Furniture are both exploring the possibilities of Internet selling. Once it was considered preposterous to sell furniture online, but a flurry of competitors are establishing Websites. Furniture.com and Furniture Online.com are among the larger Internet sellers. In the beginning, Ethan Allen will try to sell merchandise such as tables, bookshelves, and beds as well as a limited offering of upholstered sofas and chairs. Whether or not old-style retailers such as Ethan Allen can thrive on selling furniture over the Internet remains a matter of conjecture.

Levitz pioneered the warehouse-showroom concept by establishing the first warehouse-showroom in 1963 in Allentown, Pennsylvania. By 1997 Levitz served customers in twenty-two of the largest metropolitan statistical areas. However, Levitz sought protection under the bankruptcy act in 1998. Levitz offers the brands of some of the finest furniture manufacturers including Broyhill, Ashley, Bassett, Simmons, Stratford, Thomasville, and Universal. Levitz's new retail concept includes offering a broad selection of competitively priced nationally advertised brands of furniture and accessories, which is immediately available to the consumer. Both Levitz and Heilig-Meyers have established strong partnerships with manufacturers to monitor inventory levels.

The Bombay Company has become one of the success stories in the retail furniture business in the 1980s and 1990s. Nearly all of its stores were converted to superstores in the 1990s and are situated in busy locations. A comparison of Bombay's furniture is not possible since most of its accessories are exclusives made predominately in Taiwan. Generally, prices are at least one-third below competitors; however most items sell for less than $200.

Williams-Sonoma is a direct competitor of Bombay and is a specialty retailer of fine quality cooking and serving equipment and home furnishings. The company has five divisions: Williams-Sonoma, which offers culinary and serving equipment; Pottery Barn, which features casual home furnishings; Hold Everything, which offers innovative household storage products; Gardeners Eden, which provides home gardening equipment; and Chambers, which offers high quality bed and bath products. Williams-Sonoma experiences seasonal variations in demand. Historically, its strongest period is from October to December.

La-Z-Boy sells to a great many stores including its own and others. It is known primary for its main product, recliners. Its biggest problem was in expanding its product line beyond chairs and sofas.

IKEA is a fifteen-store chain in the United States, but it has captured the imagination of the entire furniture industry. IKEA, a Swedish retailer, uses store design to improve its sales of housewares and accessory items. The company" image is that of the consummate self-service home furnishings retailer since most of its furniture can be assembled at home.

SHOPPING GOODS AND THE FURNITURE INDUSTRY

Although most types of furniture are classified as shopping goods, there are some types (such as patio furniture sold by various discounters) that could be classified as convenience-shopping goods and other types of furniture and accessories (such as Stiffel lamps) that may be viewed as specialty goods. Consumers are likely to spend more time shopping for furniture and comparing specific characteristics because they are involved with the product. As a result, a process of extensive decision making is likely, requiring a protracted information search. In contrast to convenience goods, the purchase of furniture arouses high levels of pre-purchase anxiety related to whether or not the purchase is appropriate. Consumers may diminish this anxiety by evaluating product features, warranties, performance, options, and other factors.

There are two types of shopping goods that are referred to as homogenous (or price-based) and heterogeneous (or attribute-based). Price-based shopping goods include patio furniture, dinette sets, or television sets. Attribute-based shopping goods are products that are compared for style, color, and appearance. These attributes are usually more important than relatively modest price distinctions among stores. Moreover, a shopper is unlikely to find exactly the same furniture item in several stores, so price is a precarious variable to evaluate. Since there is a search for unique items with special characteristics, consumers usually shop in more stores for heterogeneous than for homogenous shopping goods. It is important to recognize that the same item could be a convenience, shopping, or specialty good since products are classified on how consumers view them.

When consumers shop for homogenous shopping goods, brands are usually compared in making the product selection. Consequently, price can be measured using this process. The lowest possible price available for the product selected can be determined if enough time is given of the search. Non-price competitive features, such as warranties, free delivery, or choice of colors provide consumers with an additional basis for comparison. In contrast, consumers consider heterogeneous shopping goods to be different from one another, and price may be the least important evaluative criterion when considering these goods. A shopper seeking tables or lamps to match a living room decor may visit several stores to find the right style, color, and design. Consumers, in this instance, prefer a wide assortment to satisfy individual tastes and appreciate sales personnel who can provide information and advice.

Retail furniture stores that sell heterogeneous shopping goods must provide a variety of colors, sizes, and designs to make their products appear unique to their customers. Since a large assortment should be carried, expenses increase, and this is one reason why markups are generally higher for attributes-based furniture than for price-based furniture. Retailers, therefore, should be concerned that there be sufficient floor space to display and to store the wide variety of items consumers expect. Retail furniture stores should also be located in or near malls or larger shopping areas so consumers may make comparisons in their search for desired attributes. Industry problems continue to be delivery, service, and the establishment of good customer relations.

THEORY OF POSTPONEMENT AND THE FURNITURE INDUSTRY

Bucklin examined the impact upon the distribution structure of the interaction between the risk of owning a product and the physical functions employed to move the product through time. The principle of postponement holds that the minimum cost and type of distribution system are determined by balancing the costs of alternative delivery times against the cost of using an intermediate, speculative inventory. The appearance of such an inventory in the distribution system occurs whenever additional costs are more than offset by net savings in postponement to the buyer and seller.[2]

Product postponement in the furniture industry can take two major forms. The first is maintaining inventories at a bare minimum and delaying the order until the last possible moment to reduce inventory-carrying costs. The second is to differentiate the product, not at the manufacturer's plant but closer to the point of sale or even after the sale to reduce physical distribution costs and to more exactingly target market demand.

Marketing efficiency is promoted through the policy of postponement of buying. For example, furniture retailers carrying sample stocks might replenish these stocks only after obtaining orders from their customers. Naturally, some adjustments are made for unexpected variations in demand. This policy reflects the postponement of changes in inventory location until the anticipated time of purchase. Sample stocks of lamps, to illustrate, might be kept on the selling floor, allowing for a wide selection for the buyer. When the customer has placed an order, the manufacturer, wholesaler, or warehouse must be contacted to complete it. Coordination is necessary on all institutional levels with fast order processing and product delivery. Otherwise this distribution system could be detrimental to all parties.

Another policy that reduces risk is delaying differentiation of the product as long as possible while the product passes through the distribution system. The greater the degree of product differentiation in the distribution system before customer purchase, the more risk is assumed in the buying and stocking of the product. The postponement concept can be applied to encourage the purchaser to complete the differentiation of the product such as the sale of unfinished furniture to consumers. These consumers can give the furniture pieces identities and distinctive appearances. The do-it-yourself market of assembling furniture not only lowers the costs to the distributor but to the buyer as well. The main limitation of this concept is that it is not necessarily applicable to all types of furniture. Moreover, the concept of postponement considers the time dimension as a basis for reducing risk to some members in the distribution system. The distance between seller and buyer, the size of the product, and available inventory space are factors to be considered when applying this concept to practical situations.

ETHAN ALLEN: APPLYING AN ADMINISTERED SYSTEM

An administered vertical marketing system is in reality a conventional distribution system characterized by effective interorganizational management. The members of this system are more closely aligned than would be the case for the conventional distribution system. The feature distinguishing an administered system from a conventional one is the degree of inter-organizational management, which is much more pronounced in an administered system. Armstrong in floor coverings, Sealy in mattresses, and Ethan Allen in furniture have all effectively applied an administered marketing system.

Ethan Allen manufactures most of the furniture sold through its distribution system of more than 300 owned and franchised retail stores. The physical appearance of the stores, ranging from architecture to layout to lighting and display, is controlled by Ethan Allen. The retail stores do not carry competing products from other manufacturers. The promotional program consisting of advertising, special events, and sales are developed and coordinated by Ethan Allen. Thus Ethan Allen, with a carefully administered system, is able to compete on the basis of quality, service, and customer assistance rather than price as is so common in the furniture industry.

Interestingly, large retailers such as Wal-Mart or Federated Department Stores do not always practice interorganizational management, even though they frequently have the power and resources. Instead, large retailers seem more concerned with obtaining specific types of concessions, such as new product introductions and promotional and inventory allowances. Usually these giant retailers concentrate their efforts on selecting and maintaining an appropriate merchandise assortment and providing merchandising services. In contrast, in situations such as the furniture industry, where retail outlets provide significant sales assistance and the retail stores are selectively located, these retailers will attempt to dominate and practice various dimensions of interorganizational management.

Ethan Allen has been practicing various aspects of interorganizational management for more than sixty-five years. The consumers of furniture products consider the purchase relatively important and therefore, as with shopping goods, expenditure is made in shopping and comparing products. Therefore, Ethan Allen exerts influence over the consumer's purchase decision. Although promotional efforts will bring the customer into the store, comparisons will still be made with other brands by shopping in two or more retail outlets. Ethan Allen, by developing its own niche in the furniture industry, has attempted to negate the effects of comparison shopping. As Ethan Allen's influence on product differentiation increases, bargaining power also increases. Other furniture retailers, such as the Bombay Company and IKEA, have also influenced product differentiation as a means of influencing the purchase decision and negating the impact of comparison shopping.

Ethan Allen has experienced higher growth rates than other furniture retailers where growth rates are relatively small. Success is attributed in large part to the company's chief executive, Farooq Kathwari. The company underwent an extensive change from 1992 to 1997 inasmuch as Ethan Allen was no longer tied to a single style. The image of selling only Colonial furniture changed by selling casual and classic styles of European and American designs. The stores were changed into one-stop shopping centers where customers could purchase wallpaper, drapes, framed prints, and even outdoor furniture. Ethan Allen also placed increased emphasis on opening company-owned stores, gaining even more control over the situation.

Ethan Allen devotes considerable financial allocations to training personnel. Ethan Allen "College" trains and develops sales associates and provides regional trainers to work with each retailer. Not only is product information disseminated but sales psychology is emphasized. Prices are not inflated so that product value and service receive primary attention.

Ethan Allen owns about 20 percent of its 300 stores and is fully integrated with about twenty manufacturing plants and three sawmills located throughout the United States. Instead of Colonial furniture, the company's most popular category is casual contemporary and more than 85 percent of its products did not exist in the 1980s. Ethan Allen has strengthened its organization and has maintained a decisive competitive advantage entering the 21st century.

LEVITZ: SUCCESSES AND BLUNDERS WITH WAREHOUSE RETAILING

Furniture warehouses were pioneered by Levitz and featured a no-frills warehouse and a location that consumers perceived would be indigenous to low prices. A large inventory of furniture, most still packed in factory cartons, was displayed for immediate sale. The first furniture warehouse stores were enormously successful. An analogy was made that furniture warehouse stores were the new supermarket of the furniture industry. However, the cost savings failed to happen. Since the furniture had not been removed from its original cartons and had not been inspected, consumers found many items either poorly made or even damaged in transit. Levitz was forced to return to many of the basic services including delivery. Although Levitz experienced early successes, the growth of warehouse furniture stores slowed markedly.

Levitz innovated in the furniture industry by opening the first warehouse-showroom in 1963 in Allentown, Pennsylvania. The warehouse-showroom / satellite furniture retailing concept targets value-conscious consumers by offering nationally recognized brands, competitive prices, and the immediate delivery of merchandise. The service of providing immediate delivery of merchandise addressed a major criticism of practices in the furniture industry. However, customers were expected to provide their own delivery services. Growth was phenomenal and Levitz grew from two stores in 1964 to fifty-five stores by 1974. A lack of central controls over inventory, advertising, and purchasing caused problems, and a professional manager was hired. A recession and excessive inventory caused Levitz to reconsider its strategies.

A change of policy caused Levitz to increase prices and to offer higher quality merchandise. This change in strategy correspondingly resulted in the process of changing the image of Levitz. A struggle within the organization took place, with one side desiring to revert to the original discounting practices and the other desiring to appeal more broadly to an affluent group of homeowners.

Suppliers realized that Levitz might blur its image and feared that the desire to upgrade its image might cause Levitz to flounder, much like another discounter, Korvette's. Image refers to how the retail organization is perceived by customers and potential customers. A firm may be perceived as upscale, discount-oriented, specialized, or broad-based. To be successful, a retailer must create and maintain a distinctive, clear, and consistent store image. Once the image and/or positioning are established, the retailer is placed in a niche relative to competitors, and it becomes very difficult to change the consumer's perception of the firm. Levitz had an image as a discounter but found that for some reason customer demand was diminishing. In any event, disagreement over the reason and how to remedy the situation caused suppliers to become alarmed and to carefully consider extensions of credit.

The hope was that satellite stores utilizing the warehouse and delivery functions of nearby warehouse showrooms would enable Levitz to serve existing markets more cost-effectively. The strategy was to display more merchandise in a large selling space than competitors. Because of the strategy of immediate merchandise availability and delivery, Levitz would be more able to competitively purchase merchandise in truck-load lots.

However, a number of blunders caused Levitz to file for bankruptcy in 1997 and to sell substantially all of its assets to Heilig-Meyers in 1998. In 1996, Levitz agreed to pay $1.2 million to settle charges that it falsely advertised sales prices in Florida. In 1997, Levitz agreed to a $10 million settlement of charges brought about by California customers who were tricked into purchasing credit card insurance, although wrongdoing was not admitted.

Although the furniture industry had experienced slow growth in the last decade, many blame outdated business practices for the downfall of Levitz. Levitz had simply been unable to change with the times. Its inventory was outdated, and the company waited too long to respond to a changing consumer demand pattern. In 1999, Levitz opened its first new store, the Levitz Lifestyle Gallery. The store features room settings arranged by lifestyles such as traditional, contemporary, and casual/country in a store less than 20,000 square feet in size. Levitz now operates 105 stores nationwide. It has freshened its product assortment and makes stores in each market more responsive to local style preferences. Specialty chains such as Crate & Barrel and Pier 1 Imports compete with traditional furniture stores with a merchandise assortment that is generally contemporary and appealing to consumers. Levitz failed to introduce fresh new styles and made the situation worse by blurring its image.

HEILIG-MEYERS: TARGETING SMALL-TOWN U.S.A.

The company operates four primary retail formats under the names Heilig-Meyers Furniture, Rhodes, the RoomStore, and Mattress Discounters. The Levitz organization was acquired in 1999, and it is still uncertain about the role that will be assumed by this purchase. Heilig-Meyers furniture stores are usually situated in small towns with populations of less than 50,000 that are at least twenty-five miles from major metropolitan areas. The merchandise assortment is approximately 60 percent furniture with the balance including bedding, consumer electronics, appliances, and floor coverings. The non-furniture categories help to reduce seasonal and cyclical aspects of furniture retailing in small towns. The typical store averages 25,000 square feet.

Rhodes was acquired in 1996, and its stores are typically located in midsize metropolitan markets carrying furniture and bedding. The acquisition of Rhodes makes Heilig-Meyers the largest furniture retailer in the United States. The more than 100-year-old retailer is attempting to express a fashion-forward image toward women who desire to express themselves in the appearance of their homes. The acquisition allows Heilig-Meyers to trade up in image and size. An average Rhodes store in 34,000 square feet and generates sales between $4 and $5 million on an annual basis.

Mattress Discounters is the largest specialty-retailer of bedding in the United States with more than 200 outlets. These stores are typically situated in highly visible, high-traffic sites frequently in close proximity to regional malls in metropolitan markets. Emphasis is placed on an aggressive promotional program, low prices, and knowledgeable sales personnel. The average store is between 3,000 and 4,000 square feet and generates approximately $1 million in sales on an annual basis.

The RoomStore offers home furnishings in complete room packages, which are coordinated by professional interior designs. Stores are usually located in large metropolitan markets and target middle income consumers. The typical RoomStore averages 25,000 square feet and generates approximately $6 million in sales on an annual basis. The RoomStore division was acquired in 1997 and numbered 107 retail units (while Rhodes numbered 99). RoomStore is based in Dallas/Fort Worth and Rhodes primarily in the southern, mid-western, and western regions of the United States.

Heilig-Meyers has gone the Wal-Mart way in some respects. The company's strategy is to offer a broad selection of competitively priced home furnishings, including furniture and accessories, consumer electronics, appliances, bedding, and other items such as jewelry and seasonal goods. Initially the company succeeded by locating its stores in small towns and by offering its customers long-term financing. The credit program has been very successful for those cv stomers who desire a long-term payment plan and who have already borrowed elsewhere up to their credit limits. Since Heilig-Meyers is situated in small towns, competition with Levitz and Circuit City, both with a large-city orientation, is not a factor. However, unlike Wal-Mart, Heilig-Meyers has grown by acquisition. The RoomStore, Mattress Discounters, Rhodes, and the core operation of Heilig-Meyers will have different store formats and in some respects different target markets. This is especially true of Rhodes with an image change to an upscale chain.

Heilig-Meyers, in light of its recent acquisitions, will need to restructure. Heilig-Meyers understands the changing lifestyle needs of small town consumers well, but the organization now has a presence in much larger markets. It is still uncertain if the company can succeed in these other markets. Brand awareness, economies of scale, and a national distribution network are strengths, but integration with diverse store formats may prove difficult. Moreover, the company does not have the training expertise of Ethan Allen and consequently may find relatively inexperienced personnel detrimental to the operation. Heilig-Meyers may have expanded too quickly for the company to position itself for continued rapid growth.

Heilig-Meyers is endeavoring to innovate by working to establish an automatic replenishment inventory system and embrace its use of a "just-in-time" delivery system. The company has not been known for innovation, and leadership in this direction is uncertain. Another challenge for Heilig-Meyers is to respond to changing consumer lifestyle trends. The company may find these lifestyle changes difficult to respond to—especially with the Rhodes operation. Small-town dominance has been its strength, and entry into other locations will present new challenges.

THE BOMBAY COMPANY: ADAPTING TO CHANGE

The Bombay Company has effectively developed a niche in furniture retailing that has helped to block imitators, and the constant reinventing of the company has helped in adapting to change. Bombay's 412 stores are located in regional shopping malls, secondary malls, and selected urban and suburban locations. The company also sells through E-commerce and catalogs. Initially Bombay sold replicas of 18th- and 19th-century English furniture such as tables, plant stands, and nightstands. The merchandise was ready to be assembled, and generally all the customer had to do was screw on the legs. The major limitation of this company strategy is that its stores are overloaded with mahogany-stained reproductions. The Bombay Company was founded in 1980 and has successfully grown to more than 400 retail units. A decision was made in

1993 to convert all outlets to superstores as desks and larger furniture pieces were added to the merchandise assortment.

The superstore conversion strategy was important in changing the organization's merchandising policies. Another innovation was to add the Alex & Ivy line that would feature not Bombay's formal English styles but French and American country and casual furniture and accessories. Price is another determinant of a successful operation. Bombay tries to sell furniture for under $500, naturally to be adjusted by future inflation. The average item is priced under $100, and consequently Bombay has earned a low-price image for selling quality furniture. The company designs its own products and has established contract factories, mostly situated in Asia. This policy is in contrast to many furniture retailers that make purchases mostly in the United States. Costs are held down by working hard on ready-to-assemble technology so that shipping and distribution costs are lowered. Cost control is maintained by shipping products in standard forty-foot containers. Competition comes mainly from Williams-Sonoma and Crate & Barrel so that careful site location in shopping malls is important. Customer return policy is liberal and designed to promote customer loyalty.

Constant change has been one of the keys to the success of the Bombay Company. In a single year 25 percent of the furniture, 50 percent of the wall decor, and 70 percent of the decorative accessories are new products. Each marketing period has a different furniture theme. More than a million catalogues are mailed out each period. Bombay tries to buy from medium-size suppliers to that comparison will be difficult for customers. The simplicity of strategy concerning change, preventing imitators, and designing its own products has helped Bombay to become successful. Continued success will depend upon its quickness and capability to identify changing environmental conditions.

IKEA: A FOREIGN MYSTIQUE

IKEA is a global retailer targeting the same type of customer in each country. A strategic decision was made not to adapt its merchandise to different regional markets. IKEA includes more than 140 stores in twenty-five countries, ranging from the United States to Europe, Saudi Arabia, and Hong Kong. Originally the company was conceived as a mail-order catalog furniture retailer in Sweden in 1949. Economies of scale, vertical integration, close attention to costs, standardized products, and minimal customer services allow IKEA to extend deep discounts to its customers.

IKEA has fifteen stores in the United States with half in the Northeast, another five on the West Coast, and one in Chicago. In the last few years IKEA, known primarily as a furniture retailer, has expanded its housewares, tabletop, home organizers, and home accents merchandise lines. The IKEA catalog features not just a moderately priced, do-it-your-self concept but also a candle assortment of great depth and breadth. Even with closet storage, IKEA has provided a new innovation by offering soft-sided storage bags in an alternative material (nylon) as opposed to the traditional vinyl or canvas. Their colors range from orange to blue and green. Even though IKEA is located in different parts of the United States, its transportation costs are reduced since ready-to-assemble furniture is less expensive to ship than fully assembled pieces.

The IKEA image is a light, natural wood, which is crisp white. Signature colors are yellow and blue and are ubiquitous. The furniture retailer reinvents itself about every ten weeks. To illustrate, a theme such as IKEA Cooks features kitchen cabinets, pots, pans and other cookware items. Other themes could be anything from IKEA Sleeps to IKEA Works to IKEA Dines. Moreover, the firm is endeavoring to create brand differentiation by concentrating on Swedish lifestyle furniture and offering high value products. IKEA is striving to develop a furniture brand identity comparable to Honda in automobiles. Quality control is exacting on all products and standards are higher than those of other furniture retailers.

IKEA has joined the ranks of category killer stores by expanding its breadth and depth with its merchandise assortment throughout the home. Current strategy is to develop its own niche by targeting young singles and young families. These category killer stores offer their customers wide selections and steeper price cuts than even traditional discounters such as Kmart. Half of IKEA's products are self-service items that are flat-packed in a rectangular box ready for home assembly. Approximately 9,000 items are offered to consumers. About 75 percent of its merchandise mix consist of furniture, and the other 25 percent are home furnishings such as textiles, housewares, kitchen cabinets, floor coverings, and accessories. Examples of category killer stores are Circuit City, Home Depot, and Barnes and Noble.

IKEA, with its marketing expertise, has cast a spell over consumers. The Swedish retailer was awarded the first ever Advertising Age Retail Marketing Campaign of the Year Award in 1998. IKEA is attempting to develop a brand that will almost become a generic term for sophisticated furniture. The thrust is on making furniture that is universally attractive, and therefore IKEA does not focus on regional tastes. The chief criticism directed against IKEA is its lack of customer services and lack of personal contact. IKEA does not appear to conduct customer research to learn about how to address complaints. Some of these complaints might be easy to address if only IKEA was interested in identifying them.

PIER 1 IMPORTS: EFFECTIVE USE OF IMAGE AND MARKET SEGMENTATION STRATEGIES

Pier 1 Imports appeals especially to college-educated working women between the ages of twenty-five and forty-four. Pier 1 Imports has more than 750 stores worldwide and has completely changed its image from the 1960s as a store catering to the college crowd to a furniture store comprised of furniture with more than 70 percent that is exclusive to them and purchased primarily from China and India. The typical customer has a much higher income than the average U.S. household and more than one-third have a college education. Major merchandise categories are furniture, decorative accessories, bed and bath, and housewares. A new image has emerged as pricey wicker settees, French stemware, and decorative Italian tables have replaced the 1960s psychedelic pillows.

Pier 1 Imports dominates a niche that it created with exotic imported furniture and housewares. Innovation has been a keynote as furnishings reflect the customer's taste for tradition. Pier 1's furniture and furnishings reflect an image of the establishment but are at the same time distinctive. A frequent-shopper program has reinforced this segmentation strategy. Customers who charge at least $500 annually with at least two transactions on the store card qualify for a Pier 1 Imports gold card. Benefits include a 20 percent off coupon at Pier 1 and a discount at Carnival Cruise Lines or other partner organizations. Customers who charge at least $1,000 in three or more visits in a year obtain a platinum card and benefits equal up to 10 percent of charge volume. Differential charge cards are not yet approved of by many retailers but nonetheless Pier 1 Imports is pioneering this strategy.

Pier 1 is placing great emphasis on hiring, training, and retaining quality associates. The chain believes that the development of human resources is instrumental for growth. Employees are trained to believe that effective service to customers is a higher priority than fulfilling a task, such as stockkeeping. Moreover, corporate culture reveals that employees believe in the store's merchandise and that an effective environment is present that promotes teamwork and excitement and encourages freedom. A corporate culture that is focused on the customer holds the company together and permeates the training program.

Although Pier 1 has done an admirable job, behavioral drift has caused the company to upgrade its products and its image over the past decade. While it was thought that this strategy was successful, Pier 1 priced itself out of the market for basic products like glassware. Therefore, Pier 1 has left itself vulnerable to new discounters such as Cost Plus Inc. Carrying more expensive products has modified Pier 1's image in certain merchandise lines. Pier 1 has been doing well but needs to address these new challenges.

Presently, Pier 1 operates stores in forty-seven states and has achieved a national presence. Regional distribution centers are maintained in Baltimore, Columbus, Chicago, Fort Worth, Los Angeles, and Savannah to better serve customers. Quick delivery is emphasized in an industry plagued by slow delivery problems. There is a continuous program to

remodel and re-merchandise all store interiors to improve visual merchandising of its products.

LA-Z-BOY: DUAL DISTRIBUTION

La-Z-Boy distributes its furniture to a network of more than 20,000
locations. The company is a manufacturer with patents on its reclining
chair and rocking chair mechanism, and also owns retail stores. La-Z-
Boy is the world's leading manufacturer of reclining chairs, the largest
manufacturer of upholstered furniture, the third largest producer of residential furniture, and in the late 1990s entered the office / home industry.
The company now sells everything from dining room sets to entertainment centers. However, recliners account for one-third of its revenue.

A strategy of dual distribution has been utilized with some selective
distribution dimensions. Dual distribution typically describes a marketing situation that is present when the same brand or the same product
line is sold through two or more competing distribution networks at any
stage in the production and distribution process. La-Z-Boy, much like
Sherwin-Williams, distributes its brand or line of products not only to its
own retail stores, but also to independent dealers. La-Z-Boy has had a
distribution arrangement with Montgomery Ward and other prominent
retailers. Consequently, the same market for recliners and other pieces of
furniture made by La-Z-Boy is served through competing distribution
networks. Dual distribution is common in many industries, including
shoes and clothing.

Dual distribution is an effort by manufacturers to find more profitable
methods of distributing their products. Manufacturers increasingly resort
to dual distribution as a means of accomplishing adequate distribution
in selected markets. This is used to maintain market position and to cover
a market that has expanded rapidly. At other times, the manufacturer
uses dual distribution as a means of gaining initial market penetration
and then to expand its market coverage. If this strategy results in greater
profitability it probably will become more widespread in the future.
There is no doubt that this policy, if misused, could be a source of conflict
between manufacturers and resellers.

La-Z-Boy in some instances has restricted distribution to sellers who
have been licensed to exclusively sell La-Z-Boy recliners and to large
resellers such as Montgomery Ward and Sears Homelife stores that agree
to specific arrangements. Dealers receive certain benefits. This selective
distribution policy emphasizes that retailers will give preferential treatment to the brand because of limited competition (since not all retailers
will be allowed to stock La-Z-Boy recliners). Moreover, because of the
reputation of the brand, retailers may find it advantageous to sell in

the local community. The retail dealer with likely join in cooperative advertising campaigns, thereby reducing costs.

La-Z-Boy was founded in Monroe, Michigan, in 1927. A full line of upholstered furniture including sofas, chairs, sofa beds, modular furniture, and leather upholstery was manufactured by the end of the 1980s. By the late 1990s annual sales reached $1.2 billion. La-Z-Boy has used consumer research to learn about consumer purchasing motives. As a result of this research, the company is creating more styles that appeal to women, particularly to those under fifty.

The distribution mix is 43 percent from proprietary stores. Proprietary stores consist of outlets that include La-Z-Boy Furniture Galleries stores and Showcase Shoppes. These stores sell only the La-Z-Boy brand. About 16 percent of the distribution pattern is to major dealers such as Montgomery Ward and other department stores. The remainder of the product line is sold to general dealers. The major problem for La-Z-Boy, with a dominant market share of the recliner business, is to generate additional growth from a narrow recliner market. Repositioning itself is not easy since there is a risk of diluting a powerful franchise and becoming just another furniture company. Since recliners are a narrow product line, there is a classic image problem with expansion and the La-Z-Boy brand name does not readily lend itself to brand extension.

WILLIAMS-SONOMA: A NICHE RETAILER

The quality of its 4.5 million customer database accounts for much of the success of Williams-Sonoma. The database includes 150 informational attributes for every customer who has made purchases from each of the firm's five catalogs. The catalogs include Williams-Sonoma (cooking utensils and accessories), Pottery Barn (household accessories); Hold Everything (home-organizational products); Gardeners Eden (gardening supplies and outdoor furniture); and Chambers (bedding and bath products). Three of these mail-order businesses also involve retail store operations: Williams-Sonoma, Pottery Barn, and Hold Everything. The database has been instrumental in determining potential store locations.

These five different organizations focus upon five concepts reflecting different areas of the home. The concepts aid customers in satisfying their home-centered needs from the kitchen and garden to the bedroom and bath. Retail sales accounted for approximately 65 percent of the revenue, while mail order comprised the remainder.

Williams-Sonoma was founded in 1956 in Sonoma, California. Innovation was an important variable as Williams-Sonoma was one of the first retailers of fine quality cookware in the United States. The chain includes Williams-Sonoma stores, the Pottery Barn, and Hold Everything outlets.

Most of the Williams-Sonoma and Pottery Barn stores use the large format stores, accounting for almost 60 percent of sales.

Williams-Sonoma is a niche retailer with 298 retail stores in thirty-nine states that has chosen where and when to compete in various markets. Williams-Sonoma has determined the scope of the market to serve and concentrates on one or more key customer segments—called niches. Williams-Sonoma offers culinary and serving equipment for those consumers interested in furnishing their kitchens. The Pottery Barn features items in casual home furnishings, flatware, and table accessories for either dining rooms or kitchens, and Hold Everything offers innovative storage products. These retail stores serve niches for different areas of the home. The development of a positioning strategy for a targeted market segment is an important dimension of niche strategy. There are other aspects of niche strategy that differentiate it from market segmentation strategy:

- The company designs differentiated products and services to satisfy the needs of the niche segment.
- Market opportunity is closely tied to the innovative process, and therefore change is encouraged. The objective is to find new and hopefully better ways to do things.
- A growth environment is fostered.
- Since the focus is on satisfying specific target markets, efficiency is maximized.

Companies that adopt niche strategies are customer driven, carefully observe trends, and are creative marketing strategists. Research is emphasized and valued. Consequently, the consumer database of Williams-Sonoma is constantly monitored. Niche strategy is a broader concept than market segmentation, encompassing management direction, overall marketing strategy, and product differentiation.

SUCCESSES IN THE FURNITURE INDUSTRY

Successful retail furniture organizations have added an exciting and dramatic environment to the consumer shopping experience. In particular, the newer retail furniture companies such as Bombay, IKEA, Pier 1, and Williams-Sonoma have captured the imagination of consumers. The Bombay Company is constantly reinventing itself by introducing a new furniture theme each marketing period. A successful niche strategy emphasizing change has helped to screen out imitators. IKEA has successfully used a universal strategy as a global retailer. Its foreign mystique adds excitement to the shopping environment. Pier 1 has successfully changed its image and dominates with a niche strategy promoting the sale of exotic imported furniture and housewares. Williams-Sonoma started as a niche retailer satisfying the needs of the kitchen market.

All of these retailers have effectively used niche strategy to target untapped markets. These retailers determined the basis for competitive advantage in serving the fragmented furniture market. Through competitive analysis each was able to identify existing or emerging opportunities for competitive advantage while other successful retailers, such as Heilig-Meyers and Ethan Allen, have followed a market segmentation strategy.

MISTAKES IN THE RETAIL FURNITURE INDUSTRY

Retail organizations that have tried to satisfy all the facets of the retail furniture market have not performed well. The strategy of endeavoring to be "all things to all people" can be deadly in targeting a fragmented market such as the retail furniture industry. Store positioning is of paramount importance to a successful marketing strategy. A distinctive niche or a market segmentation strategy must be selected.

Low prices cannot be matched unless they are accompanied by low operating costs. Niche retailers, by using a do-it-yourself policy, were able to undercut traditional furniture stores. Traditional furniture stores were slow to respond to the new niche retailers and were unable to solve their problems of slow delivery, high prices, and poor quality control. A broad market segmentation strategy was needed to offset the niche retailers, and the strategy was lacking.

Levitz reflected elements of both the traditional furniture store and the discount store. Levitz, in order to compete with a revamped Ethan Allen and the niche discounters, tried to upgrade its image by carrying higher quality furniture. Since there was internal dissension within the chain over this change in image, suppliers were left in a quandary. Customers were confused by the store's unclear market positioning and as a result, Levitz found itself with no sustainable competitive advantages and a blurred consumer image. To further complicate the situation, Levitz suffered from a lack of controls over inventory, advertising, purchasing, and other functions.

MANAGING CHANGE

The success stories of yesterday may become the failures of tomorrow in the furniture industry. Already, the Bombay Company is endeavoring to push "femininity" in its mahogany-heavy stores. Heilig-Meyers may find that expansion into other merchandise lines and geographical areas does not emphasize its strength. Heilig-Meyers has developed an intricate knowledge of market segmentation in small towns throughout the United States. The company lacks expertise in other geographical areas, and the acquisition of Rhodes may present pitfalls. Dowdiness and the inability to adapt to competitive changes in the retail furniture industry destroyed

Levitz. Williams-Sonoma, a purveyor of $400 toasters and other preten-
tious gadgets, may find its organization vulnerable to recessions even of
a temporary nature. The flexibility to adapt to environmental change may
be needed within this company.

A major challenge of the furniture industry is service. When consumers
purchase automobiles, appliances and clothing, these items are often delivered immediately, but furniture delivery may take months. In many
instances, the furniture may be damaged or incompletely assembled. Because furniture manufacturers and many retailers have not developed
any overwhelming advantages in efficiency, it is relatively easy for small
competitors to enter the market. A furniture retailer with the ability to
solve many of these problems will become successful in the furniture
industry—as witnessed by the phenomenal growth of IKEA and the Bombay Company with the strategy of flat packing and the sale of ready-to-
assemble furniture.

A customer service strategy must be carefully conceived. Many pitfalls
can be avoided by segmenting the market by the service level desired.
To illustrate, a furniture retailer could offer a sofa for sale at $1,000,
decorating advice would be $50, delivery would be $50, and pickup and
disposal of old furniture would be $50. Thus the customer could pay
anywhere from $1,000 to $1,150 for the sofa depending upon the desired
services. A further segmentation of the market could be based upon the
requested delivery date. Regular delivery date—no charge; two weeks
sooner—$50; or one week sooner—$100. Innovation and change are
needed in the retail furniture industry. Perhaps a limitation of styles,
colors, and fabrics might improve performance.

5

Shoe Stores: Targeting Lifestyle Characteristics

Environmental Challenges

- Emergence of athletic shoes
- Generational acceptance of sneakers versus leather shoes
- High costs of shoe repair
- Decline of shoe purchases

Successful Specialty Shoe Store Strategies

- Location in shopping malls
- Emphasis on fashion leadership for specific target markets
- Effective use of new technology
- Increase in the size of the stores
- Purchase of shoes from China, Taiwan, Hong Kong, Italy
- Brand development
- Shoe restoration services such as recrafting

Specialty Shoe Store Mistakes

- Price competition
- Reliance on past patronage loyalties
- Poor image of shoe stores
- Inability to shift strategies
- Vulnerability to discounters
- Failure to keep up with changes in design
- Lack of inventory controls leading to liquidations

An older generation was brought up believing that leather shoes were of much higher quality than sneakers. Leather shoes, regardless of quality, were purchased in specialty shoe stores or department stores. Sneakers were deemed inferior in quality and subsequently purchased in variety stores such as Woolworth and other stores known as five and dime stores. Even leather shoes targeted to lower socio-economic classes, tied together and tried on one at a time, were considered of higher quality than sneakers. Motives of status and prestige were intertwined with the purchase of leather shoes regardless of price. Sneakers were to be worn over a brief period of time and then discarded.

A younger generation was brought up believing that sneakers, the major part of the athletic shoe market, reflected position quality. This generation wears sneakers not only for athletic events but also for walking and for fashionable styling effects. Prices for sneakers are often higher than those for leather shoes, with most sneakers being sold in the summer and back-to-school seasons.

Once consumers spoke of "shoe wardrobes" and the adult's closet contained from eight to ten pairs of dress, casual boots, sport, and fashion shoes. Much of the footwear approaching the new millennium has crossover purposes, and the same pair can be used for multiple occasions. To illustrate, walking shoes can be used as dress shoes. Thus, shoe consumption has decreased in the 1990s.

Once the shoe industry was dominated by consumer brand insistence. This brand loyalty, along with store loyalty, has largely vanished. Much of the footwear is look-alike, and few stores are providing distinctive service with well-trained personnel. Cross-shopping behavior is prevalent as consumers cross the lines of brands, stores, and products. Dominant shoe chains such as Thom McAn, Edison Brothers, Regal, and Kinney have withered. The children's shoe business has declined, as has the men's and women's dress shoe business. What remains is largely devoted to selling sneakers. Lower-priced leather shoes are generally not repaired but discarded since shoemaker labor costs are prohibitive. Lower-priced shoes have gradually become a throw-away commodity and an integral part of consumer purchasing patterns.

The consumer behavioral shift from purchasing primarily leather shoes to sneakers has caused restructuring in the shoe industry. Woolworth, with its Foot Locker stores, has dominated the retail shoe business in the past decade. Perhaps it is the firm that operates outside of the existing structure and has little to lose through accident or design that becomes an innovator and disrupts the present situation. Retailers such as Thom McAn were insiders and desired to maintain their status and position in the industry. This group did little to disrupt or change the retailing environment. There were other retailers that were not dominant but wanted to become leaders and dominate the retail shoe business. These firms were strivers and did not want to cause significant change since this would diminish their opportunities for gaining access to accepted manufacturers. Still other retailers, known as complementors, carried other merchandise lines in addition to shoes and were not interested in becoming either insiders or strivers. Another group might be called transients and sold shoes only when they could gain special concessions from manufacturers. Therefore, in the final analysis, it was the firms outside of the retail shoe business that innovated and changed accepted practices.[1]

Woolworth, previously known for its five and dime stores, is a good example of a retailer largely outside of the shoe business that emerged as an innovator. Woolworth's capability to recognize emerging consumer trends has propelled its Foot Locker chain of stores. Later, Woolworth segmented the market by establishing Lady Foot Locker in 1982, Kid's Foot Locker in 1987, and finally World Foot Locker in 1992. Woolworth also acquired Champs Sports in 1987 and has targeted its merchandise, athletic footwear, and apparel to young, sports-conscious males. Rapid expansion of Champs Sports has multiplied store units by more than eight times since its acquisition.

Woolworth has segmented its target markets. This segmentation has carried the development of specialty store retailing even further than Wexler, the innovator of the Limited. Woolworth develops concepts that focus on a specific category of merchandise with a high gross margin. To illustrate, its San Francisco Music Box Company sells music boxes priced from $10 to $3,000 and its Best of Times carry only watches and clocks.

The Woolworth organization has chosen to use a multiple-segment approach. Thom McAn defined its market target broadly by offering a wide assortment of medium-quality shoes sold at popular prices. Woolworth, on the other hand, provides a narrow, deep products assortment at above average prices. Woolworth has accomplished this objective with a different strategy mix for each segment. A decision was made to operate more than one kind of retail outlet. Each retailer, when deciding upon a target market, would need to consider its goods and services mix, its goals, and its resources. The external environment including the size of various consumer segments, the efficiency of prevailing competition, and other factors are also important considerations of target market selection.

The specialty shoe retailer needs to understand consumer lifestyle characteristics. These lifestyle characteristics in the retail business sector have changed considerably in the past decade. Demographic factors such as family life cycle, geographic region, city size, occupation, education, and other variables need to be related to the firm's store location, prices, and goods and services mix. Purchase decisions may involve high or low consumer involvement depending upon the situation. The concept of competitive advantage, the distinct competency of the specialty retailer relative to its competitors, is paramount. The key to success is the ability to define the organization's customers and to serve these consumers either better or differently than the competition. Once the purpose of the organization is established, this purpose needs to be reconciled with the firm's mission. A number of questions should be presented—such as what products are currently sold in the store, what products could be sold in the store, and what must the specialty retailer do to effectively sell and promote its products to its selected target market. The missions as devised by Woolworth and Thom McAn were different, but each mission was tailored to its own organizational resources. This was also true to Genesco which made a sound decision to develop multidimensional brands such as Dockers and Nautica.

The vast majority of shoes sold in the United States are produced in other countries. even Nike and Reebok have most of their manufacturing done in Korea or Taiwan, where production costs are lower. Despite the obstacles of hard work and labor costs, a firm like Allen-Edmunds has managed to carve a distinctive niche for itself in world markets. New styles can be designed in hours, instead of months, because of computer-aided designs for a full range of sizes. Allen-Edmunds enhances the quality of its shoes by carefully controlled hard work and custom tailoring. This allows for a full selection of sizes and widths. In contrast, many mass-marketed shoes come in only a few widths for women and men. Major parts of the Allen-Edmunds shoe are sewn to a leather strip stitched between the shoe's sole and upper for a combination of strength and flexibility.

The retail footwear industry can be divided into high-, moderate-, and low-price segments. The high-price segment is dominated by department stores such as Neiman-Marcus, Allen-Edmunds, and Ballys. The moderate-price segment includes specialty shoe chains and junior department stores. The low-price or value-price segment is dominated by Payless Shoe Source and Wal-Mart.

Many of the specialty shoe stores such as Florsheim and Johnson and Murphy with their retail stores have targeted the middle market. Physical resources are reflected in store layout and fixtures and are targeted to cultivate appropriate market segments. The high-end market demonstrates service, appropriate shoe measurement and fittings, and customer comfort. Human resource management, training, and deployment are satisfactory in the retail shoe industry but are not on a level with that of the home improvement stores, the electronic stores, or the specialty clothing stores.

Structure

Table 5.1 indicates a diverse group of specialty store retailers such as Edison Brothers, Ventacor (Woolworth), Johnston and Murphy Shoe

Company (owned by Genesco Inc.), Payless ShoeSource, Footstar, Florsheim Group, and Nine West. The structure of the retail shoe industry is different than the drugstore, bookstore, apparel, home improvement, and electronic retail store environment in that chains do not dominate. Instead, the retail industry is fragmented.

In Table 5.1, Edison Brothers serves the teenage market with specialization in targeting the female segment. Ventacor (Woolworth) with its various Foot Locker stores sells primarily sneakers. Those who desire sneakers for athletics are given special attention. Kinney, once a family shoe chain controlled by Ventacor, has withered. Johnston and Murphy specializes in making shoes for other manufacturers. Thom McAn, once a dominant shoe chain owned by Mellville (now CVS), went out of business in 1997. In turn, Footstar, which was spun off from Melville with its Footaction stores, has specialized in targeting the young adult market. Their Meldisco division has leased space in Kmart and has targeted the discount market segment. Florsheim, a retail chain that has been around for a number of years, has focused attention on the adult market. Their John Deere boots, Frogs, Joseph Abboud, and @Ease brands are well known. Nine West, Easy Spirit, Calvin Klein shoes, Amalfi, Calico, and Bandolino brands have targeted an upscale market. Mail order or online has targeted primarily the male upscale segment (with Wright Shoes and Allen-Edmunds brands that are well known for quality) and the market for special shoe needs based on size and use. Ballys and Allen-Edmunds target the upscale markets.

Once E. T. Wright could not keep up with demand. The firm founded in 1895 was known for producing the best shoes on the market. However, by the 1980s department stores, which once accounted for 30 percent of distribution, had lost interest in stocking the expensive brand because of inventory costs. The Wright brand appealed mostly to an aging group of affluent men who purchased them only when an old pair wore out. Wright manufactured only dress shoes and declined to broaden its merchandise line until the 1980s.

E. T. Wright moved into mail order and competed with its dealers. While dealers withdrew from the distribution network, the decision paid off and Wright became a successful mail order manufacturer. Since the Wright brand of dress shoe was not enough to carry the operation, such brands as Hush Puppies, Rockport, New Balance, Sebago, and Sperry were offered. Moreover, Wright began to manufacture sneakers. This strategy worked and soon younger professionals and executives became customers.

The retail shoe industry is comprised of a number of regional and local chains. Some of these retail shoe chains such as Nine West also sell to department stores. Thus, they are much like Sherwin-Williams (in the

Table 5.1
An Overview of the Retail Shoe Industry

Company	Brands/Stores	Target Market	Number of Units 1998
Nine West[1]			1499
	Nine West	"Upper Moderate" /Contemporary Styling	281
	Easy Spirit	"Upper Moderate" Casual, Comfort, Active Styling	224
	Enzo Angiolini	Upper Scale	81
	9 & Co.	Juniors	63
	CK/Calvin Klein	Middle-Upper Market	6
	Nine West Outlet	"Value-Oriented" Consumers	164
	Easy Spirit Outlet	"Value-Oriented" Consumers	35
	Banister	"Value-Oriented" Consumers	129
	Stein Mart	"Value-Oriented" Consumers	86
	International Stores	N/A	430
Edison Brothers			449
	Baker Leeds	Juniors/Young Women (12-24)	289
	Precis	Contemporary Women	4
	Wild Pair	Teens/Young Men & Women	156
Florsheim			351
	Florsheim	Men, Mid-Price	
	Comfortech		
	Florsheim Imperial	Men, Mid-Upper Price	
	FLS	Men, Mid-Price	
	Magneforce	Men, Mid-Price	
	@ease	Men, Young Professionals	
	John Deere Boots	Men, Mid-Price	
	Joseph Abboud	Men, Upper Price	

Company	Brand	Segment	Stores
Venator			3625
	Foot Locker	Athletic, Middle Class	2008
	Lady Foot Locker	Women	649
	Kids Foot Locker	Kids	274
	Champs Sports	Athletic, Middle Class	657
	Colorado	Active/Outdoorsy	37
	Eastbay	Middle Class	N/A
Genesco			674
	Journeys	Teens/Young Adults (13-22)	258
	Jarman	Men (18-35)	244
	General Shoe Warehouse	Damaged/Overruns	16
	Johnston & Murphy	Business Professionals (25-54)	132
	Nautica	Young, Active, Upper Income	24
	Dockers	Men, Middle Class	N/A
Footstar			572
	Footaction	Teens/Young Adults (12-24)	572
	Meldisco	Discount	N/A[2]
	Thom McAn	Middle/Discount	0[3]
Payless ShoeSource			4570
	Payless ShoeSource	Discount	4357
	Parade of Shoes	Women, Moderate Pricing	213
Mail Order/On-Line			
Allen Edmunds			
E.T. Wright			

Table 5.1 (continued)
An Overview of the Retail Shoe Industry

Manufacturers		
Adidas	*All*	
Nike	*All*	*123*[4]
Reebok	*All*	*175*
Reebok	*Athletic*	*125*
Greg Norman	*Golfers*	*2*
Rockport	*Middle*	*34*
Ralph Lauren	*Middle*	*19*
Footwear		

1. Nine West Brands: Amalfi, Bandolino, Calico, CK/Calvin Klein (under license), Easy Spirit, Enzo Angiolini, Evan Picone (under license), 9 & Co., Pappagallo, Pied-à-Terre, Selby, and Westies.
2. Sold through 2,161 K-Marts, 357 Payless and Thrifty Drug Stores, and 20 Tesco department stores.
3. All Thom McAn stores either closed or converted to Footaction stores in 1998.
4. Includes 63 outlets that carry primarily B-grade and close-out merchandise, 35 Cole Haan(R) stores, 12 NIKETOWN stores, and 10 employee-only stores.

paint and home improvement industry) in that they utilize dual distribution channels. Dual distribution typically describes a marketing situation that is present when the same brand or the same product line is sold through two or more competing channels in the distribution process. The Stride Rite brand, a well-known shoe targeted for children, does a splendid marketing job using dual distribution.

The retail shoe industry is not without its price-fixing probes. Manufacturers of branded products under the Fair Trade Laws, the Miller-Tydings Act of 1937, and the McGuire Act of 1952 were allowed to establish prices that distributors and retailers charged for products. These statutes were repealed in 1976, and in essence the decision had the impact of also repealing all state fair trade laws. The casual and athletic shoe industry has been under the scrutiny of the Federal Trade Commission since 1992. Cases were lodged against New Balance Athletic Shoes, Inc., Reebok International Ltd., and Stride Rite Corporation and its Keds subsidiary. These organizations signed consent decrees with the Federal Trade Commission and fines were levied. In 1999, the Federal Trade Commission was investigating Nine West for the alleged practice of pressuring its retailers to maintain prices rather than discount.

Retailers in the retail shoe business are under pressure to continue to carry the most-coveted fashion brands. Brand names such as Nike and Reebok are in demand by consumers. An independent retailer selling athletic shoes would find it difficult to compete successfully without carrying these well-known brands of athletic shoes. Any suggestion by the manufacturer to cut off shoes would constitute coercion. Although Reebok and its subsidiary Rockport did not admit guilt in 1995, they did agree not to threaten retailers with termination of delivery if they did not adhere to suggested prices.

Manufacturers such as Adidas and Nike have vertically integrated. These existing stores are intended primarily to sell off excess inventory at a discount. However, Adidas has been considering a move into higher-end retailing which would represent a change in strategy and possibly change the distribution structure in the footwear industry.

Independent shoe store operators will need to be more efficient and creative in the new millennium in order to survive. Competition from shoe store chains is growing fiercer. Independent shoe store organizations find it easier to compete with shoe chains, large department stores, and mass merchandisers on the basis of image rather than price. By capitalizing on service, personnel, physical characteristics, atmosphere, and location, independent retailers can differentiate themselves and develop favorable customer relationships. Creativity that embodies innovation will be another important variable as independents compete in the 21st century.

Just For Feet shoe stores was an example of an independent shoe organization that emerged as a result of innovation and the development of a positive image for its target market. In 2000, Just for Feet was purchased by Footstar and will keep its name and locations. Just For Feet started as a single store in 1984 and at the end of the 1990s has grown to about 300 retail units. A typical Just For Feet big box store averages from 15,000 to 25,000 square feet compared to its competitive Foot Locker rival which averages from 4,000 to 6,000 square feet. Store size enables Just For Feet to make purchases in bulk and to carry 4,000-odd styles, ten times as many as most competitors. Just For Feet targets the athletic shoe market and, in contrast to the rest of the retail shoe industry, which has stagnated, is growing. Speed and agility in recognizing consumer shifts in taste have been the foremost reasons for the success of the company. To illustrate, in 1996, Just For Feet offered a great number of styles linked to the Olympics and made certain that it was the widest selection stocked compared to its rivals. The following year, in 1997, when hiking boots were in demand, most sneaker chains lost out, but Just For Feet had anticipated this demand pattern. In addition, a thorough training program for managers has been established that is the envy of the industry. Management selection and training had in fact helped Just For Feet stay ahead of its competition.

For small companies to compete with chains like Foot Locker and Florsheim, the speed to anticipate and react to change is imperative. Moreover, there is a certain image associated with independent shoe stores that chains find difficult to duplicate. That is the image of a friendly, personalized retailer who takes particular care in the customer's comfort and provides a congenial atmosphere in which to stop.

SATISFYING CHANGING LIFESTYLE CHARACTERISTICS

Determining why people buy and why they make the purchase choices they do is complex. Various product features such as status, prestige, economy, price, style, color, comfort, customer service, and return policies may appeal to different market segments. Purchasing n:otives are not permanent and change throughout the life cycle. Motivation is influenced by the performance of other members of the group to which a person belongs and by that of reference groups. Consumers are actively learning and acquiring new wants that subsequently modify lifestyle characteristics.

Shoe store operators are not waiting for customers; they are going to the customer. For example, some retail shoe store managers are developing a team-sports business by catering to school athletic programs. Other retailers are motivating their own employees by offering bonuses and better commission programs. More stores are appealing to consumers who desire crossover uses—the same pair of shoes for multiple occasions such as walking shoes that can be worn for casual dress.

The focus in the 1990s has addressed casual lifestyles and comfort. The growing maturity of the consumer has been a factor as well as price and design consciousness. Consumers will go into a shoe store twelve times a year, and if they see the same product over and over again they will lose interest. Manufacturers are becoming more customer focused and are moving away from traditional shoe products to more designer types of shoes. The 21st century will focus on better service and a greater polarization in the retail shoe business. Brand awareness will be paramount, but value shopping at stores like Kmart will also be present. Many consumers will patronize both specialty shoe stores and discount stores. Catalogs selling shoes by Nordstrom and manufacturers selling, for example, Wright Shoes will also gain in popularity as consumers become more pressed for time. The sale of outdoor boots will increase as consumers enjoy the environment. Retail shoe stores will constantly need to target changing consumer lifestyle characteristics.

Specialty store shoe retailers might be able to improve market segmentation of age groups by using cohort analysis. Whether it is the marketing of outdoor boots or athletic sneakers, market segmentation strategies are directed to some aspects of generational marketing and to shoppers with certain lifestyle characteristics. Cohorts are formed by significant external events that occur in later adolescence or early adulthood such as economic booms and busts, wars, or social changes that redefine values, attitudes, and preferences. For example, there are the "depression-scarred cohorts" who are concerned about financial security and therefore desire their shoes to last for long periods. These consumers value leather over sneakers and need to be convinced that sneakers can be of high quality. In contrast, there is "generation X" that came of age between 1984 and 1994. This cohort accepts cultural diversity and places its interests ahead of the team or company. This group will respond favorably to shoes for special purposes such as running, hiking, or walking.

The segmentation of purchasing habits is the process of dividing the whole into a number of smaller groups. For specialty store retailers the segmentation of consumers according to their lifestyle and attitudes can help define groups that are prone to be store loyal. To illustrate, habit-bound diehard consumers are old-fashioned and scornful of trendy fads. This group is brand loyal, store loyal, and habitual in its behavior. In contrast, the comfortable and contented consumer group is the most open-minded and store loyal. This group, when confronted with a good buy, tends to purchase more than a single pair of shoes. Each specialty shoe retailer needs to define its own patronage store motives and to appeal to varying consumer attitudes and preferences.

FLORSHEIM: SEGMENTING THE NON-ATHLETIC SHOE MARKET

Florsheim was founded in 1892 and since this period has targeted the American businessman. The decade of the 1990s has been a period of expanding the target market. Specifically, Florsheim has developed a comprehensive line of gold shoes and has launched the @Ease merchandise line to attract the younger consumer. The high-end or more affluent consumer has been appealed to by an alignment with American fashion designer, Joseph Abboud. The work boot market was developed and the John Deere line introduced to satisfy this market. Florsheim has not attempted to target the athletic market with sneakers. However, the merchandise line has been expanded to include business-casual, casual styles, and designer footwear.

Florsheim introduced a video monitor, since shoe stores cannot carry all of the thousands of styles and sizes in which shoes are available. Customers at Florsheim stores were able to order shoes in any size and color of styles available. Usually shoes were delivered to customers within a week. This technological innovation made shopping easier for Florsheim customers.

Florsheim sells its shoes through more than 350 company-owned specialty stores and more than 6,000 specialty and department store locations worldwide. In the early 1990s, Florsheim reorganized under Chapter 11 of the Bankruptcy Code and has become a profitable operation. A multi-brand chain-wide strategy denoting such brands as Florsheim Frogs golf shoes and John Deere work boots has contributed to the growth of its retail business. In 1998, Florsheim agreed to sell its shoes at JC Penney. Since JC Penney is one of the largest retailers in the United States, it is considered that Florsheim has successfully expanded their target base. This allows Florsheim to promote brand recognition and at the same time to add revenue to its operation. As long as Florsheim is careful not to compete directly with the department and specialty stores that it services, Florsheim should prosper with this strategy. The promotion of the Florsheim brand should help not only Florsheim but also the retailers through which it sells. Sherman-Williams also is a manufacturer with its own stores and sells its brands to department and specialty stores so that this distribution pattern is not unusual in the retail sector.

Store decor of new additional units reflects a more casual, contemporary look to make the store more inviting. Sub-labels such as @Ease permit the company to continue targeting the lower price-point categories. Sales promotions and consumer advertising has been significantly increased as an integral part of this new strategy. Even the mission statement of Florsheim has been revised to reflect a consumer-oriented, marketing-driven organization. The company is committed to a worldwide global penetration of its brands.

The goal of Florsheim is to maintain its traditional customer base while reaching out to younger customers. New concepts have been introduced with John Deere in the work boot market and a golf shoe collection with the Frogs brand. Joseph Abboud will make Florsheim more upscale. Repositioning both brands and stores is a formidable task. Florsheim has chosen not to add a limited line of sneakers or athletic shoes. As its traditional customer base matures there may be more of a tendency to embrace walking or other forms of exercise. The decision not to add an athletic line of a limited nature might be viewed as a mistake or even a blunder in the future.

FOOT LOCKER: TARGETING THE SNEAKER MARKET AND MAKING MISTAKES

Foot Locker, Lady Foot Locker, and Kid's Foot Locker are owned by Venator, previously known as Woolworth. Other operations include Kinney Shoe, Champs, a chain of athletic shops, Colorado (which sells outdoor gear), Footquarter, eVenator / Eastbay (internet commerce and direct markets of footwear), the Northern Group (includes 940 stores), World Foot Locker, and 1,424 specialty stores not including shoe stores. Sneakers are the biggest problem for the company. Foot Locker, for some years, has dominated this market because of its paramount position at the mall with Nike products. However, in the past few years the demand for Nike shoes has diminished. Instead, other sneaker brands such as New Balance, skateboard shoes, and hiking boots, which Foot Locker has been slow to stock, have caused a decline in sales. Competition, such as Finish Line, opened up larger stores than Foot Locker with a more varied merchandise selection, frequently in competitive locations. Moreover, Foot Locker has less space for markdowns than competitors. Families desire these markdowns.

The Kinney Shoe operation has had its share of problems, and efforts have been made to reposition these stores. One aspect of the problem has been addressed by remodeling the physical appearance of these stores with a new design. Kinney, in 1997, halted the operations of the shoe departments in Wal-Mart Canada stores, and attempts have been made to redefine its merchandise assortments to better attract target customers. However, a clear definition of the target market for Kinney has not emerged. Thus, the perception of its image by customers is that significant change has not happened. Eventually, the Kinney Shoe operation in Canada was closed.

Kinney Shoes has attempted to reinvent itself in the United States by catering to fashion-conscious female customers. The picture of a store's image is both functional and psychological. Variables such as clientele, location, promotional emphasis, convenience, and store fixtures are among the factors that constitute a store's image. Once that image is intact, it is difficult to change. Kinney's attempts to develop an upscale image have not been successful. The company did not reinforce its new image with the added budget allocation needed to change promotional directions.

Woolworth for many years was more interested in its "five and dime" operation than its shoe divisions. In 1997, Woolworth closed the last of its "five and dime" stores after 118 years of operation. Woolworth treated Foot Locker like a cash cow and invested little in the maintenance of the stores, using its cash flow to support other operations. This policy has changed, and there is a new strategy to concentrate on athletic shops such as Champs and the Sports Authority. Foot Locker mostly carries licensed apparel and has added private-label lines to its merchandise mix to leverage its name and logo. Venator has improved its inventory systems, which were considered noncompetitive, and has changed its mission to become an athletic goods business. Hopefully, this change in strategy to develope athletic sports stores and focus on the organization's crown jewels—Foot Locker, Lady Food Locker, and Kid's Foot Locker—will rejuvenate this company.

Foot Locker is already in danger of losing market share as such rivals as Finish Line, Sneaker Stadium, and Footstar's Footaction chains have established stores that are much larger and more attractive. The company has been slow to expand its store size to compete with the latest trend which is the development of shoe superstores. Sneaker sales are reportedly sluggish, and rivals such as Finish Line have added apparel to their merchandise assortment. Finish Line has more than 300 stores and shows signs of becoming a dangerous competitor.

In an effort to compete with larger stores, World Foot Locker stores have been established with an emphasis on store fixtures that will be movable and enhance the image of the store. World Foot Locker evolved from a mega-store concept and is approximately 10,000 square feet. There is an extensive merchandise assortment placed in a high-tech, high-energy environment. Shoes are displayed in a system of clear acrylic shelving, establishing "invisible walls." The stores' façades are nontraditional inasmuch as they do not feature storefront walls, glass windows, or entry doors. The open entry is flanked on both sides by two imposing metallic giants holding large acrylic globes. Moreover, there are three tiers of fixtures that rotate and display twenty-four hats that sit on translucent head blocks. Obviously, the fixtures enhance the appeal of World Foot Locker, but the downside is the expense, and only the future will reveal its profitability.

In an effort to compete Foot Locker has redesigned some of its outlets, notably Foot Locker, Lady Foot Locker, and Kids Foot Locker. These designs have been praised by the Institute of Store Planners and *Visual*

Merchandising and Store Design Magazine. Another plus has been to broaden its brand assortments with New Balance and Adidas and to carry some types of apparel. A strong negative has been the selection of the Venator name as a replacement for the Woolworth name. Venator does not have strong positive associations for many consumers and does not enhance the image of Footlocker stores. Moreover, Venator has been slow to use Internet selling.

Venator's strategy is focused on driving sales through its existing footwear stores, with more targeted assortment, better inventory control systems, and private branding. Some of the new footwear stores, namely Foot Locker, will be larger in size and designed to make shopping more fun. The company plans to use its relationship with key suppliers to bring about shorter buying lead times to improve speed to market and reduce fashion risk. The Merchandise 2000 program at Foot Locker streamlined the company's merchandising processes in the way goods are purchased, instituted, and merchandised so that customers get the shoes they want faster than ever before.

POWER IN THE SNEAKER INDUSTRY

Power is a major determinant of the behavior of members of the distribution system. Firms attempt to influence the behavior of their cooperating distribution system members through a prior relationship. In this instance, Nike is the leader with the ability to prescribe marketing policies to other members of the distribution system.

The process of negotiation between buyers and sellers involves power relationships. Generally, the two negotiating parties are of unequal strength, and furthermore, institutional strength has a way of shifting from one institution to the other. The use of power by one firm to influence another firm in the distribution system can be a source of conflict. Conflict takes the form of tension and disagreements between distribution members. The management of the conflict is not only essential but can result in better performance of the distribution system. For the distribution system to operate successfully a spirit of cooperation must be maintained between the distribution members.

Power in many specialty merchandise lines has shifted from the manufacturer to the retailer in areas such as specialty clothing, drugstores, bookstores, and home improvement. In contrast, Nike, because of the demand for its branded shoes, has the power to tell retailers how much they can order and even how to display the sneakers. However, in the last few years the demand for Nike shoes has diminished. New Balance, Reebok, and other brands have taken away market share. Outdoor boots became popular and Nike not only lost market share, but retailers began to rebel. Foot Locker has been slow to realize this change in the distribution system, but other specialty retailers have seized the opportunity and the power relationship is in continual flux and transition. The attempt by Foot Locker to add store-label or private brands to its merchandise is an effort to change the balance of power that favors Nike.

One large obstacle blocking the growth of sneaker superstores has been the formidable opposition of Nike and Reebok, the two largest sneaker producers. Both have retail outlets of their own and disapprove of discounting. Sneaker Stadium and Just For Feet are developing superstore formats but have not yet implemented a discounting strategy. However, book publishes in the past opposed discounting, but Barnes & Noble and Amazon.com overcame their opposition. Internet selling in the shoe industry has not gained strength, but it will be interesting to observe the power struggle of potential retail discounters and manufacturers in the future.

EDISON BROTHERS: TARGETING THE YOUTH MARKET AND MAKING MISTAKES

Market segmentation is the process of dividing a market into a number of smaller groups. Edison Brothers has accomplished this objective with its 5-7-9, Bakers/Leeds, Wild Pair, and Shifty's stores that carry shoes as part of their merchandising mix. Edison operates 449 specialty stores that target the youth market, but not all of their stores such as J. Riggings, JW/Jeans West/Coder, Oaktree, or REPP Ltd. stock shoes.

The tweens and teens are a significant target market for Edison Brothers. Although age boundaries are not precise and overlap, the tweens are roughly between the ages of nine and thirteen while the teens are between fourteen and nineteen. These markets are important to shoe retailers because they present opportunities. For example, Edison Brothers, with its 5-7-9 stores serves girls ages eleven to fifteen and has expanded its merchandise mix by introducing footwear in 1997. Shifty's serves teenage boys and girls and carries an assortment of apparel, footwear, and accessories and even stocks extreme skate gear. Wild Pairs' stores provide cutting-edge footwear that appeals to young men and women. Three popular brands of footwear are offered—London Underground, Robert Wane, and Skechers. Bakers/Leeds, with 289 units, sells "hip" affordable footwear for juniors and young women. Edison Brothers has emerged from financial difficulties and has made changes that have transformed the organization into a stronger, more focused specialty retailer.

A difficulty in segmenting the youth market is that teenagers are no more alike than adults and are actually a diverse group with a variety of motivations, pressures, and concerns. Teenagers can be socially driven. Expenditures can be made on shoes that enhance their drive for status.

Moreover, socially driven teenagers are brand conscious. Purchase motivation is reflected by their perception of brand images. Peer approval is paramount, and there is a tendency to shop in upscale or prestigious retail stores.

A less precise or delineated segment of teenagers is the diversely motivated market segment. This group is energetic and adventurous and has an appreciation of culture. This group is interested in pursuing intellectual activities such as exploring rain forests. Shoes that aid in participating in environmental activities would be welcome. Another market segment enjoys solitary activities. Walking or jogging might be of interest. Therefore, walking and jogging sneakers would be of interest to this group. The largest segment of the teenage market is the sports-oriented. Sports activities such as skiing, skateboarding, and bicycling are very expensive, and consequently teenagers and parents may share the expenses. Both teenage girls and boys in this market segment can be reached by retailers and manufacturers through sponsorship of tournaments for specific sports such as girls' volleyball or track and field.

Edison Brothers will have problems in targeting the youth market. First of all, markets must be identified by the products that they currently use or need. Teenagers have multiple demands for footwear. The market must also be measurable, and this means that market potential may be of significant size. Whether or not there is a demand for Shifty's apart from Wild Pair stores is questionable. It might be better to segment this market together rather than separately since ease of measurement of each market is not present. Another requirement of the marketing strategy is that the market segment be accessible. Trading area and transportation facilities are important factors to consider for each market segment. It is doubtful that both variables will be highly favorable for the size of these potential markets. Store proximity and transportation are very important for teenagers. Finally, the market segment should favorably respond to the marketing mix tailored to a specialized need of the segments. Low prices featured by discount stores are a fundamental appeal to a wide audience, but the needs served by Edison Brothers stores would not appear to target a wide enough market with a fundamental need. Combining the appeals of some of these stores might be more in the interests of consumers and the chain.

THOM McAN: BLUNDERS

Thom McAn was a traditional shoe store that defined its market broadly. Thom McAn carried a wide assortment of medium-quality shoes sold at popular prices. Thom McAn was established in 1922 and after seventy-four years of business, closed it doors in 1996 having the image of selling boring, unattractive shoes. The company was once a highly respected leader in the footwear industry.

The steady growth of brands like Nike and Reeboks as everyday footwear compounded the problems of Thom McAn. Although McAn sold its own version of athletic footwear, it just didn't seem to matter. Another problem was that discounters like Wal-Mart and Kmart captured a sizable market share for good but inexpensive shoes. From the 1930s to the 1960s, Thom McAn was the best-selling shoe brand in the United States, but in the 1970s and 1980s it became displaced. In 1992, half of its 700 retail stores were closed and the traditional family shoe store was indeed challenged.

Stores like JC Penney and Sears, besides the discounters, benefited from the closing of Thom McAn. About ninety of the Thom McAn locations were converted to Foot Locker stores. An advertising campaign to change its image had failed. Fierce competition especially from Wal-Mart and Payless ShoeSource had been Thom McAn's undoing.

Thom McAn had not carefully monitored consumer behavior trends. Shopping behavior can be changed or modified by either adverse or favorable economic conditions. Strong price competition can only be countered if there are economies of scale or pronounced competitive differentials.

Thom McAn was unable to respond effectively to the emergence of discounters, changing footwear-purchasing patterns, and a tarnished image based on its merchandise assortment. Continuous experimentation is a vital for success. Thom McAn was guilty of complacency. Store positioning was growing more important to shoe retailers in order to differentiate and try to gain a competitive advantage, but Thom McAn lacked the managerial vision to accomplish this.

NINE WEST: BLUNDERS

Nine West sells not only shoes but fashion items as well. Although Nine West has well-known brands such as Enzo Angioline, Easy Spirit, Pappagallo, and Bandolino, the company Nine West lost ground to competitors and posted financial losses. This situation has led Jones Apparel Group to tender an offer for Nine West in 1999. Nine West would appear to be guilty of overexpansion. Nine West has operated over 1,499 stores worldwide and markets footwear and accessories to over 7,000 retail accounts outside of its own stores. Another aspect of Nine West's difficulties is the rampant discounting in the industry and the popularity of casual clothing.

Nine West had diversified beyond shoes to encompass sunglasses, hosiery, and jewelry. The strategy was to develop multidiminensional brands that could be sold along with Nine West or Easy Spirit shoes. U.S.

Shoe Corporation was acquired in 1995 with the well-known Easy Spirit brand, and this was viewed positively. But Nine West was also confronted with a Federal Anti-Pricing Legislation suit for illegally setting prices for retailers that could be costly. The multi-dimensional brand strategy would appear to have been sound. However, rapid overexpansion of store units, retail prices that were too high, and slowness in responding to a changing fashion cycle caused difficulties for Nine West.

GENESCO: AN INTEGRATED FOOTWEAR COMPANY

Among the brands owned by Genesco are Johnston & Murphy, Nautica, Dockers, Jarmen, Volunteer, and the Journeys. Genesco operates on manufacturing, wholesaling, and retailing levels. Johnston and Murphy has 132 retail units and sells dress, dress casual, and casual footwear for men ages twenty-five to fifty-four. Jarman retail shoe stores number 244 units and sell casual footwear to men ages eighteen to thirty-one. Jarman leases shoe departments in department stores. Journeys is a fast growing retail chain of more than 250 units and markets casual footwear for men and women ages thirteen to twenty-two. Genesco also operates warehouse stores, boot factory outlets, and leased departments.

Genesco, in its manufacturing role, has developed brands such as Dockers and Nautica. In 1991, Levi Strauss granted exclusive license to Genesco to market footwear under the Dockers brand. Dockers shoes are sold in many stores that also carry Dockers slacks and sportswear. Not only is footwear marketed under the Nautica brand but also belts, jewelry, gloves, and hosiery. The company manufacturers principally footwear under the Johnston and Murphy, Dockers, and Nautica brands. Genesco operations appear successful but are not designed to assume a leadership role in the retail shoe store industry. Genesco has responded to changing lifestyle consumer characteristics by replacing rugged outdoor styles in the company's collection of Johnston and Murphy shoe stores. Johnston and Murphy, established in 1850, is one of the oldest retail shoe organizations in existence. Another response to changing consumer patterns is the physical store changes from a formal atmosphere to one that is more elegant, yet casual. This involves a more open feeling and full but soft lighting. The shoe-box design was changed to distinguish dress from casual footwear.

Recycling has become a significant trend in the footwear industry. Johnston and Murphy and the Allen-Edmunds Shoe Corporation offer recrafting and repairing services to their customers. Knowing that the shoes can be returned for repair makes a high purchase price a good value. This service provides the consumer with an incentive to buy more expensive shoes.

FOOTSTAR: A TEENAGE AND YOUNG ADULT FOCUS

In 1996, Melville divested itself of its Thom McAn division of shoe stores, and Footstar was spun off with the Footaction brand of athletic shoes. Footstar also comprises Meldisco, an operator of leased footwear departments in approximately 2,500 Kmart stores. The Footaction stores carry such major brands as Nike, Adidas, Reebok, and Converse.

Footaction stores target teens and young adults. Stores sell not only shoes but apparel as well. A consolidated distribution network and a centralized, shared management information system enable Footaction to better manage inventory, satisfy customer demands, and maximize cash flow. More than half of the products sold are available only at Footaction stores. More fashion-oriented labels like Fubu and Dada create interest. Footaction stores range from 4,000 to 6,500 square feet. The Meldisco line of private labels for Kmart also carries the Cobbie Cuddlers line from Nine West and the Thom McAn line of men's casual shoes. Meldisco is profitable but is dependent upon the success of Kmart.

Footaction has stores in forty-three states and plans to increase penetration on the West Coast and in Hawaii and Puerto Rico. Footaction monitors costs and should be able to compete well. Footaction is not a fashion leader, nor does it have its own strong brands. Essentially, Footaction is a me-too operation serving the young adult market and lacks a strong image and innovative ideas. Footstar represents a stable organization in the middle of an industry where retailers are in financial difficulties.

PAYLESS SHOESOURCE: DISPOSABLE SHOES

As consumers demand more convenience, an increasing number of goods, once considered durable, now include disposable products. Another variable influencing the disposable category is cost, which in the case of shoes, includes repair cost. Razors with blades, to illustrate, are sold in both the disposable and the more permanent varieties. Kodak and other companies manufacture disposable cameras. Since shoe repair costs have escalated, shoes are generally worn, not repaired, and discarded because the cost of repairing shoes is often more than the cost of buying a pair of new shoes. During 1997, Payless ShoeSource stores sold a pair of shoes for an average retail price of $11.35. Inexpensive shoes sold at stores like Payless, Wal-Mart, or Kmart are used and then thrown away. Payless and the discounters target the low. end of the shoe market in contrast to Florsheim, which cultivates the middle market and the quality department stores such as Bloomingdales and Neiman-Marcus that target the high end.

Traditional shoe stores are organized to extend service with staff control over the merchandise, but Payless offers self-service. A shoe operation that uses a self-service strategy is standardized with buying being centralized, since there is relatively little variation from store to store. Minimal or no on-the-floor assistance is provided. Customer contact in many instances occurs at the checkout counter. An array of merchandise is offered, but there is minimal selection in a product category. The self-service strategy consumes a lot of space, and this reduces selection. Frequently, this situation results in simpler and faster decisions on the part of consumers.

Payless ShoeSource is one of the largest shoe companies in the United States, with 4,570 stores. Payless ShoeSource was established in Topeka, Kansas, in 1956. Originally called the Volume Shoe Corporation, it was acquired in 1979 by the May Department Store Company of St. Louis, Missouri, and its name was changed to Payless ShoeSource in 1991. As a result of a spin-off, Payless became an independent company in 1991. The average size of a retail unit is approximately 3,400 square feet, and each store stocks approximately 9,000 pairs of shoes in more than 600 styles. Stores are situated in each of the fifty states, but the highest concentrations are in California, Texas, Florida, New York, Pennsylvania, Illinois, Ohio, Michigan, New Jersey, and Washington. The target market is all members of the family and all age groups. Payless sells more children's shoes than any other U.S. footwear retailer. The company does not purchase seconds and does not own any manufacturing facilities. Shoes are manufactured in Taiwan, China, and Brazil. Payless and national discount mass-merchandisers dominate the low-priced market segment of the retail shoe industry.

Lifestyle changes are not always so minor. Although the Puritan ethic forbade wastefulness, the relatively new concept of impermanence has become acceptable to present society. The market for disposable products is much more acceptable. Among the disposable products now sold are tablecloths, diapers, and a host of other products. Cultural forces and lifestyles are changing so rapidly that it is difficult to adjust to the needs of the market. Already low-priced shoes, watches, and cameras are discarded after use, causing a change in consumer purchasing patterns.

MANAGING CHANGE

Although fads, fashion, and styles are related concepts, some distinctions can be made among them. Fads are of shorter duration than fashions, seem to be more personal, and tend not to respect themselves. Styles are permanent and do not change, whereas fashion does change. Colonial furniture is a distinctive style. When styles become popular during a period, they become fashion. Not every style becomes a fashion because it may not be popularly accepted. Fashion evolves from sociological and psychological factors and is cultural in character. Basically consumers are conformists.

The fashion adoption process reflects influences on consumer purchasing behavior. The fashion adoption process is a series of buying waves that develop as the given style is popularly accepted in one group and then travels to other groups until it finally falls out of fashion. These wavelike movements are divided into maturity duration and finally the decline of the market's acceptance of a style. Three theories of the fashion cycle can be advanced:

- Trickle-down, where a fashion cycle travels downward through several socio-economic classes. For example, Allen-Edmunds and Bally's are known for quality stylish shoes. Both Allen-Edmunds and Bally's have their own retail outlets and sell to other specialty store retailers. The shoe styles then trickle down to department stores such as Lord and Taylor and finally to discounters such as Wal-Mart.

- Trickle-across, where the cycle travels horizontally and simultaneously within a number of social classes. For example, a style with different gradations of quality is introduced at the same time in exclusive high-price specialty boutiques, medium-price specialty and department stores, and discount stores. Price and quality mark the differences in the shoes sold on the three different levels. However, the style is basically the same. The trickle-across concept best demonstrates the adoption process for most fashions.

- Trickle-up, where the process is initiated in lower socio-economic classes and moves upward among higher-income and social groups. T-shirts for example, once the domain of blue-collar workers are now designed by Yves St. Laurent, Calvin Klein, and others. Shoes, like "Skeeters" also moved up the socio-economic ladder.

Another perspective has been advanced by Reebok. In the early 1990s, Reebok International designed its Blacktop series to develop its image as a performance rather than a fashion company. Blacktops were targeted at sandlots and playgrounds where the vast majority of basketball games in the United States are played. Reebok continues to refine its image and focus on quality of performance. Reebok has grown from an aerobics-shoe marketer in the 1980s to the second-best selling brand of athletic footwear by the start of the 21st century. Nine West has run afoul of the fashion cycle in shoes because of its slowness in responding to changes. Kinney Shoes at first did not respond to fashion-conscious female customers. Thom McAn developed an image of selling stodgy shoes since the shoes did not reflect any excitement or interest. Since retailers' shoes are subject to the fashion cycle, management must know what stage the cycle is in at all times. Retailers must make the decision as to when to enter the cycle and when to exit profitably.

Accurate forecasting is extremely difficult in achieving success, since the fashion cycle is rooted in the prevailing culture. The retailer and the manufacturer frequently operate largely on intuition and past experience.

Generally, the retailer cannot successfully participate in all the stages of the fashion cycle—introduction, accelerated development, maturity, and decline—at the same time. A high status specialty shoe store should enter at the start of a fashion trend. A specialty store appealing to the middle-income market should plan to enter the cycle in time to market the style as it is moving to its popularity peak.

6

Home Improvement Stores: Targeting the Do-It-Yourself Market

Environmental Changes

- Do-it-yourself trend
- More women customers
- The changing home building market
- The home remodeling market
- The installation business

Responses to Environmental Changes

- Home centers versus home improvement centers
- Scrambled merchandising
- The warehouse concept
- Efficient, personalized service
- One-stop shopping strategies
- Geographic cluster segmentation strategies
- Appropriate products
- Flexible credit programs
- Customized delivery services
- Staff product knowledge

Home improvement centers have successfully targeted the do-it-yourself market which has been the basis of the phenomenal growth of such chains as Home Depot and Lowe's that now compete with Sears. The do-it-yourself customer changes over time. Aspirations tend to grow with achievement and decline with failure. As baby boomers grow older, fewer have the stamina, patience, or time to assume home projects. Accordingly, home improvement centers such as Home Depot now offer home remodeling services and installation of some products. Remodeling revenue for Home Depot, Lowe's, and Sears is expected to accelerate in the future.

The home improvement center market is affected by environmental trends. Economic trends in the 1980s reflected recession, fewer housing starts, and a slowdown in do-it-yourself remodeling work. The economic recovery in the mid 1990s released considerable pent-up demand. Baby boomers, although marrying at a later age, are in a better financial position and are likely to increase spending on home decor. Home ownership has been the American dream in the past and this attitude is likely to continue. Home ownership has become more affordable as lower interest rates prevail. Moreover, the upward spiral in home prices has declined with median prices rising no more than 3 to 4 percent a year. Thus, the potential home improvement center market appears much more promising in the future than it was in the past.

The home improvement center market, a market with sales of more than $140 billion a year, is composed of individuals and organizations with the interest, the desire, and the purchasing power to obtain products that will enhance their home. Therefore, the demographic factors of markets and the lifestyles of the people who comprise these markets are important considerations. Microwave ovens with built-in features such as higher standards for insulation and energy efficiency have become important elements of value. The extent of the purchasing power of target markets and how they desire to spend their discretionary income are paramount considerations for understanding the home center market.

More female shoppers are patronizing home improvement centers as they participate in home decorating tasks. Women increasingly are making purchasing decisions that were once made jointly with husbands or by the husband alone. This larger role is a reflection of the gains made by women in higher education and of the emergence of economically independent women in higher work positions. It is also a reflection of new living arrangements that emphasize the role of women as heads of households. There has been a blurring of gender roles as more women perform home decorating tasks and more men perform household management and family care tasks.

There is a vital link between geographic preference and economic opportunity for home improvement centers. The Sunbelt states have attracted population growth from other regions with harsher climates. The housing market in the Sunbelt states consequently has provided much better market opportunities for home improvement centers. Geographic mobility is a potentially useful market segmentation dimension. From 17 to 21 percent of the population moves at least once a year. This market segment generally has more income and lives in costlier homes. The mobile segment tends to be an attractive market for furniture, appliances, paint, garden and yard equipment, and other home maintenance supplies.

Regional distribution of population is important to home center retailers since regional differences lead to variations in the demand for many products. These differences develop because of climate, social customs, and other factors. For example, the sale of outdoor furniture will soar in the Pacific states as this region increases in population. Because of the climate people in the Pacific states spend many more hours outdoors than those in the Eastern states.

Although there have been differences in regional growth rates, distribution of the total population has only slightly altered. The states with the fastest growth rates, with the exception of Texas and Florida, still remain very small. For example, the Mountain states have developed more rapidly than any other region, yet constitute only 5 percent of the nation's population. There are a number of well-known reasons for the growth of more popular regions: the attractiveness of climates and lifestyles of Sunbelt areas, the lower costs of establishing business organizations in the South, the energy production boom of the Midwest and Southwest regions, and the increasing expenses of energy in the Eastern states. Slow population growth is an important implication for home improvement center retailers inasmuch as they will not be able to count on a rapidly growing population to increase their customer base. Instead, home improvement center retailers will need to take customers away from the competition. Retailers who will grow are those who can best anticipate and respond to changing customer demand patterns.

The most notable trend concerning age distribution and projections is the aging of the U.S. population. The elderly consumer represents an attractive market for housing. Many elderly consumers who are selling their homes in harsher climates and reestablishing themselves in warmer geographical locations desire home remodeling performed by home centers or other retailers. Home centers that can provide household items for this market will stand to profit. This market may even furnish new homes with the help of professional interior decorators and therefore constitute, in some geographical areas, an upscale market.

Short-term trends in disposable personal income, savings, and discretionary spending can disguise but not reverse long-term trends. Home ownership is an integral part of the American dream. The traditional family may not necessarily remain the target market as singles and other nontraditional units also desire housing appropriate for their needs. The concept has been advanced that even if conditions do not warrant the purchase of new homes, consumers will still remodel.

Lowe's, Black & Decker, Color Tile, Masco, The Stanley Works, and W. R. Grace have formed the Home Improvement Research Center. This organization provides reports to the home improvement industry on future developments, trends, and changes in demand patterns such as consumer savings, housing and construction, population, and American household characteristics.

Home Depot and Lowe's have dominated the home improvement center market and are known as "big box" home centers. A trail of casualties have either been sold, acquired, or have vanished from the scene. Organizations such as Payless Cashways, Rickel, Hechinger, Moore's, and Grossman's have been affected by fierce competition. In fact, Hechinger decided in September 1999 to liquidate its 117 stores to maximize value for its creditors due to continued losses and stiff competition. Hechinger includes Home Quarters and Builders Square stores. Home Depot and Lowe's have been able to do things either better or differently than the competition.

Five key ingredients in the home improvement center industry are important for success: innovation, target market segmentation, image, physical environmental resources, and human resources. Innovation in the home improvement center industry developed when Home Depot effectively implemented the warehouse store concept and when Lowe's instituted scrambled merchandising. The warehouse concept was to revolutionize customer service, and the policy of scrambled merchandising broadened the merchandise offerings so that home centers, previously called lumberyards, could be referred to as home improvement centers.

Both Home Depot and Lowe's have developed effective strategies of market segmentation and have promoted clear store images to consumers. Home Depot targets consumers who desire low prices and a high level of service. Home Depot has promoted an image as a destination store that serves as a magnet for customers because or merchandise assortments, displays, price, and other unique features. Lowe's segments customers in small towns, satisfying their wants and needs. Lowe's has effectively promoted an image as a one-stop home improvement center through its policy of scrambled merchandising.

Home Depot has used physical environmental resources to effectively create its image as a low-price store. Merchandise is displayed on the selling floor in cut cases, on floor-to-ceiling open shelving, or on pallets. Bernard Marcus of Home Depot, with his outstanding leadership qualities, has also used manpower resources effectively. Marcus participates in the training of store managers, is very tolerant of mistakes, encourages initiative, and avoids the red tape of bureaucracy. He has been compared favorably with Sam Walton as a people motivator.

The strategy to segment the do-it-yourself market has been responsible for the growth of the home improvement center industry. The ability to educate consumers who are not knowledgeable about home improvement techniques has been extremely successful. Home Depot and Lowe's have both successfully responded to environmental changes.

STRUCTURE

What constitutes a home improvement center? The stereotypical picture was an operation that carried hardwood and lumber and sold primarily to building contractors. The modern home improvement center sells primarily to the do-it-yourself market sector of homeowners and combines the traditional hardware store and lumberyard with a self-service home improvement center. The typical home center carries a wide variety of building materials, hardware, paints, power tools, garden and yard equipment, plumbing and heating equipment, electrical supplies, and other home maintenance supplies. Some home improvement centers have expanded their offerings to include home furnishings and household appliances. Home centers offering upscale merchandise have favorable niche market opportunities. Sears and other mass merchants sold power tools; specialty stores, such as paint and floor covering retailers, sold decorating items. All of this changed as the home center sector underwent a revolution. The home improvement center market is dominated by Home Depot and Lowe's, although the market is fractured. Sears, Sherwin-Williams and other firms are formidable indirect competitors.

Table 6.1 depicts the leading chains, some of which are prospering while others are in reported difficulties. The decade of the 1990s has witnessed the phenomenal growth of Home Depot and Lowe's. While the home improvement market has grown, the growth of indirect competition has caused varying difficulties for some home improvement chains. The market is fractured as stores like Sears, Sherwin-Williams, True Value, Wal-Mart, and others sell some of the merchandise carried by the home improvement chains. Consequently, Payless Cashways, Grossman's, Moore's, and Wickes have all experienced restructuring or have sought shelter under the bankruptcy act and then reemerged.

Scrambled merchandising has broadened the appeal of home improvement centers. The selling of major appliances such as refrigerators, washing machines, dryers, stoves, and home entertainment centers has further developed the image of one-stop shopping. Some home improvement centers also carry unpainted furniture, lamps, and floor tile. Home improvement centers are already preparing to carry other types of merchandise that consumers will desire such as security devices.

Table 6.1
An Overview of Home Improvement Center Chains

	Number of Units 1998
Home Depot	761
Lowe's	484
Hechinger's	244[1]
Menard	135
Payless Cashways	154
Wickes	101
Indirect Competitors	
Sherwin-Williams	2378[2]
Sears	918[3]
True Value (TruServe)	10,500[4]
Ace Hardware	5039

1. By 1999, Hechinger's had 117 stores.
2. Includes 2,259 paint stores and 119 company-owned wholesale automotive coating stores.
3. Includes 653 Sears Dealer Stores and 265 free-standing Hardware stores.
4. In 1997, True Value merged with ServiStar and Coast to Coast hardware to form TruServ.

Internet selling may not prove lucrative for home improvement center chains as it has been for other retail, book, or apparel store chains. It would seem unlikely that consumers will buy hammers, drills, and kitchen sinks online. However, Home Depot and Lowe's have started to experiment with online sales. A drawback to Internet purchasing would be the shipping costs added to the total price for consumers. It is possible that commercial organizations such as hotels and apartment buildings may buy staples as door hardware, towel bars, and tools by computer. The do-it-yourself consumer market desires help and education at point-of-purchase, and the fundamental purchasing motivation has been at the core of home-improvement center chains' success.

The primary growth sector is the warehouse home improvement center concept, pioneered by Home Depot. Stores buy direct from the manufacturer and are technology driven through advances in the latest scanning equipment and bar coding. Home improvement centers usually maintain large showrooms that display sample merchandise. Customers purchase merchandise by placing merchandise requests at the order desk, and a clerk pulls the order from adjacent warehouse stock. Customers also serve themselves with showroom stock. Since home improvement centers provide customers with information and advice on the use of materials and equipment, there is a strong possibility that a customer loyalty base can be promoted.

As the 1980s unfolded, it became apparent that pronounced changes would occur in the home improvement market. New store formats developed to satisfy rapid growth. The warehouse store with its huge breadth and depth of merchandise assortments, self-service, and high sales volume became a formidable competitor. Superstores proliferated in the

1990s and drive-through lumberyards were tried. Some retailers attempted to combine different store formats, while others tried to defend their market. Retailers that failed to adapt to the changing environment have lost market share.

Many large retailers, such as Sears, have integrated backward in the distribution system and now own manufacturing or processing companies. Firms such as Firestone and Sherwin-Williams have integrated forward and own or franchise many retail outlets. Consequently, vertical integration is a structure commonly found in the retail sector. However, vertical integration is not a panacea, and Evans Products was to learn, as outlets under the names of Grossman's and Moore's were established, that integration presents problems.

The vertical marketing system has a number of characteristics that are different. First, vertical marketing systems consist of interconnected units which, through coordinated efforts or ownership, develop strategies and programs to determine the best combination of functions to be performed by specific units within the system. Second, the vertical system is designed to benefit from economies generated from systems analysis. Third, the vertical system has greater control and member loyalty than may be forced through contracts, and thus more stability. Fourth, there is more staff and operating support to ensure coordination and implementation of strategies. Fifth, there is emphasis on total volume, costs, profits, and investment relationships for the total distribution system. Sixth, the vertical marketing system relies on decision making by specialists.

Evans Products Company was an integrated manufacturer, wholesaler, and retailer of building products. Operations included manufacturing building materials such as lumber, plywood, hardboard, and particle board and the production of specialized building products such as interior paneling, cedar exterior siding, wood and plastic moldings, metal bifold closet doors, and mobile home air conditioners. These products were distributed through the company's wholesale and retail distribution networks.

Evans Products Company integrated forward when it decided to control its own retail outlets under the names of Moore's and Grossman's. Grossman's, situated predominately in New England, was about the sixth largest home improvement center in sales volume and about the fourth largest in number of retail stores. Eventually, Grossman's and Moore's vanished from the scene because of management and financial decisions. Evans purchased wholesale lumber distributors in order to market its products more aggressively. However, overextension is an important cause of financial difficulties, and Evans unfortunately had overextended itself. On the other hand, successful vertical marketing systems have been developed by Sears and Sherwin-Williams who are among the many manufacturers actually owning part if not all of their vertical system components. Tandy, with its Radio Shack stores, operated many of its manufacturing facilities but recently has been separating itself from this operation. Sears is successful in appliances with its Kenmore brand and also in other areas such as paint.

The possible disadvantages of the vertical marketing system include the inability of some marginal firms to operate profitably in a vertically integrated setup. Although savings can be exacted, greater financial resources need to be committed to cover the higher fixed costs. Possible managerial limitations include failing to closely monitor increased inventory holdings and placing restrictions on the variety of merchandise offerings. All of this might lead to an inflexibility of operations, which could be detrimental.

The home improvement industry is made up of a large number of small competitors with a few large competitors such as Home Depot, Lowe's, Menard, Payless Cashways, 84 lumber, Carolina Holding, HomeBase, Sears Hardware, and Lanoga. The aggressiveness and effectiveness of competitors are important determinants of the level of competition for a market area. Generally, the home improvement centers combine warehouse and showroom facilities. Warehousing fundamentals are used to reduce operating expenses and thereby offer discount prices as an important customer appeal. Evans Products, a manufacturer that used vertical integration strategy to compete in the home improvement sector, was unsuccessful. Wickes still maintains some manufacturing operations and Lowe's has forged a partnership approach with selected manufacturers, but most home improvement centers operate primarily in the retail sector. As Home Depot experiments with opening smaller stores, independents will be confronted with increased competition. The independents have survived with inherent competitive advantages of service and convenience, and now Home Depot will challenge these strengths.

INDIRECT AND REGIONAL COMPETITORS

Competition for Home Depot and Lowe's is coming from indirect and regional competitors rather than other national organizations. Several home improvement centers such as Payless Cashways, Grossman's, and Moore's either are just a shadow of their former selves or have been casualties in the competitive wars. There are indirect competitors such as Sherwin-Williams and True Value and regional players such as Menard which can be more of a threat.

Sherwin-Williams has more than 2,000 stores selling primarily paint throughout the United States. The company has been in business over 130 years. TruServ sells primarily hardware and paint and is the largest co-op in the industry. There are more than 10,000 members of this organization, but retail units tend to be small and nowhere near the size of individual Home Depot and Lowe's superstores. TruServ stores not only serve customers but janitorial suppliers as well. Ace Hardware, while not as large as TruServ, added lumber and building materials to its merchandise lines. Ace stores have remained successful because of their focus on convenience and service and their ability to establish strong market niches. There are more than 5,000 independent Ace Hardware stores nationally and hundreds of them are lumber and building materials retailers.

Home Depot has announced that in the 21st century an important strategy will be the establishment of medium- and small-size stores to combat the competition of such organizations as True Value, Ace, and Sherwin-Williams. Home Depot believes that this target market desires personalized service and convenience and that it will be better able to serve this market with medium-and small-size stores. Consequently, while True Value and Ace are presently indirect competitors, Home Depot will become a direct competitor in the future.

Menard is a regional home improvement center with 135 store units situated in nine upper-midwestern states. Its supermarket style stores are smaller than those of its rivals but they offer a similar selection by keeping a smaller quantity of items on store shelves and restocking them quickly from adjacent warehouses. Menard also has a manufacturing facility that makes doors and picnic tables which helps to keep prices down. Menard competes with smaller stores that appeal to more do-it-yourself consumers. The belief is that the sheer size of Home Depot stores is the weakness in attracting do-it-yourselfers who desire to shop in a smaller, friendlier atmosphere. Home Depot's strategy of establishing medium and small stores to compete in this market means that the future of Menard and other regional firms is uncertain.

ENVIRONMENTAL CHANGE RESPONSES

As the 21st century begins, there are indications that consumers will focus more on the home in the future. Concerns about increased crime and more stressful lives have led consumers to desire a home where they can relax in comfort and security. As a result, consumers are spending more on products that will make the home more enjoyable. To illustrate, home remodeling and fiber-optic systems to monitor lighting, security, and fire protection are future growth markets. Home entertainment products such as digital and computerized television and camcorders are also predicted growth areas. Consumers are generally more demanding in the marketplace, desiring comparative information about products, levels of service, product warranties, and other proofs of dependability.

Home improvement centers have innovated by implementing two important concepts in response to environmental change. Scrambled merchandising has had a profound impact on the merchandise offering, and the warehouse concept has had a significant impact on merchandise display and inventory management. Each concept has complemented and reinforced the other to make home improvement centers a viable and functional force in retail trade.

SCRAMBLED MERCHANDISING

Whether the home improvement center is large or small, policies must establish the type and assortment of merchandise it will offer for sale. The nature of the marketplace and competitive forces will influence and determine these policies. Customer characteristics will also guide these merchandising initiatives. The conventional home centers offered lumber for sale. The merchandise assortment was narrow but deep. Lowe's follows a scrambled merchandising policy, offering both the traditional merchandise lines and a broader assortment of related merchandise for the home such as television sets, VCRs, stoves, refrigerators, washers, and dryers. Frequently, these nontraditional merchandise lines carry higher margins and profits. For the customer, scrambled merchandising provides the benefit of one-stop shopping convenience.

Many of the independent home improvement centers cannot compete with Home Depot, Lowe's, and others in buying power and financial resources. Therefore, the growth of these independents may come from an expanded assortment of product lines or the implementation of scrambled merchandising. This merchandising policy may not only increase customer traffic but may also provide increased revenues and profits. In the future, expansion will probably include carrying such items as tile, carpeting, yard, and patio furniture, and everything for the home. Lowe's plans to expand into the lucrative home-office market by selling computers, fax machines, and cellular telephones.

The decision for a home improvement center to implement the concepts of scrambled merchandising depends upon a broad customer base and a large retail trading area. The frequency of customer patronage and their preference for one-stop shopping is another factor in the decision process, along with the nature and extent of competition in the retail trade area. Financial resources, stock turnover rates, and investments in inventory become crucial.

The merchandising policies of home improvement centers have been unpredictable. Lowe's has made effective use of scrambled merchandising but some other home improvement centers have not made effective use of this policy, perhaps believing that their situation and conditions do not warrant it. The decision for home improvement centers to implement scrambled merchandising depends upon target market requirements, the nature of the business, competition, and customer expectations.

THE WAREHOUSE STORE CONCEPT

Home Depot has revolutionized home improvement center retailing by effectively implementing the warehouse store concept. Its business strategy is to offer a broad assortment of high quality merchandise at low "day-in, day-out" warehouse prices. The warehouse store concept was first used in food retailing but has been applied by Home Depot successfully in its operation. Home Depot is a discounter, pricing items way below competitors in a no-frills setting. The warehouse emphasis is placed on the sale of national brands sold at discounts. Decor is inexpensive and promotion is done primarily through direct mail catalogs and newspaper advertising. High ceilings allow for stacking lumber and other products. While some warehouse stores in other retail areas may not provide service, Home Depot is known for effective and efficient customer service. Because of this service policy, Home Depot has built a very loyal customer base.

Home Depot is a new type of specialty store known as a category killer store. For example, Home Depot's 100,000-square-foot stores carry 30,000 different items of lumber, tools, lighting, and plumbing supplies with prices up to 30 percent below those of traditional hardware stores.

The limitations of implementation of the specialty warehouse concept in home improvement centers are that they can be adversely affected by a recession in the housing market. There can be a decline in store patronage due to a decline in the popularity of its product category because its offering is so concentrated. The category killer store may not appeal to customers interested in a small store setting. Home Depot maintains wide, uncrowded aisles to avoid the cramped feeling customers experience in other types of warehouse stores. Home Depot is really a superwarehouse carrying 40,000 to 50,000 products that is a combination of the superstore and warehouse store. This operation carries a full line of high-volume, low-price merchandise.

HOME DEPOT: EFFECTIVE USE OF HUMAN AND PHYSICAL RESOURCES

There are many who maintain that Bernard Marcus, chairman of Home Depot, is the Sam Walton of home improvement centers. Home Depot, with its constant innovation and effective use of human and physical resources, has dominated the home improvement center scene. This is a far cry from the 1979 opening of the first Home Depot store in an abandoned 72,755-square-foot Treasure Island Discount site outside of Atlanta, which turned out to be a disappointment. Learning from this mistake, in just ten years Home Depot still became the largest warehouse home-center retailer in North and South America with 761 stores. Partially responsible for this growth has been the strategy to employ a sales force with a background of home maintenance and knowledge of lumber, tools, paint, and remodeling planning. While Bernard Marcus remains as chairman, Arthur Black has become CEO and president and is now responsible for operational strategies. The question remains if Black can motivate employees as well as Marcus and envision future innovation as well.

Home Depot stores serve three primary customer groups:

- D-I-Y (Do-It-Yourself) Customers: These customers are typically homeowners who purchase products and complete their own projects and installations. To complement in-store expertise, Home Depot offers D-I-Y "how-to" clinics taught by associates and merchandise vendors.
- B-I-Y (Buy-It-Yourself) Customers: These customers are typically homeowners who purchase materials themselves and hire third parties to complete the project and/or installation. Home Depot offers the B-I-Y customer installation services for a variety of products through third-party contractors.
- Professional Customers: These customers are professional remodelers and commercial users. For these customers, Home Depot offers commercial credit programs and delivery services.

Home Depot stores are situated in high density shopping areas. Stores average 70,000 square feet of enclosed space and 8,000 square feet of outdoor garden area. Some stores stay open twenty-four hours a day. The key to the merchandising strategy is the warehouse concept. Fork lifts and dollies are used to move merchandise directly from the receiving area to the selling floor through wide aisles. Purchases are made mostly direct from manufacturers in large quantities. Merchandise is warehouse-priced, typically 15 to 30 percent below conventional home improvement centers. National brands are emphasized in displays. In 1999, Home Depot began test-marketing a new store concept, mom-and-pop style stores, which are a third of the size of typical Home Depots. These stores cater to the small project do-it-yourselfer.

Although the warehouse merchandising philosophy prevails, Home Depot is a service-oriented operation. Management considers its employees' expertise in merchandise and home improvement techniques essential to achieving merchandising strategies. A formal employee orientation and training program provides the full-time staff with essential information and techniques. Authorities claim that Home Depot employees are far superior to their counterparts in rival stores in explaining information to novice repairers.

The company pays significantly higher wages than does its competition. Salespeople are not paid commissions. Management desires to make certain that if a seventy-five cent washer will suffice, sales personnel will not be tempted to push a more expensive part because of a commission system. Managers are constantly trying to select employees who can be promoted to operating stores. Once employees become assistant managers, they are eligible for lucrative stock options.

Home Depot merchandising is innovative. Managers are encouraged to try new techniques and in return are tolerant of mistakes. Store managers have ample latitude in selecting merchandise and have direct access to top management. The overriding practice of Home Depot is to avoid the pitfalls of bureaucracy. Initial purchasing decisions are made at the corporate level by merchandise managers, and reorders are usually handled by store management personnel.

Service and customer satisfaction are more important in the 21st century than in the 1990s because in a slow-growth economy, companies survive by retaining customer patronage. Home Depot is known for customer service and among industry consultants is known as one of the best service providers in the service industry. The Home Depot culture encourages employees to build long-term relationships with customers. Employees are trained in home-repair techniques and can spend as much time as necessary to educate shoppers. High-pressure sales tactics are not used. Bernard Marcus still prowls the stores and often asks customers if they found what they wanted. With its service philosophy, Home Depot has delivered to investors the second best ten-year return among the Service 500 firms and ranks number one in ten-year growth in earnings.

Home Depot has a strategy to be the leader in a merchandise category and was one of the largest sellers of unfinished wood furniture, developing it into an $80 million-a-year business. IKEA, the Swedish retailer with fifteen stores in the United States, devoted the majority of its store space to selling unfinished wood furniture offering a much larger selection. Home Depot could not match the prices of IKEA since the product occupied only from 2,000 to 7,000 square feet and therefore volume selling was not possible. Because Home Depot could not be the power retailer in selling unfinished furniture, the item was discontinued and was replaced with an expanded selection of floor tile and wallpaper.

Similar to Wal-Mart, Home Depot has upgraded its computer order and inventory systems which complement and reinforce customer service. This change affords Home Depot data flexibility to satisfy changing merchandise demands of many independent customers and the need for rapid feedback to quickly satisfy changing customer service needs. This special order system automates what had been a manual process involving thousands of special orders. The continuous adaptation to changing needs and demands is an advantage of this new special order system. Although Home Depot has followed Wal-Mart in outstanding customer service and the implementation of advanced computer systems, Home

Depot has chosen to penetrate large urban markets in contrast to Wal-Mart's and Lowe's targeting of small urban markets.

Warehouse stores typically offer customers large discounts with minimal service and little decor. Home Depot stores have the charm of a freight yard but provide outstanding customer service. Warehouse retailing appears simple but in reality is very complex. Home Depot must carefully monitor buying, merchandising, and inventory cost as discounting diminishes the gross profit margin. Home Depot, in the home improvement center industry, has been a market champion in successfully offering low prices and high service.

Since the environment of the 21st century will be much more dynamic than of the 1990s, retailers will need to develop and enact adaptation strategies. Home Depot has endeavored to develop what is known as a destination store—that is, a retail unit where the merchandise assortment, presentation, price, or other unique features act as a magnet for customers. Approximately 30,000 people walk through a Home Depot store in a week, half of whom are women. Instead of selling toys or other items, Home Depot sells only items intended for home use. Management wants the perception to be that when people consider a do-it-yourself project, they think of Home Depot. Home Depot succeeds because it staffs stores with knowledgeable sales help who can advise customers with their problems. Therefore, customers perceive Home Depot as worth a special shopping trip when considering a do-it-yourself project.

LOWE'S: A ONE-STOP HOME IMPROVEMENT CENTER

Lowe's is oriented toward locations in smaller communities and is second to Home Depot in size in the industry. It now operates 484 stores selling building materials and goods to consumers and commercial business customers. After acquiring Eagle Hardware & Garden, Inc., which operated thirty-eight stores in ten western states, Lowe's is the sixth largest appliance retailer and is ranked forty-first in sales among customer electronics retailers.

Stores have been renovated from within, establishing vertical displays that allow selling space to be created where inventory was once maintained. Larger stores have been constructed to replace older outlets. Lowe's has concentrated on building stores from 40,000 to 60,000 square feet, which is above the industry average. Lowe's plans to lease more sites than it has done previously in order to accommodate its expansion strategies. With increased selling space, the company has been able to expand its core consumer categories, which include hardware, tools, paints, plumbing, and home decor. Other categories, such as exercise equipment, bicycles, and soft bath merchandise, have been deleted.

Consumer durables account for only about sixteen percent of Lowe's total sales, but it is still among the industry leaders in the sale of these products. Although the home electronics offering is not comprehensive, Lowe's is among the top fifty electronics retailers in sales volume in the United States. Among appliance retailers, Lowe's is among the top ten retailers in sales volume. In these categories Lowe's competes with Sears, Circuit City, Silo, and Radio Shack. Since Lowe's customers are in small- and medium-size cities, value pricing is usually associated with urban superstores and this helps build a solid loyalty base.

Lowe's sales volume gains were led by product categories that received the greatest benefit from larger square footage or the advancement of the home improvement superstore concept. Home decor and illumination sales grew by twenty-one percent. Kitchen, bathroom, and laundry sales increased by fifteen percent. Sales of tools, lawn and garden products, and heating and cooling systems also experienced double-digit percentage growth. All of these sales gains are from home improvement center superstores rather than from the conventional Lowe's outlets. Therefore, Lowe's is now committed to building home improvement center superstores in the future, and in fact, concentrating on larger stores is at the core of their expansion plans.

Lowe's is targeting the female consumer. Women initiate the majority of home improvement projects. Research studies have found that women have an image of home center stores as messy with lumber, tools, dust, and cabinets or plumbing fixtures stacked on the floor. Lowe's is trying hard to provide an aesthetically pleasing shopping environment. Lowe's has created complete kitchen and bath vignettes for displaying cabinets, vanities, sinks, faucets, and fittings. These products in the past have been lined haphazardly along walls or on racks. Related products from nearby departments, including wallpaper, paint, carpeting, and small appliances, embellish these room displays. Tables and chairs are placed in some kitchen vignettes so that customers may relax while comparing cabinets and fixtures with samples brought over from nearby departments.

Since many women are taking greater interest in home repairs, Lowe's stores schedule microwave cooking demonstrations, decorating seminars, and do-it-yourself clinics. Lowe's believes the key to attracting female customers lies in providing them with the same type of amenities offered in department and specialty stores. Service and customer satisfaction is emphasized.

Lowe's has used a contiguous expansion strategy that locates new outlets in markets close to existing ones. Once these new markets are developed, they serve as stepping-stones to the next expansion stage. A contiguous expansion is necessary when stores are served from existing distribution centers and when tight centralized control from headquarters is required. This strategy can minimize the need for new major advertising campaigns. Lowe's has expanded from its small-town base in the Carolinas into Texas, Illinois, Pennsylvania, the Midwest, and the West, where the company finds itself competing directly with Home Depot. Lowe's so far has held its ground when competing directly with Home Depot, a fact that has surprised many industry analysts. The acquisition of Eagle Hardware will also allow for direct competition with Home Depot in states ranging from California to Montana. This rapid expansion may place added strain on the company's personnel, its information systems department, and its entire infrastructure.

Lowe's success was due in part to the decision to include a brand assortment of home products such as stoves, washing machines, dryers, and electronics. Since the home center industry was composed of small firms with limited resources, the strategy of scrambled merchandising was an aggressive method to satisfy customer demand.

FUTURE BATTLES BETWEEN HOME DEPOT AND LOWE'S

Future battles between Home Depot and Lowe's will involve multiple market segmentation as both organizations desire to provide home remodeling services to their target markets. This new market segmentation strategy necessitates enlarging the target market to include those consumers who would rather not perform remodeling tasks themselves. Both organizations are expanding their geographical segmentation base. Home Depot will have more than 1,300 stores by the year 2002 and Lowe's, which is in the process of building eighty mega-centers and targeting large urban markets in the West and Northeast, will compete directly with Home Depot.

There are differences between Home Depot and Lowe's. Everything about Home Depot is Halloween pumpkin orange and everything about Lowe's is blue. In addition Lowe's has loads of appliances and even competes with Circuit City. Lowe's has been a small market retailer and is now building 150,000-square-foot stores nationwide. Home Depot is experimenting by opening small stores between 35,000 and 40,000 square feet and will compete with independent hardware stores. Home Depot is also opening Expo Design Centers with chandeliers, antiques, kitchens, and baths targeted for the upscale market.

A number of questions remain as both Home Depot and Lowe's develop new strategies.

Home Depot Future Changes

• Can Home Depot absorb thousands of new employees and maintain its high service standards with rapid store expansion plans?

- Will Home Depot be able to successfully expand and dominate the professional maintenance industry without losing its core customer base?
- Will Arthur Black, the successor of Bernard Marcus, be able to effectively motivate future leaders within the organization?
- Will Home Depot be successful in cultivating the upscale market with its Expo Design stores?
- Will Home Depot be successful with the opening of small stores?
- Will limited vertical integration be successful, as Home Depot has acquired National Blinds, a company specializing in window coverings and wallpaper?

Lowe's Future Changes

- Will Lowe's be successful in operating mega-centers?
- Will Lowe's be able to successfully expand into large urban markets in the West and Northeast through the acquisition of Eagle Hardware & Garden?
- Will Lowe's be successful in competing directly with Home Depot in large urban markets?
- Will Lowe's be successful in satisfying the commercial and residential builders market?
- Will Lowe's be able to profit through special orders from catalogs, kiosks, and the Internet, which constitute new potential markets?
- Will Lowe's brand development strategy prove successful?

Management vision must include the adaptation of strategies to take advantage of competitive environmental conditions. A sense of showmanship that lends itself to an exciting environment will be needed in the future as more women patronize home improvement centers. Store decor and atmospherics must reflect a dramatic shopping experience. A major problem in the future will be the development of multiple market segmentation strategies as other market segments, such as professional home builders and customers who desire Home Depot and Lowe's to perform remodeling services, are included in the target market.

PAYLESS CASHWAYS, INC.: A FAILED NICHE-STORE STRATEGY

Payless Cashways has targeted an upscale market that includes serious do-it-yourselfers and professional home builders. The competitors of Payless Cashways include Home Depot, Lowe's, and a variety of regional and local chains and independents. The target markets of these firms vary somewhat. For example, income and demographic characteristics of the thirty-five to forty-year-old owner served by Home Depot differs from the target market selected by Payless Cashways.

Payless Cashways' retail stores offered a comprehensive mix of functional and fashionable goods. Lumber was made the focus of its product offerings with the thought that lumber would be purchased first for a major home improvement project. Therefore, the sale of lumber was featured in print and broadcast advertising.

Payless Cashways had varied its business format with Home and Room Designs, a 12,000-square-foot store selling home room designs, and Toolsite, a 15,000-square-foot store devoted to professional tools. Payless Cashways had pursued a niche-store strategy in contrast to Home Depot and Lowe's which offer warehouse-format stores.

There were a number of reasons for this failed niche-store strategy. Consumers and independent contractors believed that Payless' service was not comparable to other home improvement centers. Service was considered below acceptable standards. Another reason that has been advanced was that Payless was frequently experiencing stock-outs with such staples as nails. Moreover, financial ratios were ominous, and stock turnover decreased. Target markets were not sharply delineated, and as a result, the store image and its market positioning became blurred from the customer's standpoint. Merchandise lines and prices were not distinctive enough to compete.

An organization cannot operate in every market and satisfy every need. Therefore, a market focus needs to be developed. This means that the organization must find a way to serve delineated target markets either better or differently than the competition. Payless needs a definite plan of action. Reorganization plans seem to lack direction.

WICKES: BLUNDERS

An important reason for the failure of Wickes was that it did not take advantage of population growth in the suburbs and did not target its product lines to the needs of customers in different geographic locations. Furthermore, Wickes continued to serve its traditional base of customers whose purchases were directly tied to housing cycles. Wickes did not cultivate the do-it-yourself market as well as Lowe's and Home Depot. These new changes in the home improvement market might have been missed because managers were constantly shifted from one business format to another and stores were not situated in good locations. In contrast, Home Depot adopted the philosophy that even when customers are not purchasing new houses, they fix up the old ones. Wickes was very slow to cultivate the remodeling market.

In 1975 Wickes acquired more than thirty wholesale building material distribution centers in twenty states from the Evans Products Company and branched out from its basic lumber wholesaling and retailing formats into such operations as food processing, farm machinery, and furniture stores. But as Wickes grew, its profits failed to keep pace. Essentially, it was the retail furniture business that proved to be Wickes' achilles' heel. In 1975 Wickes had more than 230 building supply stores in thirty-six states. Battles in many markets with Levitz Furniture, a pioneer warehouse retailer, and other established merchants were too much for Wickes. Although Wickes was strong in urban store outlets, it incurred losses in suburban markets. Eventually, this situation led to a management shakeup, but problems were still to plague Wickes.

Wickes announced in 1980 that it would discontinue its money-losing building division, which constructed pole-frame building and commercial and industrial structures. The recession was blamed for a sharp drop in sales and subsequent losses. Finally in 1982 Wickes filed for Chapter 11 protection. This was the second largest retail reorganization proceeding since W. T. Grant went into Chapter 11 in 1975.

Wickes also owned the Gable-Skogmo department store chain, plus supermarkets, drug-stores, and various manufacturing operations. The immediate closings did not include any of Wickes's twenty-four furniture warehouse showrooms or the any of the company's three Attitude stores in Chicago, which specialized in more contemporary furniture for apartments and condominiums. Wickes was the largest stockholder in such stores as Garfinckel, Brooks Brothers, and Miller and Rhoads before these outlets were taken over by Allied Stores. Wickes also sold the Red Owl supermarkets and Snyder's Drug Stores.

In 1982, Wickes was the fourth largest retailer in the world, but its size did not guarantee its success. The acquisition in 1980 of Gable-Skogmo, a Minneapolis chain of supermarkets, drugstores, department stores and mail-order houses was a contributing factor to Wickes's difficulties. Wickes had eighteen different divisions or subsidiaries with 375 stores in the United States and sixty-five in Europe. There was also a strong link to the housing industry, which was saddled with high interest rates. Even the do-it-yourself home improvement business had faltered from the impact of the recession, and competition intensified. In summary, although untimely diversification constituted a challenge, Wickes was unable to cope with the cyclical swings in the building materials business.

Eventually, Wickes reestablished itself. The furniture division was the worst problem. Customers were now offered a five-year warranty against defects and workmanship, a full refund if the customer was dissatisfied for any reason, and a promise to match any lower price by a competitor by refunding the difference within thirty days. Wickes also needed to turn around a negative shopping experience. Shelves were now fully stocked, employees were added to insure quality service, and the more profitable stores were renovated. The new chief executive officer went on television informing customers of the changes in Wickes and promising that customers would receive full value and entirely what they had a right to expect.

In 1990, Wickes controlled the Builders Emporium chain of approximately 120 stores originally purchased in 1978. Builders Emporium owns only about 10 percent of its stores and leases the remainder. The stores average 40,000 square feet of selling space. Builders Emporium is one of the largest home improvement retailing chains in California. The store's merchandise assortment includes home and lumber products, tools, hardware, garden and nursery items, and seasonal goods. Builders Emporium stores generally provide a wider selection of items and lower prices than hardware stores, greater convenience and better service than warehouses stores. Commercial customers constitute less than 5 percent of its total sales. The average customer lives within three miles of the store and makes an average purchase of less than $20.

Primary competition was from warehouse store chains. Warehouse stores were generally able to offer lower prices than Builders Emporium because of higher sales volume. Home Depot and to a lesser degree, Home Club, and Builders Square were also competitors but not as significant as the warehouse stores. Builders Emporium featured brand name merchandise and naturally customers were able to make price comparisons that were sometimes viewed unfavorably. Eventually in the late 1990s, Wickes divested itself of Builders Emporium. However, Wickes did not leave the do-it-yourself retailing scene entirely but instead launched a Web site to sell professional-grade tools online.

HECHINGER: MISTAKES

Leonard Green & Partners purchased Hechinger, Builders Square (formally controlled by Kmart), and Home Quarters and merged them together into the industry's third-largest home center chain. Two former Hechinger store units have been reopened under the name Wye River Hardware & Home. Hechinger had entered warehouse retailing too late, expanded too late, and addressed its internal operations too late, causing the company to terminate its operations in 1999 and begin holding going-out-of business sales at its remaining 117 stores.

Based in Landover, Maryland, Hechinger initially developed an opposite strategy from Home Depot by operating stores that attract female shoppers. However, by acquiring the Home Quarters Warehouse chain in the Southeast, Hechinger decided to diversify. The Home Quarters chain was like Home Depot but second in price and service. Triangle Building Centers were also acquired by Hechinger in Pennsylvania. When pitted against Lowe's, they were a poor second.

Hechinger had benefited immensely from the building boom in the Washington, D.C.-Baltimore area. Hechinger had established superstores that carried about 40,000 items, compared with 25,000 to 30,000 items carried by its rivals. Its stores were more attractive than conventional home improvement center stores. Hechinger stores had vinyl-covered floors in contrast to the concrete usually found in no-frills warehouse outlets.

Hechinger's expansion had been ambitious. Geographic expansion was also filled with pitfalls because of the declining economy in New England and competition from Home Depot. Hechinger tried to develop a middle ground in its strategies by presenting an image known for ambiance as compared to Builders Square, a conventional warehouse store. Hechinger lacked the financial strength of Home Depot, and its sales personnel lacked the expertise with customers. It would seem that Hechinger offered good prices and good services but was a poor clone of Home Depot and found it difficult to compete with Lowe's.

The Leonard Green buyout and subsequent control of Hechinger, Builders Square, and Home Quarters seemed to lack direction toward some clear goals. Although goals may be adjusted during planning stages, some precise objectives should provide a starting point, which was lacking in this situation. Hechinger's leaving the market will send more shoppers to Home Depot and Lowe's.

MANAGING CHANGE

Home Depot and Lowe's have succeeded because they have maintained a focus on their core business, have been able to get better terms and exclusive merchandise from their suppliers, and have constantly sought new strategies to innovate in order to stay ahead of the competition. Success or failure hinges on these elements and how well they are performed.

Lowe's has changed from a traditional home center to a modern home improvement center. Home Depot has pioneered the warehouse concept applicable to home centers and is a discounter in the home center market. Moreover, employees provide knowledgeable service and advice concerning customer-building plans. Home Depot is rapidly becoming the Wal-Mart of the home center industry. In contrast to Lowe's and Home Depot, many organizations, such as Grossman's and Moore's, remained conventional home centers and this strategy proved disastrous. Moreover, in recent years the home improvement center environment has seemed to be little more than turbulent. Rickel Home Centers and Hechinger have disappeared, and Payless Cashways and Scotty's are struggling to survive. Prominent regional chains such as Wolohan Lumber and National Home Centers have downsized in order to maintain profitability, which has been eroding. The home center industry consists of many independents servicing specific geographical locations, such as Menard in the Midwest, and lacks the resources to make strategies like scrambled merchandising or the warehouse concept work effectively.

These small independent retails have formed cooperative groups allowing them to realize the economies of scale by making large-quantity group purchases. Ace Hardware and TruServ Corporation are introducing new hardware store formats in efforts to compete. Independence is maintained and efficiency improved by capitalizing on quantity and time-purchasing discounts, thereby enhancing competitiveness with chains.

Environmental changes such as the do-it-yourself trend, women interested in home repairs and remodeling, and the blurring of gender roles have caused some home center organizations to change to home improvement centers. Home centers, largely, because of competitive pressures, are experimenting with new or modified formats and also with nontraditional locations. Since customers are afflicted with poverty of time and the role of women has changed, home improvement centers have placed emphasis on convenience and service. Convenience, exemplified by extended hours, short waiting times, and other factors, makes shopping easier. Service includes some convenience factors and also friendly, knowledgeable sales staffs, easy credit, liberal return policies, and post-purchase services. Lowe's has employed convenience by promoting one-stop shopping. Consumer durable goods such as washers, dryers, and television sets can be purchased at Lowe's. Home Depot and Lowe's both stress service to women. Although not new, scrambled merchandising remains a major strategy of some home improvement centers.

Home improvement centers are constantly identifying significant trends and developing marketing strategies to satisfy consumers. Changing trends either present opportunities or pose threats for home improvement centers. One trend affecting the home improvement industry is the direction of movement in interest rates. Sales in the home improvement industry usually move in tandem with home sales. From the 1980s to the beginning of the 21st century, home improvement centers have benefited from falling interest rates, which stimulate new and existing housing sales. Rising interest rates could slow sales in the housing market and concomitantly in the home improvement industry. The home improvement industry might need to focus in the future on do-it-yourselfers who desire to remodel their present homes rather than buy a new one. Home improvement centers have continually changed and adapted to environmental trends. Therefore, the outlook for home improvement centers remains positive for continued growth in retail trade when confronted by changing environmental trends and competitive challenges. Home improvement centers have emerged to satisfy widely different consumer preferences for service levels and specific services. Home improvement centers such as Home Depot and Lowe's have learned the lessons of the past and have developed strategies for success:

- Make customers happy. Provide guidance in the use of products sold. Extend customers better values than the competition and present a wider merchandise assortment to select from. Maintain a high level of customer satisfaction.
- Maintain a low ratio of rent to sales because of volume selling.
- Motivate employees to have pride in the store's merchandise and to maintain in-depth product knowledge and if possible, to try to save the customer money. Motivated employees should help to increase customer repeat patronage.
- Strictly enforce controlling service, cleanliness, and all other aspects of the operation.
- Take advantage of favorable word-of-mouth communication thereby decreasing promotional costs. Satisfied customers are the best "advertisements."
- Identify and cultivate a growing market. The do-it-yourself market of both male and female consumers is growing.
- Maintain a clear and distinctive image as a home improvement center.

Wickes learned that while growth is possible, it needed to have sufficient managerial and financial resources to survive. Payless Cashways could not effectively motivate employees and maintain high levels of service. Home improvement centers such as Home Depot and Lowe's have learned that opportunities exist when a traditional market structure prevails and when there are gaps in satisfying customer needs by existing firms. However, Lowe's with its recent decision to compete directly with Home Depot may be exceeding the capabilities and resources of its organization.

7

Bookstores: Targeting the Educated Market

Environmental Changes

- Maturing Population
- Increasing educational attainment
- Growing double-income market
- Desire for value
- Increasing computer literacy leading to E-books
- Seasonality of business

Responses to Environmental Changes

- Product positioning
- Positive atmospherics
- Superstore format
- Development of interest stores: mystery, children, sports
- Internet selling
- Discounting
- Management of inventories

The bookselling business is growing at a slow rate of less than 4 percent a year and represents a $23 billion market for the United States book business. Profit margins are thin, and the product being sold is a commodity. As individuals acquire more education their choice of goods and services will be much more selective than those of persons with less education. More education on the part of consumers should create additional demand for such products as books, art, travel, musical recordings, and other cultural activities. Estimated book publishing industry sales have increased from approximately $12 billion in 1987 to about $23 billion in 1999. The four major sources from which adults purchase books are large chain bookstores, small chain / independent bookstores, book clubs, and E-commerce / Internet.

Many authorities predicted the decline of educational enrollments during the 1980s. However, this has not happened. Instead, college enrollments increased in the 1990s. There is every prospect that this trend will continue in the decade of 2000. The younger generation has realized that workers without skills will become marginal workers in the future economic environment. This will become increasingly evident as new technology requires broader training of workers and professionals in order to be effective. It is interesting to note that these educational gains have developed in spite of increasing tuition and expenses for room and board.

Another enrollment trend is that more and more college students are age twenty-five and above. This indicates that increasing numbers of people are learning that the value of an education cannot be underestimated and that books are an integral part of the life experience. The college-educated consumer generally has more discretionary income than the rest of the population and has more of a propensity to read and purchase books.

Educational achievement can be used to distinguish among market segments. For example, specialized book clubs target consumers interested in science fiction, history, business, and other reading categories. General book clubs such as Book-of-the-Month target readers with a wide array of interests. Consumers are invited to select books from specialized catalogues thereby gaining access to a broad selection of books. With the growth of the computer age Amazon.com is able to provide Internet browsers with a large number of titles not commonly found in retail bookstores resulting in the average online book shopper buying more books per visit than someone shopping in a bookstore.

The United States provides booksellers with a fast growing market for a number of reasons:

• Rising educational levels. High school graduation rates are high and approximately half of the graduates continue with their education. All factors equal, educated people generally buy books.

- The graying of America. Older people tend to read more than younger consumers. New book superstores with coffee shops have discussion groups that are attractive to middle-age and older consumers who have outgrown the cocktail scene.
- The growing double-income market. Two-income households have more money to spend and are able to pursue varied interests. In many instances, this means that more books are purchased.
- Profitable regional markets. There is a higher concentration of book purchasing in select metropolitan areas, cities with colleges, and the western region of the United States.

The sale of books by retail bookstores in the United States changed in 1975. To that point, the U.S. Congress had exempted retail price maintenance by manufacturers from federal antitrust laws. Fair trade laws now represent a historical curiosity as a result of the repeal of the Miller-Tydings Act and the McGuire Act, which were enacted in 1937 and 1952 respectively. Until this abandonment of fair trade enforcement by states, publishers could specify the prices at which booksellers sold their products although laws that regulate the right of sellers to sell below costs may still be in effect in a number of states. The passage of the Consumer Goods Pricing Act in 1975 made vertical price fixing illegal per se, and the subsequent abandonment of the enforcement of many individual state statutes considerably changed the practice of selling books at retail.

In 1985, the B. Dalton Bookseller chain announced a discounting program that signaled a price war that was to change the structure of retail trade bookselling practices forever. At that time, B. Dalton had more than 700 units and was discounting hardcover best-sellers by 25 to 35 percent and Waldenbooks, with more than 900 outlets, began to compete using this pricing strategy. A price war could further undermine the financial condition of many independent bookstores.

The reaction of many independents and small bookchains varied in the 1985 period. Brentanos, an elite seventeen-store chain based in Chicago, maintained that its long history of bookselling dating back to the turn of the century and its large inventory would become more competitive. In 1985 Barnes & Noble was a large seller of textbooks and had just started getting into discounting other types of books. Crown Books was already discounting all books, not just best-sellers, and therefore did not believe this change would affect its chain. The Pickwick chain, a discounter with nearly forty units, immediately halted expansion plans. Many independents realized that Waldenbooks and B. Dalton had captured about half of the general retail book business. Of particular note was that neither B. Dalton nor Waldenbooks planned to reduce service, since both chains increasingly relied on sales of audiocassettes, videocassettes, and game sales. Publishers did react adversely to these pricing policies, but retail bookselling practices were to change drastically as was the market structure of retail trade. Fair trade legislation had been repealed, and this was the basis for future change.

A consideration of the successes and failures in the retail book trade shows that many mistakes have been made, and that the organizations still viable are those that were able to make adjustments with such variables as innovation, target-market segmentation, image, physical environmental resources, and human resources.

Innovation took place when Crown Books made the decision to discount best-seller books. This strategy resulted in an important disruption in the retail book trade and had serious effects on publishers. Leonard Riggio of Barnes & Nobles innovated by introducing two important concepts. First, books should be marketed as consumer products. Second, a retail bookstore environment should provide entertainment and a relaxing atmosphere.

Retail bookstores have segmented the market by specialization. There is an audience for books in such areas as mystery, fiction, business, children's literature, religion, and other categories, and therefore bookstores have been established to target these specialized areas. These bookstores provide breadth and depth for a serious audience. Image is also reflected by atmospherics and is paramount in the superstores.

Physical environment resources have been approached by booksellers in a number of different dimensions. Amazon has pioneered ordering books on the Internet. Moreover, distribution to the purchaser has been accelerated by strategic placement of warehouses. As Barnes & Noble and others attempt Internet selling, buyers are finding it easier to order out-of-print books, hard-to-find books, and books sold by small publishers.

The use of human resources has not been overlooked. Customers who patronize superstores are given a great deal of personal attention. Those customers who purchase rare books are able to speak to knowledgeable personnel.

The biggest mistake of independent bookstores was the failure to recognize the threat of discounting. Another mistake was not to recognize the potential of the superstores. The day of the independent bookstore is diminishing with the development of large chains and the development of Internet selling. Since 1991 membership in the American Booksellers Association, which represents independents, has fallen from 5,200 to 3,300 stores. The once proud name of Brentanos has vanished from the scene as the independent retail bookstore gradually becomes an endangered species. Independents fight back by seeking strategic locations and by specializing in serving specific markets in such areas as science fiction or biography, or sports and other particular market segments.

POSITIVE ATMOSPHERICS

With the development of superstores, bookstore retailers have been able to offer much more than a mere assortment of merchandise. Successful bookstore merchants facilitate the exchange process by creating a shopping atmosphere that enhances value for the store's target customers. The physical environment of the store is an integral part of the exchange process. Superstores, with their relaxed reading and browsing environment, provide a well-thought-out marketing strategy that supports a wide offering of books on a broad variety of subjects. Book and poetry readings provide an exciting atmosphere and, in conjunction with a high level of personal service, establish a distinctive image for the store in the customer's mind. At the same time, Waldenbooks has begun a kiosk program, which will be located in malls where Walden has an outlet. The kiosks will sell a variety of motivational products under the name Successories.

Synergy between store atmosphere and merchandising philosophy is also a key to the successful operations of superstores. The designs of superstore outlets please the expectations of their customers well. There is an appeal to families with children with planned activities for young customers. The aesthetics and ambiance of the superstore along with the service it provides are integral to store image. Superstore book retailers have created a homelike atmosphere that is similar to the historical picture of the old country store before the Civil War with the men playing checkers near the old pot-bellied stove and exchanging town gossip. For example, Barnes & Noble has game night every Tuesday where patrons can play chess, Scrabble, or backgammon in the café of their store at the Inner Harbor in Baltimore. Every Wednesday from noon until 2:00 P.M., classical musicians play in the café and every Monday evening, great books such as *Dr. Zhivago, To Kill a Mockingbird,* and *All the President's Men* are discussed. Furthermore, Tattered Cover, an independent store in Denver, has created an atmosphere of trust and community that pervades its store environment. Check-writing customers are not required to furnish identification. Employees are given a key to the store and allowed to borrow available books. These policies develop more informed personnel and symbolize complete trust. Intense loyalty to the store is fostered, and this attitude transfers itself to the way customers are treated. Thus, positive atmospherics can promote a differential advantage.

Bookstore merchants are targeting sensory appeals that are conducive to purchasing. Atmospherics is the psychological impact created by a store's design and physical surroundings that are developed by the stores merchandising activities.[1]

Table 7.1
An Overview of Book Retailers

	Net Sales 1998	Number of Units 1998
Barnes & Noble (B. Dalton, Doubleday, Scribner's)	$3.006 billion	1009
Borders (Waldenbooks)	$2.6 billion	1167
Amazon.com	$610 million	N/A
Books-A-Million	$345 million	173
Crown Books	$298 million	179

MARKET STRUCTURE

Retail booksellers employ strategies of scrambled merchandising and market segmentation. Barnes & Noble, to illustrate, offers Rodin's *The Thinker* bookends for approximately $59 and the *Thai Bell* which resonates serenity for about $105. Retail booksellers also maintain music departments with a wide stack of CDs, cassettes, and educational games. Market segmentation strategies are sharply defined as some retailers specialize in selling only mystery books, children's books, or religious books.

Table 7.1 indicates that Amazon.com is the third largest seller of books in the United States in total sales. An important reason is that through the Internet, Amazon can offer consumers a much larger choice of titles than the ordinary bookstore. Consumer tastes are both specialized and varied so that the ordinary bookstore might not find it profitable to stock book titles that are not in great demand. Barnes & Noble, B. Dalton, Crown, Waldenbooks, and Books-A-Million discount either all or a part of their inventory.

Another dimension of the prevailing market structure is the decline in the number of independent bookstores. Retailers that provide coffee shops, literary discussions, and guest speakers among other types of activities are seizing market share away from small independents that cannot afford these amenities. The growth of Barnes & Noble—with the acquisition of six Marboro Books stores in 1979, 796 B. Dalton stores in 1986, three Scribner's Bookstores in 1989, twenty-three Booktop stores in 1989, and thirty-nine Doubleday Book Shops in 1990—has helped to further consolidate the industry.

Since the early 1980s, retailers have evolved in two different directions. One trend has been a continued movement toward highly specialized merchandise lines. Examples include Waldenbooks for Kids and bookstores targeting mystery and detective story readers. The other trend has been toward a general merchandise annex, with broad assortments represented in superstores. Barnes & Noble, Borders, and Books-A-Million are all concentrating on developing the superstore structure.

Table 7.1 does not depict the vertical integration of the industry economics. Colleges and universities maintain bookstores that take market share away from Barnes & Noble, Borders, and other booksellers. The market is further diversified with drugstores, discount stores, and department stores also selling books. Nonetheless retail trade is still dominated by book superstores such as Barnes & Noble, Borders, Books-A-Million, and Crown Books with Amazon.com making exciting inroads.

Book superstores provide the customer with the convenience of one-stop shopping along with a wider range of products and services. The superstores draw patronage from a wider trading area than conventional bookstores and increase the productivity per square foot of selling space. The increased profitability in book superstores is especially attractive to giant book chains such as Barnes & Noble and Borders who are currently experiencing declining profits.

Because consumers' educational and income levels have increased, they tend to have more leisure time with a growing range of alternative ways to spend that time. In order to attract consumers, the typical superstore offers a comprehensive title base, a café, a children's section, a music department, and a calendar of ongoing events, including author appearances and children's activities. Customers can relax and read in the café, which serves a variety of exotic coffees, teas, and beverages with savory entrees, light lunches, and pastries and desserts. Many feature national authors for book signing and discussion group meetings.

Superstore sales have increased in the 1990s, but costs have also escalated. Books are ordered in large quantities and if they don't sell, discounts from fifty to eighty percent are given. This means less profit for both the superstore and the publisher. Superstores can exert power over publishers by threatening to return books unless they are permitted to sell them at half price. Waldenbooks and B. Dalton have closed a large number of mall stores since 1995 because many malls couldn't support two major bookstores. The closings represent an opportunity to expand superstores in other locations. Competition is getting fiercer. In fact, Crown Books has sought relief under the bankruptcy act.

A recent trend in book marketing is to sell books outside of traditional bookstores allowing publishers to target precise market audiences. To illustrate, cookbooks and books about food are sold in Williams-Sonoma, a high-priced chain with 163 stores nationwide, and Crate & Barrel, which has more than sixty units. Next to cookbooks and books about food, children's books are probably among the best-selling books sold outside traditional bookstores. FAO Schwarz, an elite toy store with more than forty stores around the United States, stocks several thousand books. Disney Stores, with 713 units in the United States, also stocks a large inventory of books.

The Metropolitan Museum of Art in New York City stocks from 8,000 to 9,000 titles and has fifteen satellite stores. Rand McNally, noted for travel and entertainment books, has more than twenty outlets and a title base of about 5,000 books. The sale of books outside of traditional book-stores has eroded market share. This trend has exerted pressure upon independent book retailers who lack the resources of the large chains.

By purchasing books over the Internet consumers have forced compa-nies to change the way they sell. Amazon.com has accumulated a cus-tomer base of approximately three million, but profits have eluded it. Book sales are increasing but so are costs, and competition is fiercer. In efforts to diversify and confront competitors, Amazon entered the music business and almost overnight has become successful in this sector. Since Amazon.com does not order titles from a distributor until an order is placed, Amazon is able to turn over its inventory about ten times as fast as Barnes & Noble. Although sales are rapidly increasing for Amazon, promotional costs are diluting profits and causing losses. Barnes & Noble and Borders have also entered Internet bookselling, as have other compet-itors. Books-A-Million will supply books and book-related merchandise to the Wal-Mart online store. This alliance should help both Wal-Mart and Books-A-Million to more effectively challenge Amazon.com.

The growth of superstores has challenged the existence of independent book retailers. Barnes & Noble and Borders have begun to write a new chapter in book retailing with their superstores. These superstores have economies of scale, lower advertising costs, a wider selection, and an improved ambiance compared to independent book retailers. Superstores stock between 80,000 and 100,000 different titles, provide extended hours, and offer an atmosphere favorable for browsing. There is no question that superstores generate increased sales. Although Books-A-Million, Barnes & Noble, and other booksellers are investing heavily to open new superstores, it is questionable whether sales per square foot productivity generated by superstores significantly increases profitability. Meanwhile independents fight back by emphasizing superior customer service, capi-talizing on long-established first-name relationships, and targeting select niche markets. Using a scrambled merchandising strategy, they are plac-ing a greater emphasis on the sale of calendars, videos, toys and sales of books to school libraries. Independents may have an advantage in servic-ing casual readers and the market segment that may find superstores in-timidating.

BRENTANOS BLUNDERS

Brentanos was founded in 1907 and became a cultural center, selling art objects and sometimes jewelry as well as books. Store image and the perception of store image by consumers was to make Brentanos a legend in its own time. For someone to explain that he or she had made a purchase at Brentanos in Chicago, New York, Boston, or any of its branches was virtually analogous to having announced a purchase at

Neiman-Marcus in Dallas or Tiffany's in New York. Yet, on July 31, 1995, Brentanos closed its doors.

The fundamental lesson that can be learned from the Brentanos situation is that a firm cannot stand still. Market opportunities and threats are ever present in the environment and adaptable behavior should be the basis for strategy development. A continual reassessment of the environment, including industry structure, is needed, and this may require a shift in strategies.

Brentanos sold noteworthy books and numbered among its customers Andrew Carnegie, Henry Clay Frick, J. P. Morgan, Theodore Roosevelt, and other celebrities of the period. However, this successful operation was hit hard in the depression, and in 1933 the firm was sold to Stanton Griffis and Adolph Kroch. All store outlets were sold, with the exception of the main store in New York and branches in Washington, D.C., Chicago, and Paris. Three years later the Chicago branch was given to Kroch and the operation was known as Kroch's and Brentanos.

In 1962 the organization was purchased by the Crowell-Collier Publishing Company and operated very successfully until the 1980s. In 1981, Crown Books moved into the Chicago area with its discounting policy. Kroch-Brentano had sufficient lead-time to discount but refused. A lack of managerial vision maintained the belief that Brentanos excellent service and knowledgeable staff would suffice and that discounting was unimportant. Much of Bretanos' durability had stemmed from its employees who were remarkable both for their learning and loyalty. Human resources were an integral part of its past success, but obviously the competitive environment had been misjudged and price was more important than the Brentanos management had considered. Management had considered it a competitive strength that its foreign book collection and periodicals were unobtainable elsewhere. Its rare book collection and first editions and its series of cultural events that attracted hundreds of people were held in high esteem by management and customers. However, in the final analysis, the lack of a discounting strategy and other factors became its undoing.

Location was also a factor. Location is of paramount importance to the success of a prestigious specialty bookstore. The inability of stores to adapt to urban development, changing traffic patterns, and population shifts will cause casualties in the future as they have in the past. For example, in the 1980s Brentanos, like other retailers in Chicago, watched the shopping traffic shift to North Michigan Avenue. The firm was also hurt by the movement of superstores into the area and the decade of bookstore vulnerability in suburban shopping malls. The flagship store had been caught in an old downtown area and was not a destination location. Customers targeted by Brentanos were no longer shopping for books in suburban malls. Instead, North Michigan Avenue became their destination.

Another reason for the fall of the once revered giant was its slowness in realizing the importance of new technology. Computer technology which Brentanos was slow to adopt, has placed a much greater emphasis on cost control and inventory management. The need to integrate financial planning with merchandising programs has changed the way business was previously done, and Brentanos lost opportunities because it did not sufficiently realize the long-term benefits of effective financial analysis, planning, and control. The time for Brentanos to computerize was in the mid-1980s, but by 1993 technical difficulties caused the company to abandon a computer inventory program and start over again. Early computer inventory studies were largely ignored.

Under-capitalization left Brentanos unable to battle the competition. Discounting was not used until 1991, ten years after Crown Books had innovated this strategy. Ten percent was offered off every book in its stores, 30 percent off *New York Times* best-sellers, and a frequent buyer discount was offered through its Good Sense Card. Management had suffered from marketing myopia, however, and the discounting made the company's financial position worse rather than better.

Management must consider the marketing environment as dynamic and constantly changing. Instead, management often concentrates on maintaining a clearly delineated business operation. Crown Books instituted a discount policy in 1981, B. Dalton in 1985, and Brentanos in 1991. While other retailers were computerizing, Brentanos as late as 1993 was unsuccessful in its efforts to do so. There was a lack of vision and resources. Brentanos environmental analysis and contingency planning strategies appeared to be nonexistent. Managerial vision should focus on decisions that have long-term implications rather than on objectives focused on a one- to two-year period.

THE PORTER THEORY

According to Michael Porter, three strategies are used to attain competitive advantage.[2] First, a differentiated offer in the form of a product or service can be directed to consumers. Second, the organization may become a low-cost producer among a group of competitors. Third, the organization can operate in a protected market segment. The Porter model identifies three generic strategies: cost leadership, differentiation, and focus. A cost leadership strategy appeals to a wide market and offers goods or services in large quantities. Retailers are able to minimize per-unit costs and extend low prices through economies of scale. On the other hand, with a differentiation strategy, the retailer aims at a large market by offering goods or services viewed as distinctive. Some view these offerings as unique by virtue of design, features, or reliability: price is not an important variable. Finally, a focus strategy aims at a narrow target segment through low prices or a unique offering. For Porter, above average performance in an industry is related to a firm's ability to select a strategy that is sustainable relative to competitors.

To illustrate this theory, Crown Books entered the market using a cost leadership strategy against Brentanos and other traditional bookstore retailers. Crown maintained a low overhead and sold national best-sellers and other popular books at a substantial discount. Then Crown Books was confronted with competition from more differentiated discounters, such as Barnes & Noble and Borders, that were creating fun and relaxing environments for book lovers. These focused discounters have not only compromised Crown Books' competitive advantage but have also challenged the positions of conventional bookstore retailers.

BARNES & NOBLE: SEGMENTING FUN AND CULTURE

One of the fundamental distinctions between the large chain bookstores and the independents has been an underlying philosophy. The independents believed that their function was a transfer of culture between the store and its customers. The chains—with coffee shops, book signings by noted authors, and browsing and reading space—tried to make reading books fun. Barnes & Noble developed a philosophy that segmented a market by combining fun and culture.

Barnes & Noble is the world's largest bookseller, with more than 1,000 stores including 481 superstores located in forty-nine states and the District of Columbia. Barnes & Noble's share of book sales has climbed from 7 percent in 1992 to 15 percent in 1999 at the expense of independent bookstores. Barnes & Noble became a leader in the retail book business with the 1974 opening of its discount trade bookstores, which later evolved into superstores. B. Dalton was acquired in 1986, which increased Barnes & Noble's exposure to mall retailing while the acquisition of Scribner's and Doubleday moved the company into upscale malls. In 1990, the new superstore format was introduced. Before the 1970s Barnes & Noble was a large seller of new and used textbooks, particularly targeted at colleges and universities. The company now operates MBS textbook exchange, the largest seller of wholesale college textbooks in the industry. In 1971, Leonard Riggio purchased Barnes & Noble.

Barnes & Noble had advanced into other areas of the cultural world by publishing its own books (through an affiliation with Marlboro Books), by a mail-order subsidiary, by operating college bookstores, by establishing the Discover Great New Writers program, and by sponsoring the Writers Harvest, an annual series of readings conducted throughout the country by Share Our Strength (an antipoverty organization) and developing an online Website. The Website has more than 720,000 customers in 175 countries. The leadership of Leonard Riggio, the founder and chief executive, has been instrumental in advancing Barnes & Noble from a modest-size discounter into an industry leader in less than a decade.

The current strategy of Barnes & Noble is focused on three areas. By acquiring B. Dalton, Scribner's, and Doubleday, it absorbed shopping mall stores into the chain. However, profits in shopping mall stores are limited, and therefore Riggo is downplaying the mall stores in favor of developing superstores. Many of these superstores are as large as small-town department stores and contain benches for browsers, children's reading corners, a café selling cappuccino and snacks, and gift shops to enhance book lovers' collections. Superstore sales are much higher than the mall stores, but a possible negative has been high costs that swallow up profits. The last strategic area has been to develop online selling. Amazon.com has usurped the market share of book sales, and Barnes & Noble is responding to this competitive threat by moving aggressively onto the Internet. Barnes & Noble also operates its own giant distribution center, giving it a cost advantage over online booksellers. The retailer stocks 600,000 titles in its New Jersey warehouse. Barnes & Noble provides speedier delivery for Internet orders than Amazon.com. Moreover, Bertelsmann AG, the world's largest book publisher and owner of Random House, has purchased a 50 percent interest in Barnes & Noble's Internet bookselling unit and should help to bolster this operation. More recently Barnes & Noble began focusing on a customer segment that was ignored in the past—namely, teenagers. The company purchased Babbage's Etc., a chain of 495 stores, aimed toward teenagers interested in software and technologically based educational games.

In 1998, Barnes & Noble became the exclusive bookseller of Disney Books with the creation of a Disney book boutique on both the Disney site and the Barnes & Noble's online site. Disney will have a button on the Barnes & Noble home page, and both sites are linked. Offline, Disney gets the added value of retail promotion in Barnes & Noble stores. This arrangement is an extension of Barnes & Noble.com's Affiliate Network, which already includes sales relationships with CondeNet, Sports Zone, and Time Inc. News Media.

Riggio has developed two important fundamentals that have permeated retail trade. When Riggio determined that buyers of books also desired entertainment, sales exploded. Barnes & Noble was born again in the 1980s with superstores. The physical environment reflected a high visibility, an upscale ambiance, and usually a suburban location close to the target market. The ambiance demonstrated a woody, traditional, soft-colored library atmosphere, modern architecture, and stylish displays.

Shopping in a bookstore for consumers was a social activity. The children had puppet shows, and the adults had lectures and author signings.

The second fundamental advance by Riggio was that books are consumer products. The underlying philosophy was that people buy books for what the purchase says about them. The purchase reveals the buyer's taste, cultivation, and trendiness. As a consumer product, books can be sold with an emphasis on the glamour of the book as an object and the fashionableness of a trendy author. Melvin T. Copeland first classified consumer products as a three-category system of convenience, shopping, and specialty products, which is still used.[3] The system is based on consumer awareness of alternative products, their characteristics, and the degree of search considered necessary. The consumer products system recognizes that customers may view the same products differently. Bucklin was to extend the classification system to retailing, developing a product-patronage mix that Riggio has successfully used at Barnes & Noble.[4]

Barnes & Noble was in the college book trade years ago and not only has maintained this presence, but with Follett College Stores, its chief competitor, dominates college store leasing. Barnes & Noble leases more than 350 college stores and Follet leases more than 500. Each company serves more than 3 million students and is aggressively adding more college bookstores. Each organization custom publishes concise packs, and Barnes & Noble also publishes some of its own books under the Dorset Press imprint, which is similar to Brentanos in past years.

Barnes & Noble is the only book retailer in the United States operating through all four channels of distribution: retail stores, the Internet, 1-800-The-Book, and mail order. Barnes & Noble, in an effort to enhance its physical distribution strategies, has announced plans to open two massive distribution centers in Reno, Nevada, and Atlanta, Georgia, to serve both its superstores and the burgeoning online operation. This move is viewed as a positive long-run strategy that should increase the company's capability.

Barnes & Noble is the largest operator of superstores in the United States but the organization is not without its mistakes. Site location has presented a challenge. For example, in Berkeley, California, in Ann Arbor, Michigan, and other locations stores have not been successful. In some instances, the reason has been congested traffic arteries, or an over-saturation of competition, or a poor choice of location.

BORDERS: A ME-TOO COMPETITOR

Borders was founded in 1971 by Tom and Louis Borders. The objective of the organization was to create the environment of a community center where customers could get together for book and poetry readings, workshops, and sociable coffee and tea. Borders acquired Waldenbooks from Kmart in 1994. Waldenbooks carries anywhere from 15,000 to 48,000 titles depending on the size of its store, which ranges from 3,300 to 8,000 square feet. Borders and Waldenbooks are separate companies with distinctly different personalities. Although Borders structured its stores in a manner similar to that of Barnes & Noble, a competitive differential has developed. Borders is among the top sellers of classical, jazz, and new age music titles in the United States. Waldenbooks, unlike B. Dalton operated by Barnes & Noble, focuses upon selling videos and toys. Borders, in an effort to further develop a competitive differential, also operates a number of Planet Music Superstores. Borders is the world's second largest retailer of books, music, and other information educational, and entertainment products. The company operates 204 superstores, and Waldenbooks has 904 stores. Borders carries a combination of more than 200,000 book, magazine, music, video, and periodical titles in its stores.

Borders's challenge is to innovate and develop a distinct image. An analogy can be made between Sears and Montgomery Ward, and Barnes & Noble and Borders. Sears became the innovator and Montgomery Ward a "me-too" organization. The lack of genuine innovation in merchandising strategies gave Wards an image of a nonprogressive store, a relic of the past. Poor positioning and foggy target marketing gave Wards an image of a "me-too" store that did not do things as well as Sears. If Borders is not careful, this analogy may come true in the future.

More than 200 Borders stores have been situated throughout the country and their offerings in music have been strengthened. Borders has noted that music stores have not targeted an adult audience very well and therefore has added this offering in its bookstores. Borders has increased the scheduled monthly calendar events at its stores and is more community oriented than Barnes & Noble. The Internet is an exciting new area for retailers, but Amazon.com and Barnes & Noble have developed their Internet offerings much more than Borders, and therefore the company may flounder in the future.

Borders has brought in Robert DiRomualdo and the company seems to be undergoing a cultural change. Many of the new executives did not come from bookstore retailing. Yet there seems to be little emphasis on innovation. Although Borders was the first to provide coffee and espresso bars in its superstores and the first to sell music CDs along with books, innovation is not a high priority. A lack of innovation in bookstore retailing is a danger signal for the future.

Borders has revamped the Waldenbook's operation. There is an enlarged Kiosk program, and while some stores have been closed larger ones have been opened. These larger stores are more profitable than the smaller units. In an effort to innovate and remove its "me-too" image,

Borders will eventually print high-quality paperbacks in its stores in approximately fifteen minutes' time. A positive advantage of this print-on-demand is immediate access to older or more obscure titles. Another immediate advantage is that this new use of technology will help Borders become more competitive with Amazon.com.

Borders, Barnes & Noble, and a number of major book publishers have been sued by the American Booksellers Association because the book publishers granted discounts to the large retailers that were not given to independent book stores. The suit was filed under the Robinson-Paterson Act, a 1936 federal antitrust statute that forbids price discrimination. California state statutes have also been involved and the resolution of this case is pending.

CROWN BOOKS: RETAILING MISTAKES

Crown Books believed that past success guarantees continued success. Crown was the pioneer bookstore discounter and maintained that customers desired books at lower prices and not coffee shops. The typical Barnes & Noble and Borders stores have almost double the titles of Crown, but Crown offers a larger discount on best-sellers, such as 40 percent off hardcover *New York Times* best-sellers. Crown also believed that customers liked to browse and therefore was late in developing a Website on the Internet. The persistence of a traditional corporate culture without adaptability to change has weakened Crown Books considerably. Unfortunately, the traditional strategies of Crown Books have placed Crown in the middle between Amazon.com, which can offer to sell at deep discounts, and higher-service stores such as Barnes & Noble and Borders. Crown Books looks at each of its stores as a "neighborhood" store and has focused on developing this image.

In 1997 Crown introduced the Muse for Books kiosk, an interactive system able to cross reference books by author, title, or subject, that provides customers with more than 300,000 critical reviews, synopses, and recommendations. Crown Books operates in Chicago, Houston, Los Angeles, San Diego, San Francisco, Seattle, and Washington, D.C. Operations are confined to metropolitan areas, which limits its national recognition even though there are more than 160 bookstores. The Dart Group controls Crown Books. Because of disappointing profits it has made efforts to sell the company, but these attempts have not been successful. In the meantime, Crown has tried to enlarge its customer base, modernize its information system, and initiate employee-training programs to enhance the customer's shopping experience. While Crown Books has been sinking, Barnes & Noble, Borders, and Books-A-Million have been operating profitably.

BOOKS-A-MILLION: USE OF DIFFERENTIAL ADVANTAGE

Books-A-Million operates 173 stores in seventeen states predominantly located in the southeastern United States. At least two-thirds of these outlets are superstores. Efforts have been made to develop a differential advantage by establishing an Imaginative Department, which carries children's computer games, science kits, microscopes, books on insects and dinosaurs, and puzzles for children. Other attempts to establish a differential advantage include stocking collectible sports cards and comic books and creating a museum section that features art books. Some of its stores feature a coffee bar, a regional and local interest section, a newsstand with a TV monitor tuned to CNN, and a Hallmark card and gift shop. It is uncertain whether or not these innovations will be introduced in all Books-A-Million outlets or if they will be successful.

Books-A-Million has exceeded Crown Books as the third largest retail book chain in the United States. The chain offers a broad spectrum of categories including books, magazines, gifts, music, and video. Much of the organization's profitability occurs in the Christmas season. There would not seem to be any strategies to spread out sales during the course of the year, and a lack of such planning might be seen as shortsighted. However, many of the Books-A-Million outlets are situated in the South, and the chain is strong in targeting regional reading tastes. An alliance has been established between Wal-Mart and Books-A-Million to sell books through the Wal-Mart online store. This alliance should not only challenge Amazon.com but help Books-A-Million become more competitive with Barnes & Noble.

AMAZON.COM: THE LEADING ONLINE RETAILER

Although Amazon.com was founded in 1994, the company is the leading online retailer of books with sales of over $600 million a year and has rapidly moved into the sale of other types of products. The objective is for Amazon.com to be the place where you can find anything. The company sells CDs, videotapes, audiotapes, and other products. Amazon.com views its marketing programs from a long-range perspective rather than concentrating on quarterly earnings as most organizations do. This long-range perspective appears to underlie the philosophy of becoming the Wal-Mart of the Web. Amazon.com will also add greeting cards and rare books to its merchandise lines. Purchasing stakes in other dot.com retailers, such as pets.com and even toys, are already taking place. In 1998 and 1999, Amazon's costs rose faster than its sales growth, making unlikely the company's prospect of turning a profit in the immediate future. Amazon is an innovator, having pioneered the sale of books online and taken advantage of speed by getting the customer's order delivered quickly.

Customer book selection and discounting are key marketing appeals. Amazon.com offers its customers more than 4.7 million titles to select from, with discounts of up to 40 percent on many hardcover books and 20 percent on paperbacks. Amazon.com stocks a limited number of best-sellers. In an effort to speed delivery, Amazon.com has expanded its Seattle distribution center and opened a second distribution center in New Castle, Delaware. Amazon.com depends on the Ingram Book Group, which is the leading book supplier to online retailers. Ingram ships direct to consumers in the retailer's name.

Amazon.com has worked out promotional deals with American On-line, Yahoo! and Excite, which will draw more customers to the book-seller. Amazon has more than 1.7 million customers on the Internet compared to 250,000 Barnes & Noble Internet customers. Repeat custom-ers currently account for over 50 percent of Amazon orders with interna-tional sales representing 25 percent of net sales. Of the $23 billion in books sold in 1999 in the United States, only $38.3 million were purchased online. That's more than triple the $11.4 million in 1995. It is expected that this market will reach $225 million by 2000. The company spends about 26 percent of its total sales on marketing and advertising. With the introduction of its music store in June 1998, the company has become the number one online music seller. The company has also introduced its video store and an enhanced gift store, which includes personal electronic and toy products.

The competitive environment for Amazon is indeed formidable. Bor-ders and Barnes & Noble have effective distribution systems for stocking superstores, but these are of little use in cyberspace. However, with brand identification that is stronger than Amazon.com. Barnes & Noble is inten-sifying online selling and is an immediate threat. However, a larger threat to Amazon may come from booksellers online that target specialized audiences. For example, Pandora's Books, which sells out-of-print science fiction and mysteries, can offer more expertise in its subjects than a full-source book retailer like Amazon. It is in these specialized subject areas that Amazon's market share may erode. Other competitors include Book Stacks Unlimited, Inc., and Wordsworth Books. As Amazon aggressively expands into other product categories such as compact disks, video, and toys, other specialty retailers are becoming alarmed and are fighting back. To illustrate, CD Now, Cyberian Outpost, eToys, and Reel.com have joined together to form an online shopping network. Since Bertelsmann announced that it would buy a 50 percent interest in the Barnes & Noble online operation, it would appear that the competition might be closing in on Amazon.

Amazon points shoppers to bargains, staff recommendations, and books in areas related to the one they're browsing. It notifies customers by e-mail when new books are available. Although sales are in the hundreds of millions, Amazon's high expenses have resulted in a net loss while it maintains high expectations of success. Competitive threats are increasing as other sellers such as Borders enter the market.

SUCCESS DOES NOT GUARANTEE CONTINUED SUCCESS

Brentanos and other conventional retailers were once major players in the retail bookstore industry. Unfortunately, they did not foresee the success of discounters. While personalized service was important, it was not as important as conventional retailers envisioned. Moreover, conventional retailers failed to grasp the importance of entertainment and just plain fun. Barnes & Noble, a seller of college texts, realized that entertainment and a serious reading environment were strong consumer motivators.

Successes in Bookstore Retailing

- Using of entertainment as a consumer motivator.
- Marketing books as consumer products.
- Using scrambled merchandising strategies with categories such as music.
- Using technology with online setting.
- Broadening offerings by including titles from small publishers.
- Segmenting retailers with such categories as mystery and children's bookstores.

Mistakes in Bookstore Retailing

- Reacting slowly to discount retailing.
- Responding slowly to superstore strategies.
- Relying on past consumer loyalties.
- With the exception of Amazon, failing to recognize early the potential of online selling.

MANAGING CHANGE

Social and cultural patterns in the United States are changing rapidly, and many of these changes are reflected in reading behavior. An analysis of emerging lifestyle trends has provided three trends that have a bearing on the marketing and merchandising of books. The first trend, which has been called voluntary simplicity, has its roots in material simplicity and the ecological ethic. The second trend has its roots in self-fulfillment. The third trend is reflected in the changing status of a mature population.

One important value of voluntary simplicity that has a bearing on reading behavior is personal growth. Self-help books and books that develop an individual's inner self sold in record numbers in the last half of the 20th century, a trend that shows every evidence of continuing. A broad assortment of book titles is necessary in satisfying needs of personal growth, and Amazon has grown tremendously with only a few years of product offering on the Internet. Riggio's contention that books should be marketed as consumer products is another dimension of satisfying personal growth desires.

Another aspect of lifestyle trends in the latter half of the 20th century that shows every indication of continuing is the consumer's quest for self-fulfillment. The lifestyle of self includes the psychological as well as the physical. The lifestyle suggests an individualistic orientation. Those who subscribe to this philosophy want to purchase many diverse services as they seek to enjoy life and find adventure. Books on travel and adventure are paramount. Readers may find self-expression vicariously by attending book and poetry readings and participating in discussion groups. In the future these consumers will have a tendency to disassociate themselves from conspicuous consumption and will be more concerned with meaningful symbols that express who they are and what they would like to achieve. Leonard Riggio's insight that reading behavior reflects the individual's desire to make a statement would seem to reflect this lifestyle trend.

Still another lifestyle trend is reflected in the changing tastes of a mature population. The aging, or graying, of the population calls for greater attention to the needs and wants of an older generation and a corresponding reduced emphasis on the youth culture. The growth rate of the elderly market is expected to be twice that of the population rate. Another consideration is the large number of baby boomers who will begin to join this market segment in large numbers in the beginning of the 21st century. Both of these markets derive great satisfaction from reading and read much more than their counterparts did in a previous generation.

Managing change in consumer behavioral reading habits has been an important part of book marketing and retailing. Books have become consumer products and are subject to sale not only in bookstores but also in drugstores, supermarkets, and on the Internet. Bookstores specializing in mysteries, religious works, children's literature, and even cookbooks have developed to service diverse markets. Superstores with coffee bars serve consumers not only with food but also entertainment and book and poetry readings that stimulate intellectual curiosity and enthusiasm. Specialty bookstore merchants are making efforts to bring a measure of total satisfaction to consumers. More stores are selling specialty books, such as wine dealers offering books about wine to their customers and travel agencies selling books about travel. Competition is expected to be fiercer in the 21st century, with Internet selling having an impact on independent and superstore book retailers in the future. E-books, digital bits injected into a handheld device with an intrasharp display, will become an important product in the next decade and further seize market share away from retailers.

8

Electronics Stores: Technological Segmentation

Successful Electronics Store Strategies

- Use of sophisticated inventory control strategy
- Effective merchandise selection, service, and pricing
- Pressure on suppliers for lowest prices
- Selling brand name merchandise below traditional prices
- Maintaining high merchandise turnover
- Promoting innovation
- Maintaining a high level of advertising

Electronics Store Mistakes

- Vulnerability to lower-priced discounters
- Poor inventory control management
- Departure from cost leadership
- Disregard of competitive forces
- Lack of concern for store image
- Reliance on past patronage loyalties
- Introduction of new product technology categories without consumer acceptance

Technological discoveries such as computers, transistors, digital products, cellular telephones, high definition televisions, and videocassette recorders are responsible for the development of the electronic store. There is no doubt that additional technological discoveries consumers can use will develop opportunities for retailers in the 21st century. Technology affects the way consumers interface with the market. The video cassette recorder allowed consumers to tape their favorite programs for later viewing and to see motion pictures in the comfort and privacy of their homes and thus paved the way for such chains as Blockbuster. The personal computer gave consumers access to a large amount of information and allowed them to shop and handle financial transactions at home. Circuit City, Best Buy, and Radio Shack are leading the way in bringing the latest products developed by technology to the consumer.

Electronics stores need to target market segments based upon consumer knowledge and acceptance of products developed by new technology. Consumers differ in their readiness to purchase new products. In each new product category, there are consumption leaders and early adapters. Other consumer groups adopt new products much later. Therefore in developing strategies, electronic retailers need to understand the diffusion process.[1] The diffusion process describes how different market segments are likely to accept and purchase a product over time. The adoption process consists of the decision-making stages consumers go through before buying a product or service—namely, awareness, interest, evaluation, trial, and adoption.

During the awareness stage of the adoption process, an individual becomes conscious of the innovation (let's say a VCR) but lacks information about it. During the interest stage need is stimulated and information is sought. During the evaluation stage, the individual weighs the advantages and disadvantages of the purchase. The trial stage consists of the initial purchase to determine how well the purchase satisfies those unfilled needs. Adoption follows a satisfactory trial, and subsequently the product is used on a regular basis.

The individual in the trial stage of the adoption process endeavors to reduce risk. A one-week or thirty-day free home trial is an effective strategy for videocassette recorders, as is a warranty. Another determinant of the trial stage would be the relative advantage of the product. The relative advantage criteria represent the degree to which an innovation is perceived as better than any possible substitute. Finally, the ability to communicate the attributes of the new product is also a strong determinant.

There are two important implications of the consumer adoption process for electronic retailers. First, since adoption is a process, consumers must progress through the awareness, interest, and evaluation stages before entering the trial and adoption stages. Second, different consumers will be in different stages of the adoption process over time. Therefore, a major challenge is presented when directing marketing communication and promotion to consumer.

The diffusion process demonstrates when different market segments are likely to purchase the new product. Innovators are the first market segment group to purchase a new product. They are willing to accept risk and are often opinion leaders. Early adopters are the second group of consumers to buy a new product. This market segment enjoys the leadership, prestige, and respect that accompany early adoption of new products. The early majority is the first part of the mass market and has status among its peers. The late majority is the second part of the mass market to buy a new product. This group is less responsive to change than the early majority groups. Finally, the laggards will not adopt a new product until the product reaches maturity.

Product characteristics can be used to predict and explain the speed and diffusion of a new product. The more complex the product, the slower its diffusion. For example, before personal computer functions were simplified, primarily professionals purchased them for home use. Another product characteristic is that of relative advantage. The word processor with its storage function has a clear relative advantage over an electric typewriter. The degree to which the product can be tried on a limited basis is also an important inducement. Demonstrations are helpful but cannot be substituted for in-home trial as a risk reduction method. Electronics retailers need to understand the consumer adoption and diffusion processes in order to develop sound strategies to facilitate consumer patronage.

Currently electronics retailers will find that cellular phones are going through the diffusion process. Specialty electronics retailers will need to establish their target market segment and develop strategies to reach consumers in each stage of the adoption process. This involves establishing a relative advantage of the cellular phone to communicate its attributes to the target market. Strategies will also need to be developed to reach appropriate market segments such as early adopters or early majority. The community in which the retailer is located may be in a different stage of the diffusion process than other parts of the United States and even adopters in metropolitan areas may be different than in small towns.

The impact of technology does affect electronic retailers in different ways. Consumers' technological knowledge will influence their selection of goods and services. Electronics retailers must be aware of these influences and especially the customer's level of knowledge in order to provide appropriate retailing strategies that satisfy consumers. Technological developments can provide many new market opportunities. For example, thirty years ago such products as solar-powered pocket calculators, small personal televisions, laptop computers, and cellular telephones were not available to consumers. The 21st century will offer digital versions of satellite TV systems, camcorders, cameras, and video players that will stimulate a broader interest in consumer electronics.

Electronic retailers have expanded their strategic role by developing market driven business strategies. Presently electronic retailers operate in a complex and highly competitive business environment. It is important for the specialty retailer to guide the mission, objectives, and strategies of the organization on the basis of the needs and wants of the marketplace. A strong market-driven strategy is a starting point. The Tandy Corporation with its Radio Shack chain follows a market-centered strategy by uncovering customer needs. Alliances with Sprint and Compaq are illustrative of responsiveness to customers' changing needs. Radio Shack has listened to its customers by providing help at point-of-purchase for consumers so that the consumer can use and enjoy the benefits from new technology. Radio Shack also expanded its strategic role by positioning its line of personal computers in the eyes and minds of buyers in the early 1980s. Management had to remove the discount store image many buyers held of the Radio Shack chain. Accordingly, the company developed a campaign focused on the high-quality technology of its products. This campaign allowed Radio Shack to expand its market for selling personal computers.

A consideration of the triumphs and blunders of electronics store retailers shows that many mistakes have been made, and only those organizations that have been able to make constant adjustments with such variables as innovation, target market, image, physical environmental resources, and human resources have remained viable. The early electronics store retailers, many of whom were discounters, did not obtain high grades using all variables, but some of the variables were used in a successful manner. Radio Shack, Circuit City, and Best Buy stand out in this respect. Innovation took place when Circuit City decided that the superstore format could be effective in selling electronic merchandise. Innovation has not really been a hallmark of discount electronics retailers since they used a low-price strategy to attract customers.

Strategies of target market segmentation and image have been used effectively. Circuit City and Best Buy have successfully targeted price-sensitive consumers who also demand product knowledge in making their purchases, while Radio Shack has established a strong differential advantage in serving the new consumer

Radio Shack and Circuit City have effectively employed physical environmental resources. Radio Shack's locations and strong distribution network ease the concerns of many neophyte customers. Circuit City, with its superstore structure, makes feasible one-stop shopping for expensive durable goods. Moreover, Circuit City's strong information/computerized system makes possible a broad merchandise assortment.

Human resource management is highly effective in both Circuit City and Best Buy organizations. Both companies maintain a high caliber, effective sales staff. Circuit City believes that commissioned sales people are more effective than salespeople on a straight salary, while Best Buy maintains the reverse. Although at opposite extremes, these strategies are effective for Best Buy and Circuit City.

Circuit City and Best Buy seek total consumer satisfaction, using focus groups and surveys to measure satisfaction and to ease post-purchase doubts. These techniques have proven to be effective when the purchase of expensive durable goods is involved.

Many of the failures among discounters developed from their inability to identify and respond to changing needs of consumers. The failures were due to fierce competition, product saturation, inept management, changes in the way products were sold, and, in cases like Crazy Eddie fraud. Whatever the reason, Incredible Universe, 47th Street Photo, Crazy Eddie, Trader Horn, and others have disappeared from the retailing scene.

MARKET STRUCTURE

Electronic retailers carry a wide array of products ranging from personal computers to cellular telephones to pagers to digital cameras to audio products for the home and car to entertainment software and to new technology products such as Mini Disc systems and High Definition Televisions. One challenge for electronic retailers is to compete with discounters such as Wal-Mart and other mass retailers such as Sears to sell these products. These general merchandise retailers make the decision to carry these new types of technological products after consumers who are innovators and early adopters have purchased the products from electronic retailers. These general merchandise retailers then target the early majority and late majority consumer segments, which comprise the largest groups of the total population. Although it is usually a combination of causes that are responsible for store failure, this is one important reason why some electronic retailers have found it difficult to compete.

Table 8.1 indicates that Radio Shack operated by Tandy is the largest retailer in this category. Radio Shack is situated in the major forty metropolitan locations in the United States. Circuit City, the second largest electronic retailer, is concentrating its efforts in developing superstores. The Best Buy organization is situated in thirty-two states and not only carries electronic products but also stocks appliances such as refrigerators and washers and dryers. Best Buy is in the process of aggressively entering new metropolitan markets. Crazy Eddie and The Wiz are some of the casualties of the electronic store wars, although The Wiz has been reorganized under the U.S. bankruptcy law. These organizations have

Table 8.1
Leading Electronics Retailers

	Net Sales 1998	Number of Units 1998
Tandy (Radio Shack, Computer City)	$4.789 billion	5140
Circuit City	$10.8 billion	590
Best Buy	$10.08 billion	311
Rex Stores	$417 million	228
CompUSA	$5.286 billion	162

not only been competitive victims but victims of their own internal blunders. The 1990s presented a long casualty list of either store closing and/or bankruptcies. Montgomery Ward exited consumer electronics in 1996 and in that same year Best Products and Babbages got into difficulties.

An important dimension in understanding the market structure of electronic retailers is the interaction between technology and site selection. The ease of communication may especially lend itself to demonstrations, even though complex, and make it possible for consumers to perceive technology benefits in them. How compatible the new technology is with the existing attitudes and practices of those persons who are potential adopters of the innovation is another variable. Radio Shack has used market saturation aggressively to establish a strong market position and has developed a system that can open large numbers of stores very quickly by maintaining a high degree of standardization for each store unit and limiting the number of store prototypes. Radio Shack, due to its site selection strategy, can establish a preemptive position and force its competitors into a defensive position. Another advantage of this location strategy is that immediate operating economies are gained.

Rex Stores, a Dayton, Ohio, chain of more than 200 stores, has established outlets in smaller cities in the Southeast and Midwest. Rex is rapidly spreading east into Pennsylvania and other states as sales increase. Expertise shown in the development of Wal-Mart, and currently Heilig-Meyers in the retail furniture industry, is confined to small-city retailing.

Product life cycle management is an important aspect for profitability. Technological advancements challenge every electronic retailer. Diffusion of the new product technology is a natural phenomenon that can be influenced by retailers. All factors equal, heavy advertising should increase the awareness of the new product and increase the rate of acceptance. Diffusion progresses in a specific pattern, but electronic retailers can influence that pattern by the use of effective strategies.

A high level of knowledgeable service at every age of the customer relationship is essential. Ongoing training programs are needed in understanding new technologies and merchandising opportunities for sales personnel. Retailers need to carry a broad merchandise mix that spans an entire range, from entry-level products to products that are designed for the most knowledgeable consumers. Another aspect on which electronic retailers concentrate efforts is after-sale service. Strong vendor relationships are necessary for repairs, and help may be needed in advising consumers how to integrate new merchandise with products previously purchased.

Competition in electronic store retailing is at all geographic levels. Competition is becoming diverse, as discount stores such as Wal-Mart and Target enter the market. Traditional retailers such as Sears are also formidable adversaries. AT&T, Bell Atlantic Mobile, Sprint PCS, and others are aggressively establishing wireless phone stores selling wireless phones, wireless service, pagers, and accessories. Both AT&T and Bell Atlantic Mobile had more than 150 stores as of 1998. Carrier-owned stores are experiencing some difficulties as consumers complain of rushed service. Yet for all their problems, carrier-owned wireless stores are starting to challenge traditional retailers.

Rex Stores has entered Internet selling of appliances before any of its rivals. Rex Stores offers as many as several hundred products online. By late 1999 Best Buy and Tandy, owner of Radio Shack, plan to begin selling products on their Websites. Circuit City and Amazon.com began selling electronic goods over the summer of 1999. Wal-Mart also plans to sell electronic goods online in the future. Competition on the Web is growing fiercer, and it is a matter of conjecture about future winners and losers. Meanwhile, Rex Stores is taking fifty to 100 orders a day, making it the most profitable organization selling electronic goods online.

ALLIANCES AND COALITIONS

A strong alliance is a long-term collaboration combining the strengths of two or more organizations to accomplish strategic objectives. The strategic alliance can take many forms. The most informal arrangement would be for a manufacturer and retailer to work together. The manufacturer makes the product and trains the retailers' personnel; the retailer sells the product to the consumers. Sometimes there can be an exclusive arrangement in a given territory. The more informal the agreement, the more flexible and faster it can be implemented. An informal arrangement may lack commitment, but the alliance can be adjusted as the condition changes.

Radio Shack/Tandy has formed a coalition with Sprint and Compaq. According to Michael E. Porter, examples of coalitions include marketing agreements, technology licenses, supply agreements, and joint ventures.[2] Sprint and Compaq are using a means for gaining a differentiation advantage of vertical linkages without actual integration. Another aspect of the coalition is to overcome the obstacles of coordination among independent firms. Since coalitions involve long-term relationships, closer coordination ideally should be achieved with a coalition partner rather than with an independent firm.

Both Sprint and Compaq have developed products that have advanced technology and have brought new benefits to consumers. Sprint and Compaq will exercise great control over the situation as the products are sold to those consumers who are innovators and early adopters. Radio Shack, as the major customer of Sprint and Compaq. will exercise more control as the products are purchased by the mass market of early majority and late majority consumers. Radio Shack can gain a dominant position under conditions of technological diffusion, whose influence Sprint and Compaq can ignore only at substantial risk. The alternative of establishing retail stores taken by IBM and AT&T has encountered mixed results.

TOTAL CUSTOMER SATISFACTION

Customer satisfaction rests on three fundamental bases. First, the product or service must perform as expected and be backed by guarantees or warranties. Second, the product should have social reinforcement expectations. Third, the product or service should satisfy consequential experience expectations. At the core of total customer satisfaction is the effective use of human resources and the development of consumer-friendly programs.

The marketing concept stresses customer satisfaction, yet the research is still in its infancy as to understand how satisfaction is reached. Consumers develop expectations based upon past experience, acquired information from various sources, and sales presentations and promotions. When using the product, whether it is a computer or a camcorder, expectations are compared with experience to arrive at a perceived level of satisfaction. The ideal result is for experience to equal or exceed expectations. If the opposite occurs, dissatisfaction is the outcome. Because of the technological nature of the product, electronic retailers are confronted with a challenge to establish and maintain a balance between expectations and experience.

A buyer's perceptions of the product after the sale can influence repeat sales and word-of-mouth transmission to others. Products sold by electronic specialty store retailers are prone to cognitive dissonance. Cognitive dissonance is the doubt that a correct purchase decision has been made. Dissonance typically increases as the value of the item increases and the relative importance of the decision increases. For example, purchasing a computer creates more dissonance than buying a radio.

Electronics retailers, with the cooperation of the manufacturer can take measures to minimize the amount of customer post-purchase dissatisfaction. Companies can follow-up computer purchases with messages affirming the wisdom of their brand choice. Requests for suggestions for improvements and strategic locations of available services can ease purchase doubts. Instruction booklets and strategic locations of available services can ease purchase doubts. Instruction booklets and service agreements are also designed to reduce dissonance. Finally, post-purchase communications demonstrating new computer applications and providing for rapid redress of consumer grievances should also help to reduce cognitive dissonance. Focus groups, consumer panels, and consumer surveys also render important insights for better satisfying the customer.

THE PORTER MODEL AND DISCOUNT STRATEGY

Michael Porter has developed an approach to corporate strategy that focuses on competition.[3] The Porter model suggests that competitors in an industry must choose a sustainable strategy based on cost leadership, differentiation, focus, or some combination of generic strategies. The selection of a strategy is contingent upon a firm's strengths and the importance of several environmental factors, including the threat of new industry entrants, the bargaining power of suppliers and customers, the availability of substitute products for customers, and the intensity of rivalry among industry competitors. It is critical for a firm to make a clear strategic choice or it will run the risk of trying to be all things to all people. The latter is believed to be a recipe for mediocrity or even failure in an intensely competitive industry where substitute products are readily available.

Kmart, for example, began with a cost leadership strategy against mass merchants such as Sears and conventional department stores. Wal-Mart built its business on a cost leadership strategy but differentiated itself from Kmart by increasing the value added to its customers by offering more customer service and somewhat more fashionable apparel. In contrasts, Circuit City has employed a more focused strategy. Circuit City, specializing in home electronics, is an example of a retailer like Wal-Mart, which enjoys considerable bargaining power with manufacturers but, unlike Wal-Mart, has combined cost leadership with a focused strategy in narrowly defined merchandise groups. Circuit City, by carrying nationally recognized brands and offering specialized sales assistance, presents a threat to the general merchandise retailers who offer less specialization and slightly higher category prices. The cost-focused discounters are thus able to offer more value to price-sensitive consumers.

RADIO SHACK: A STRONG DIFFERENTIAL ADVANTAGE

Radio Shack (Tandy Corporation) with 5,140 stores has a differential advantage among electronic retailers because many of the items sold in electronic stores have become commodities with limited differentiation. Price is frequently an important consideration and the basis of competition in commodity markets. If the consumer is a novice, then the strong distribution network of The Tandy Corporation constitutes a strong aspect of a differential advantage.

The Tandy Corporation was established as a small leather goods company name Hinkley/Tandy Leather Company in 1918. Radio Shack was established in Boston in 1921 to sell high-tech products. After World War II, the Tandy leather-craft stores were expanded and by 1960 numbered 160. Radio Shack was purchased in 1963 and had only nine units.

Tandy not only has a distribution network but, for many years, was a manufacturer of electronic equipment. Tandy's role in manufacturing also constituted a differential advantage, but Tandy is endeavoring to diminish its role in manufacturing. Vertical integration in an industry dependent on technological change, investment, and research presents many obstacles for a retailer. Although Tandy was the first company to develop and mass-market a personal computer and thus established its leadership in the electronics and computer industry, high costs and declining sales in the computer industry caused Tandy to reassess its corporate mission. Strategic alliances with Compaq and Sprint have strengthened Tandy's position among electronic retailers. Radio Shack made Sprint its exclusive national wireless provider for ten years, and in exchange Sprint provided millions of dollars in advertising support. Compaq Computer refurbished a portion of Radio Shack's stores in exchange for its exclusive distribution agreement. Radio Shack has benefited enormously from these marketing alliances and in 1999 made another agreement with RCA, hoping for similar results.

Tandy's expansion and experimentation plans have not been successful. Tandy closed down Energy Express, a freestanding kiosk-styled store that sells batteries, and Famous Brand Warehouse, an outlet store for refurbished brand name electronics goods in the middle 1990s. Moreover, McDuffs and Video Concepts, which were designed to satisfy the needs for secondary markets, are likely candidates for closing unless their situations can be reversed.

Tandy, in an effort to segment the market, designed some big-box stores such as Incredible Universe, a seventeen-unit, mega-store consumer electronics chain, and Computer City, which targeted the experienced computer user. Radio Shack has become a telecommunications store in addition to serving its target market as a source of parts, peripherals, and gifts. The sale of telephone and cellular phones is an important part of this strategy. Radio Shack is the number one retailer of wireless telephone service in the United States.

Tandy's efforts at expansion have been flawed. The Incredible Universe store chain was confronted with a series of blunders. Competition and location were two important factors causing the demise of the chain. The mistake was to open new store units near a number of aggressive price competitors. Incredible Universe stores were unable to overcome poor location selection.

The goals of Computer City were to establish a more upscale image and to better serve the more experienced user while retraining those purchasers who were relatively inexperienced. The interior of the stores has been revamped and remodeled. The chain's bright yellow and ware-house-styled floors were replaced with a softer, more congenial color with good grain finishes and a more user-friendly layout. Computer City stores will provide an information center, Internet access, output services, and an Internet Café. New stores will feature a digital imaging center. Meanwhile it would seem to make more sense for Radio Shack to serve the more inexperienced user and allow Computer City to concentrate on the relatively experienced user, including business corporations. Computer City cannot serve all markets well, and Tandy would be well advised to serve distinct market segments.

Vertical integration had been the mission of the Tandy Corporation until the early 1990s. Tandy was the largest retailer of consumer electronics and also a major producer of electronic products. Vertical integration is the process whereby the firm acquires another firm at a different level of distribution. The manufacturer might acquire a wholesaler or a retailer, or a wholesaler might acquire a retailer. If the retailer acquires a manufacturer or a wholesaler, then this would be known as a backward vertical integration. Vertical integration is an effective means of securing increased coordination and integration of effort and commitment.

Vertical integration, on the other hand, if not implemented correctly, can create potential operating costs that outweigh operating economies. The management system could be strained, as precise coordination of functions will be necessary. Moreover, the classic method of reducing risk is to diversify, but vertical integration tends to increase commitment and investment. The firm may also discover that vertical integration can reduce flexibility. The restructuring of Tandy away from manufacturing allows it to concentrate its efforts and resources on what it does well.

Another aspect of this spin-off is that prior spin-offs included Bombay Company, a furniture retailer; Pier I, a home-furnishings firm; and Color Tile, a home-improvement products company. In the late 1990s Tandy had closed Incredible Universe, McDuff, Video Concepts, and Edge in Electronics. It is apparent that when entering the 21st century, Tandy will be able to concentrate its resources and efforts on the Radio Shack chain.

The goal is to make Radio Shack the ultimate electronics convenience chain in the United States. In order to achieve this mission, Tandy must position itself as a low-price electronics chain with a strong distribution network. Compaq, with its features of portability, good construction, and quality monitor, has added to the image of Tandy with a strategic alliance. Sprint in the telecommunications segment also promotes Tandy/Radio Shack.

CIRCUIT CITY: SUPERSTORES AND CUSTOMER SERVICE

Circuit City was founded in 1949 and is a leading retailer of brand-name consumer electronics, personal computers, entertainment software, and major appliances in the United States. Circuit City operates 590 superstores in more than 100 markets and introduced the superstore concept to the electronics retailing market in the mid 1970s. In 1999, Circuit City added cyber-shopping to its traditional retail offerings by opening its E-Superstore, *www.circuitcity.com*. The E-Superstore offers local superstore inventory access, express pickup, low prices, full freight, in-depth product features and price comparisons, factory-authorized repair services, and easy exchanges at any Circuit City Superstore location. The development of portfolio retailing has also been a significant factor in strategic planning. CarMax was founded in 1993, and plans are in the works to develop Digital Video Express and to investigate entry into furniture retailing.

Since the early 1980s, Circuit City has evolved based upon the objectives to render the best customer service possible and to offer this service at competitive prices. Circuit City has organized its marketing activity to focus on markets with similar competitive conditions and therefore uses a centralized buying organization. Merchandising mix and displays are also controlled centrally to ensure a high level of consistency from store to store. Circuit City advertises low prices and provides customers with a low-price guarantee. If a customer finds a lower price within thirty days of a purchase, Circuit City will refund 110 percent of the difference to the customer. A unique niche has been identified that targets customers who are less discount oriented and more interested in dealing with a knowledgeable sales staff. This consumer market segment is pictured as high-end shoppers who desire a greater merchandise assortment than competitors provide. Quality of service is much more than lip service as more than 300,000 customers are surveyed annually. Circuit City measures customer satisfaction using its sales staff, cashiers, warehouse staff, delivery, and product service specialists. These surveys help Circuit City provide the highest possible customer service, as satisfaction is assessed at virtually every stage of customer interaction.

Circuit City continues to serve the customer after the sale is completed. Post-purchase services include installation centers for automotive electronics, product repair, and toll-free customer service telephone numbers. Service centers are staffed with installers who are nationally certified by the independent Mobile Electronics Certification Program. Circuit City maintains a network of more than 500 technicians. A wholly owned credit card bank operation provides better control over all customer interactions.

While Circuit City has been for the most part successful in its strategies, blunders have occurred. Policies that would tend to anger customers include allegations that Circuit City misleads customers with a zero-interest-financing plan. As a result Circuit City agreed to pay ten states $25,000 each to settle the case and agreed to clarify its payment policies. Another incident occurred when the Consumer Affairs Department sought to fine the company more than $30,000 after accusing the chain of charging 15 percent restocking fees on product returns. The allegations were denied. Circuit City has also been involved in antidiscrimination cases. The NAACP in Virginia launched a selective buying campaign against the firm for alleged racial discrimination.

Although there is a slowdown in the industry due to Wal-Mart's aggressive expansion on the East Coast, Circuit City announced the intention of doubling its number of stores by 2001. Regional discounters Bradlees and Caldor filed for Chapter 11 and Jamesway, Ames, Hills Stores, and Rose's Stores are in financial difficulty. Circuit City, however, does maintain a differential advantage with a Microsoft Station, a joint effort by Microsoft and Packard Bell in their stores. Moreover, Circuit City has made a major impact on home entertainment retailing with its aggressive pricing strategies.

A broad merchandise assortment has helped Circuit City achieve positive financial results. The personal computer business has suffered a downturn but the sale of major appliances offset this situation. The sale of digital satellite systems and large-screen televisions also contributed to growth under challenging conditions to other parts of the merchandise mix. The superstore format has not only extended the merchandise assortment but has also cushioned adverse product cycles.

BEST BUY: A NEW CONCEPT

The company was started under the name of Sound of Music, an audio component systems retailer, in 1966. In the early 1980s the firm expanded into video products and appliances, and in 1983 adopted the name of Best Buy. Best Buy now has more than 310 stores in thirty-six states. Best Buy has a precise philosophy that influences the development of its objectives and goals, namely, to provide consumers with new technologies, exceptional value, and customer service. Best Buy introduced the retail format known as "Concept II," which placed all inventory on the sales floor and with the aid of noncommissioned sales personnel, offered customers low prices with less pressure. In 1995, the chain introduced Concept III, which incorporates a larger store format created to produce a more informative and exciting shopping experience for the customer. The latest concept is referred to as Concept IV, with the new layout focusing on digital products and sharper design.

The company's mission revolves around customer service and a team approach in attacking problems. Best Buy believes that customer service is enhanced by a non-commissioned sales staff. In this way post-purchase doubts can be significantly reduced. Moreover, a team approach strengthens such areas as financing, repair, in-store upgrades, and computer software training. The merchandise assortment demonstrates a reception to change, and a policy featuring customer choice in categories such as home office, consumer electronics, appliances, and entertainment software was developed.

Until recent times, Best Buy lagged behind Circuit City in establishing the superstore format. In order to remain competitive, the Gallup organization was employed to survey 10,000 Best Buy customers to better understand shopping and purchase behavior preferences. In addition, the company also uses focus groups.

Best Buy uses a retail format similar to a self-service discount store and provides a higher level of customer service and product explanation. The company provides a selection of brand name products comparable to retailers that specialize in the store's principal product categories to ensure a high level of product availability for customers. Best Buy's objective is to provide customers with the best product value available in the market area through active comparison shopping programs, daily price changes, lowest price guarantees, and special promotions, including interest-free financing, performance service plans, and home delivery.

Best Buy is led by its founder Richard M. Schulze. His belief in the accomplishment of collective goals, whether or not these goals are explicit noted or constantly accepted, has given cohesion to Best Buy and in turn made it successful. The company has made blunders. In 1996 a giant miscalculation was made on Christmas when computer inventories were understocked. Best Buy was destined to join Nobody Beats the Wiz, Crazy Eddie's and Tandy's Incredible Universe in oblivion. But Schulze (with the help of Andersen Consulting) was able to overhaul everything from marketing to inventory control and also hired a new outside management team. Since these moves took place there has been an improvement and Best Buy has again become formidable in the electronics industry. Only time will tell whether or not Best Buy has within its culture the ability to avoid costly blunders.

CIRCUIT CITY VERSUS BEST BUY

Circuit City has opened a number of stores in Chicago, an area long dominated by Best Buy, while Best Buy has expanded into Atlanta and Phoenix, considered major markets by Circuit City. This invasion of each other's territory led to a price war in the middle 1990s. Circuit City was able to undercut Best Buy by maintaining low costs via a highly automated inventory tracking system. Best Buy's strategy was to rely more on self-service then a high level of customer service (as provided by Circuit City) and thereby reduce costs. Best Buy pays its staff on a salary basis whereas Circuit City uses a commission system. Although Best Buy's overhead expenses are lower, its modified service policy makes it more difficult to sell highly profitable items such as extended service contracts that are instrumental in the success of Circuit City. Best Buy competes through its full selection of merchandise and has an alliance with Microsoft to promote its online service.

PORTFOLIO RETAILING

The concept of establishing a portfolio of retail businesses is not new. Since the 1980s, retail diversification has lost favor with a number of retailers. Yet, portfolio retailing has gained favor. Portfolio retailing blends the strategy of diversification with the strategy of focus. Focus diversification has become a growth strategy for the 21st century.

Circuit City opened its first CarMax operation in 1993 and plans to have eighty to ninety stores in 2001. Synergies with automobile retailing are linked by Circuit City's customer-service skills, knowledge of operating and financial controls, and expertise in selling expensive durable goods on a credit basis. Thus, a common set of core competencies is present. Core competencies are not capital or facilities but integral capabilities. Core competencies must provide access to markets, promise significant perceived customer benefits, and be difficult for competitors to emulate.

Portfolio retailing has worked well for those retailers with a mature and possibly vulnerable core enterprise and with adequate financial resources. Core competencies that can be transferred synergistically to related businesses are paramount. Firms like Circuit City that are in a relatively mature industry and need new growth opportunities and have the financial resources are best able to take advantage of portfolio retailing strategies. Therefore, Circuit City's entry into the used-car market seems more feasible since it is known for customer service and financial controls. Moreover, electronic products and automobiles are durable goods and have some parallels.

Portfolio retailing has been successful for Spiegel but proved unsuccessful for Walgreens. In the late 1980s Spiegel purchased Eddie Bauer, a sportswear and casual apparel retailer. Since the purchase, the number of Eddie Bauer store units has more than tripled and sales and profits have been rewarding. Innovations included the Home Collection, Northwest style home furnishings, and All Week Long, a line of women's sportswear and special occasion attire. Both concepts conveyed an image of craftsmanship and product quality. Meanwhile, Spiegel found that increasing costs and other problems diminished its core business, which was catalog retailing. However, Spiegel was successful in transferring its knowledge of customer apparel purchasing behavior and its powerful order-entry system to the Eddie Bauer operation.

Walgreens, in contrast, was unable to transfer its core competencies to acquired department stores, supermarkets, and fast-food chains. Eventually, all of these businesses were divested. Portfolio retailing had not worked for Walgreens. Walgreens, as a drugstore chain, is in a growth industry and portfolio retailing efforts stretched management and financial resources. Integration of the various businesses was not possible. During this period of portfolio retailing Walgreens was actually expanding its drugstore chain.

Portfolio retailers must know their markets well and should be able to operate multiple retail operations. Portfolio retailing means focusing investment with customer demand as well as responding to changing customer needs. The following are guidelines that can be used to successfully implement portfolio retailing:

- Build the core business so that it develops boundaries and direction for focused diversification.
- Develop core capabilities and competencies that are transferable.
- Stress concepts that are relative to the firm's resources. For example, Spiegel through the consumer bank it owns was able to offer credit to Eddie Bauer customers.
- Build for the future. For example, Circuit City, with CarMax, has entered a market by innovation with one-price and discounts price policies. The public may be tired of traditional automobile retailers and receptive to change.
- Promote innovation so that new ideas are constantly used. This is exactly what Spiegel has done with Eddie Bauer and what Circuit City is attempting to accomplish with CarMax.

Specialty retailers are especially able to profit from portfolio retailing. Many specialty retailers are niche marketers and know their customers well. A sense of timing is essential, and specialty retailers are adept in this area. These specialty retailers have also developed a strong real estate expertise so that location selection is advantageous.

ELECTRONIC STORE BLUNDERS

Crazy Eddie, a chain of forty-three discount electronic stores, finally closed its doors in 1990. The chain that virtually invented electronics retailing died as one of its founders was convicted of fraud. "Crazy Eddie" was convicted of falsifying inventory figures and securities fraud in 1993. Television commercials in the 1980s pictured a pitchmen who shouted, "Crazy Eddie's prices are insane!" Among the colorful antics used was forcing customers into deals by locking them in the store or taking their shoes. When negotiating with vendors, "Sugar," a one-hundred-pound German Shepherd owned by "Crazy Eddie" often came along for possible intimidation purposes. Crazy Eddie is a legend in electronic store retailing.

Nobody Beats the Wiz sought bankruptcy protection in 1997. Nobody Beats the Wiz was a chain of fifty-three stores in the Northeast that used bank loans to finance purchases of TVs, computer monitors, printers, and other electronic equipment from Asia. Heavy advertising spending, quick turnover, and small profit margins with prices slashed to the bone was the strategy. The stores did not have a one-price policy and was a paradise for price negotiators.

Suddenly in 1997, Nobody Beats the Wiz was confronted with intense competition, over-expansion, and the Asian crisis. Competitors were confronted with the same problems, but unlike them, the Wiz was fully leveraged and had millions of dollars worth of inventory that was sold at a loss. The Wiz had relied on fast turnover, and now goods languished unsold on its shelves. The unexpected had happened, and the Wiz was without a contingency plan. Today, the chain of stores has been restructured under the bankruptcy code and was purchased by Cablevision, Inc. for $80 million. The retailer downsized to forty locations in the New York City area.

Meanwhile, Circuit City entered the New York City market and the competition grew fiercer. Best Buy was a threat in some other geographical areas, and Wal-Mart and Target also sold TVs and VCRs. Risk increased as PCs grew obsolete faster. Competition beyond the New York region has severely damaged the Wiz, and a heavy price was paid for expansion beyond the Wiz core market.

SUCCESS AND MISTAKES IN ELECTRONIC STORE RETAILING

Technological change in the United States has been accelerating rapidly as PCs become obsolete and software changes occur frequently. VCRs, camcorders, and digital entertainment systems are also part of the rapid technological advancement that has made inventory management difficult. Competitive price slashing has made the marketing environment more volatile. Therefore, the successes in electronic store retailing have been hard earned and the mistakes have been glaring.

Successful Electronic Store Strategies

• Avoid cut-throat pricing
• Establish high level customer service
• Improve supply chain management
• Sell brand name merchandise below traditional prices
• Maintain high merchandise turnover
• Improve regional management
• Offer interactive product demonstrations

Electronic Store Mistakes

• Careless inventory control management
• Departure from cost leadership and maintenance policies
• Myopia regarding competitors
• Failure to clarify image
• Complacency
• Failure to scrap failed consumer technology products

Success in electronic store retailing has been marked by the emergence of Circuit City, Radio Shack, and Best Buy. Wal-Mart, Target, and Lowe's, although not electronic retailers, have also performed well nationally. Silo and Rex are successful regional chains. However, traditional stores like JC Penney have abandoned their electronics departments and a host of discounters such as Zayre's had a tendency to rely on price-cutting without cost consideration.

MANAGING CHANGE

Major technological discoveries such as the computer, the transistor, color television, and videocassette recorders are responsible for new types of merchants or will be marketed through existing retailers. The development of the Xerox process not only created a new company, but new channels of distribution were established to reach prospective heavy users. Copying machines are now available for the general consumer market.

The impact of technology on marketing and retailing goes beyond strategic planning because it fundamentally alters the social and economic environment for conducting business. There is a wide array of laborsaving appliances such as the microwave oven that have changed the role of the housewife and made it possible for women to enter the labor force.

Product life cycles have become shorter in recent decades due to improvements in technology. Consequently, retailers have incurred greater risks. Technological advancements will continue to present opportunities as well as competitive threats to management.

Electronics stores need to consider a number of focal points in the strategic planning process as changing conditions evolve. First, customer needs and wants must be satisfied. This means that customers should be educated as to how to properly use new technology. Second, governmental restrictions should be considered for how these products are packaged and advertised. For example, energy efficiency on electrical products and costs to consumers has become an issue in the 1990s and will continue well into the 21st century. Third, the company's current objectives and available resource expectations regarding market share, degree of risk, technological knowledge, and future growth are important considerations.

The objectives of the strategic planning process should help in establishing the merchandise assortment. The merchandise assortment will in turn influence decisions about pricing, communications, and levels of service. For example, Circuit City and Best Buy carry refrigerators and also stock washers and dryers, dishwashers, stoves, microwave ovens, and various small appliances. An assortment of products is needed to satisfy different customers and maintain loyalty. The merchandise assortment in each product line is the basis of the attraction of specialty electronic stores and pricing and service levels become differential strategies.

Many technological advances will have a profound impact on electronics store operations in the future. Already Circuit City has implemented a computerized control system in inventory management that establishes a differential advantage. Computer-to-computer linkages with suppliers have reduced ordering time and improved inventory flow. Thus, Circuit City has been able to balance its merchandise assortments more rapidly and improve its operational ratios.

Strategic alliances formed by Radio Shack with Sprint and Compaq are the basis of the future. Circuit City and Best Buy and other electronic retailers would do well to establish training procedures and perhaps facilities with manufacturers to educate consumers about technological changes. Home improvement chains such as Home Depot have satisfied consumer needs by establishing do-it-yourself classes, and electronic retailers should seriously consider this example.

Positioning market segment strategies will become more important in the future. Consumers targeted as innovators, early adopters, early majority, late majority, or laggards will be cultivated. A potential market segment such as senior citizens has been virtually ignored, and electronic retailers might do well to cultivate this growing market segment. Many electronics retailers have not survived and those that will be successful in the future must have the vision to respond to changing conditions.

9

Toy Stores: New Strategies of Niche Retailing

Successful Toy Store Strategies

- Niche strategy
- Location strategies
- Image development
- Effective use of human resources
- Partnerships with manufacturers
- Effective use of licensing

Toy Store Mistakes

- Price competition with discounters
- Rapid overexpansion
- Emulation of Toys "R" Us
- Ineffective effort to extend selling season
- Delay in using Internet selling
- Delay in taking advantage of store brands

The retail toy store industry in the United States is dominated by Toys "R" Us and Wal-Mart. Wal-Mart is the largest U.S. toy retailer in a $23 billion U.S. toy market. The business is highly competitive and competes on the basis of brand merchandise selection, superior customer service, and competitive pricing. Toys "R" Us represents 15 to 17 percent of toy retailing in the United States in 1999 compared to 25 percent in 1990. Toys "R" Us uses a retailing plan placing emphasis on physical distribution, location, brand names, and in-store returns. Although discount pricing was a prominent visible factor in the success of Toys "R" Us, so was a large product assortment of more than 18,000 products as compared to Wal-Mart's 200-item selection. Behind the scenes, the function of physical distribution, the process by which Toys "R" Us accelerated the flow of products from manufacturers in the right quantities at the right time to their stores, was largely responsible for its success as a retailer. The 1990s have witnessed the impact of other discounters such as Kmart and Target and of niche retailers such as Zany Brainy, Noodle Kidoodle, Imaginarium, eToys, and Amazon.com. Niche retailing in the toy industry has evolved from successful site location strategies. The objective is to locate store units where a group of potential customers who share common characteristics make them especially receptive for the educational products and services that toy stores like Zany Brainy sell. In the last decade, a number of toy store chains such as Child World and Lionel have failed, and the small independents have become extinct.

Charles Lazarus, the founder of Toys "R" Us opened his first store in 1957. Charles Lazarus is to Toys "R" Us as Leslie Wexner is to the Limited and Leonard Riggio is to Barnes & Noble. These merchants belong in a Retailing Hall of Fame. Toys "R" Us is one of the great success stores in retailing.

The company, through its computer system, has had the capability to implement a just-in-time distribution system. One reason why just-in-time and other automatic inventory-control systems are a source of competitive advantage is that they are cost efficient in improving customer service and thereby serve to ensure customer satisfaction. For just-in-time to operate properly, suppliers must be able to provide fast, reliable deliveries. A universal product code has been affixed to the merchandise, so that when purchased, its code is automatically scanned. Because of the information transmitted to a central computer, management can determine order quantities for each product and can maintain optimal inventory levels based on consumer purchases. Merchandise is maintained for only a short time in warehouses strategically located throughout the country. Toys "R" Us trucks transport the merchandise from the warehouse which is situated a relatively short distance from the stores. Many of the company's warehouses are large, modern automated facilities that process, store, and assemble merchandise for shipment.

The Toys "R" Us physical distribution system aids in determining product offerings to target customer needs. Distribution costs are reduced, and savings are passed on to the customer in the form of lower prices. Profits have subsequently been increased and a differential advantage has been clearly established, with increased customer satisfaction being the result.

Several trends have been observed in toy retailing that may change its future direction. Although large chains may dominate the industry, Child World and Lionel have failed and Toys "R" Us is no longer the threat it once was. A new breed of toy retailers such as Zany Brainy, Noodle Kidoodle, and Imaginarium are enjoying success as niche marketing is emphasized in conjunction with specialty items and in-store services. Toy purchasing patterns have changed and this means that large manufacturers such as Mattel and Hasbro, as well as the giant retailer, Toys "R" Us, will need to respond to these changes. The big toy manufacturers realize that they are not just toy companies but are in reality children's entertainment companies. The companies are now aiming their products at a PC-literate generation of children. Until these formidable firms learn to adjust and satisfy new consumer buying patterns, niche manufacturers and retailers will continue to capture increased market share.

A number of these changing buying patterns appear to be positive for the toy industry. First, there are more grandparents, generally with fewer grandchildren as compared to a previous generation and with more discretionary income. These grandparents enjoy indulging their grandchildren. Second, there are more double-income families. Thus, there is more money to be spent on children, and parents may feel somewhat guilty that time is limited and therefore more money is expended on toys. Next, family size is smaller. This means that much more is spent on children today than was on the children of yesterday. Another positive note is that a reward for good grades or just a weekend shopping trip has helped to extend the toy season that once was rooted in Christmas.

Whereas a number of trends are positive for the toy industry, other changes in buying patterns pose a growing problem. First of all many parents, for whatever the reason, are concerned with a lack of available time for shopping. Parents can buy other items besides toys at discounters such as Wal-Mart, Kmart, and Target. Many of these discounters have well-stocked inventories of toys. Moreover, many parents are turning to the niche retailer for toys that have educational or enrichment value. Other parents desire in-store services provided by these niche retailers. Another important trend that causes a dilemma is that children are outgrowing toys earlier, moving on to computers and electronic games. Toy spending seems to peak at age three and decline steadily for each age group. Moreover, the buying of toys over the Internet has taken market share away from the traditional retailers who were slow to adopt this method of selling. Age compression is another variable, as girls were once interested, for example in Barbie until they were nine or ten years old, and now they lose interest in Barbie at ages five or six. The problem is how to attract older children to buy toys.

Not only do parents have less time, but this is true of children too, because of the educational trend toward giving more homework to children at earlier ages. Organized sports, such as Little League, take time away from playing with toys. Finally, although children have larger allowances than a previous generation, spending is on collectibles such as baseball cards or for girls who are "tweens," on makeup and jewelry.

A consideration of the successes and failures of toy retailers shows that many mistakes have been made, and only those organizations that have been able to make constant adjustments with such variables an innovation, target market, image, physical environmental resources, and human resources have remained viable. The structure of toy retailing is experiencing new developments that have taken the form of niche marketing with emphasis on specialty items and in-store services. Innovation has taken place with strategies of niche retailing, most notably by Zany Brainy and Noodle Kidoodle. Both companies sought profits by avoiding competition from Toys "R" Us, a powerhouse in toy retailing. Zany Brainy and Noodle Kidoodle at first sought opportunities that would be unlikely to attract competitors. These educational toy retailers believed that there would be sufficient time in their niche to ensure profits before competitors could successfully enter. Both Zany Brainy and Noodle Kidoodle have chosen to define the market in which they compete according to geographical boundaries, thereby maximizing location and physical resources. This strategy utilizes both niche retailing and physical resource management. In April 2000, Zany Brainy purchased Noodle Kidoodle and created a 163-store chain under the Zany Brainy name.

Toys "R" Us has successfully developed an image as a destination toy store. Customers believe that they can find a broad selection of toy merchandise that would satisfy all preferences. In contrast, Zany Brainy has developed an image as a retailer of educational and creative toys. Store services further this image as many former educators are employed to help customers find just the "right" toys. The use of former educators makes effective use of human resources in satisfying customers at the point of purchase. These strategies have aided Toys "R" Us in segmenting a mass market that desires a wide selection of merchandise and Zany Brainy in targeting customers who desire to purchase educational toys.

The variables of innovation, image, target market segmentation, physical store decor and human resources have been used to counter the competitive presence of such discounters as Wal-Mart, Kmart, and Target all of which have seized market share away from toy retailers. Zany Brainy has rapidly positioned itself as a distinctive alternative to the discounters. Toys "R" Us with its wide selection, emphasis on its learning center, and computer games is also endeavoring to compete effectively against the discounter.

STRUCTURE

Table 9.1 presents the leading toy retailers in the United States. Toys "R" Us, the leader, has found its market share of the retail toy industry shrinking and is down to 15 to 17 percent market share from its commanding 25 percent of some years ago in a $23 billion-a-year toy retailing business. Together, Wal-Mart, Kmart, and Target have approximately 28 percent of market share and with other lesser-known discounters comprise more than 30 percent of market share. Department stores such as JC Penney have a relatively small market share of the retail toy market. While niche retailers such as Zany Brainy, Noodle Kidoodle, and Imaginarium are increasing their market share, none of these stores will dominate the retail toy industry since their niches, while sizable, will not make that much of a national impact. Kay-Bee Toy is the only survivor who has competed with Toys "R" Us and is in the process of reinventing itself. Child World and Lionel, other toy superstores, have not survived, and it is doubtful that new chains of toy superstores will emerge in the future.

Shopping patterns have changed and consumers have turned their attention to the discounters and the niche retailers. The discounters have expanded their toy assortments and consumers have purchased the standard and popular toys from the discounters. Many consumers have made purchases from niche retailers that carry a broad selection of educational toys or toys that build on a child's creativity. For example, Noodle Kidoodle offers an in-store computer center that stocks more than 600 software titles and encourages consumers to try them. A movie theater provides children with not only movies but also live performances. Moreover, Imaginarium stocks about 3,000 products, and 1,500 books and has developed an extensive line of private label items.

Niche retailers such as Zany Brainy, Noodle Kidoodle, and Imaginarium have found that new technologies are enabling them to market to individuals as individuals. The relationships between customers and retailers are returning to the "intimate" relationship that mom and pop retailers fostered some years ago. Zany Brainy, based in Wynnewood, Pennsylvania, is undertaking a national expansion program. The company is opening a number of superstores and features nonviolent, nonsexist toys. Noodle Kidoodle, part of Greenman Brothers, Inc., operates stores in the eastern United States and Chicago. The company features

Table 9.1
An Overview of the Retail Toy Industry

	Estimated Market Share 1998	Number of Units 1998
Toys R Us	15-17%	1481
KB Toys	4-5%	1322
Zany Brainy	1-2%	80
Noodle Kidoodle	1-2%	42
Imaginarium	1-2%	>40
FAO Schwarz	.05%	41
Disney	.05%	713
Warner Brothers		180
Discounters		
Wal-Mart	15-18%	2884[1]
Kmart	7-8%	2161
Target	.02%	851
On-Line		
eToys		N/A
Department Stores		
JC Penney	1-2%	1150

1. Includes 1,869 discount stores and 564 Supercenters, and 451 SAM'S Clubs stores.

games on personal computers. Imaginarium, headquartered in Walnut Creek, California, has forty stores in sixteen states. The stores, located in shopping malls, feature a wide selection of creative toys.

eToys Inc., an Internet retailer, has been eagerly embraced by Mattel, Hasbro, and other toy manufacturers. Both Mattel and Hasbro were hurt by reductions in inventory at Toys "R" Us and some other large retailers, and as a result are eager to reduce their dependence on a few large retailers. eToys, unlike some other online retailers, has had little difficulty in obtaining access to top-selling brands. Although eToys is a long way from profitability, the company is receiving the cooperation of toy manufacturers and doubtlessly will take some revenue away from traditional toy retailers. In 1998, eToys sold $23 million in toys alone. It is estimating revenue at $125 million in 1999. Amazon.com has also expanded into the sale of toys on the Internet. eToys and Amazon.com play heavily on the appeal of avoiding excitable children in toy stores. However, both Toys "R" Us and Wal-Mart have engaged in Internet selling of toys and the competition is keener. Customers will find it easier to make returns to stores and this is a plus for the retailers.

The first FAO Schwarz toy store opened in 1862 in Baltimore. The company offers a merchandise assortment of high quality, expensive toys. The target market is the affluent customer who is status and prestige conscious. FAO Schwarz maintains a high level of customer service and an exciting environment in which to shop. There are almost 100 boutiques organized around such themes as trains and the circus. Merchandise ranges from stuffed animals to customized model cars and dollhouses selling at several thousand dollars. Prime locations such as New York City's Fifth Avenue are selected. Salespeople in FAO Schwarz take particular care in demonstrating and explaining the toys to customers. Thus FAO Schwarz has selected different locations and merchandise than the toy superstores.

Supermarkets and drugstores usually stock the more popular toys during the Christmas buying season. Neither of these institutions pose serious competition to toy retailers, superstores, or discounters. The advent of scrambled merchandising, particularly in supermarkets and drug stores, has hurt the small independent toy retailers as they are confronted by toy superstores and discounters.

The making of exclusives for toy retailers including Toys "R" Us, Wal-Mart, JC Penney, and other large retailers has been a part of retailing for some years. For example, FAO Schwarz designates as much a 30 percent of its inventory as exclusives. KB Toys, a unit of Consolidated Stores, has revitalized its mall-based chain by selling exclusives. This strategy sets retailers apart from their competition. Naturally, if the exclusive line does not sell, the retailer is placed at risk. The structure of retailing has been modified as retailers pressure manufacturers for a special merchandise line of toys that will not be sold elsewhere. Traditional toy retailers have been slow to use Internet selling lest they cannibalize themselves. Moreover, no store brands are offering effective competition with national brands.

POWER IN THE TOY INDUSTRY

Toys "R" Us is one of the strongest specialty store retailers in the United States and, in turn, helps dominate the retail toy industry because of its buying power. Toys "R" Us can exert a strong impact on the product, price, and promotion activities of toy manufacturers. Child World and Lionel have left the retail toy scene, and only KB Toys remains as a distant competitor. Therefore, Toys "R" Us is in a unique position to control and administer the toy industry distribution system.

It is possible that Toys "R" Us could serve as a gatekeeper in either admission or denial of entry into the toy distribution system. Toys "R" Us in this situation could either encourage the introduction of a new product or block its entry. To illustrate, Hasbro invested millions of dollars to launch Nemo, a home video game system to compete with Nintendo but cancelled the project when Toys "R" Us reacted negatively. Moreover, Toys "R" Us has required all of its suppliers to pay a fee to have their products included in Toys "R" Us newspaper advertisements. This may place an undue burden on small toy manufacturing companies. Toys "R" Us has developed a year-round market for toys that is beneficial to the toy industry. Whereas other toy retailers tend to promote toys only at Christmas, Toys "R" Us has helped the toy industry to operate more efficiently. Furthermore, Toys "R" Us shares its market data with toy manufacturers so that immediate information on sales and the effectiveness of marketing programs is known. Therefore, there is an acknowledged interdependence. The Toy Manufacturers Association in the 1970s worked directly with banks to help Toys "R" Us when it had financial difficulties.

Through the years, Toys "R" Us has made valuable suggestions on possible design improvement and marketing improvements for toy producers. Toys "R" Us has helped manufacturers by granting credit and even prepaying bills. Toys "R" Us has recognized the responsibility and its own advantage in aiding toy manufacturers to succeed. Toys "R" Us stocks more than 18,000 different toy items in football-field size stores and needs a steady flow of successful products in order to achieve its own profitability. The development of an effective just-in-time distribution system has enhanced its strength.

TOYS "R" US: THE CATEGORY KILLER

The first category killer store, Toys "R" Us was established in the late 1950s. A category killer store offers an exhaustive selection in a single product line. Toys "R" Us features relatively low prices, and consumers are drawn from wide geographic areas. In the 1990s organizations in other specialty lines such as Home Depot, Circuit City, and Barnes & Noble emerged. The category killer store may not attract consumers interested in a small store environment or one-stop shopping. Home Depot has moved to open small stores, but Toys "R" Us has not tried to please customers interested in a small store format. Toys "R" Us would like to be known as a destination store, where the merchandise selection and presentation, pricing, and other unique features act as a magnet for consumers, but the popularity of discounters such as Wal-Mart has obscured this image in recent years. However, this was not always the case, and Toys "R" Us could have been referred to as a destination store in the 1980s.

The strategies of Toys "R" Us were very successful from 1985 to 1995. Among the factors responsible were:

- The firm maintains a year-round inventory of toys. In contrast, department stores and discount stores reduce their inventory in the "off season." Consequently, a high level of customer loyalty has been maintained and new toys are given an early introduction.
- Customers are offered an extensive selection.
- Orders are placed in the off season from toy manufacturers allowing better purchase terms.
- Space is used effectively and efficiently.
- Purchasing power gives the firm a high priority on reordering merchandise from manufacturers that consumers demand.
- Although it is not a discounter, prices are low enough so that Toys "R" Us is considered a category killer store.
- A computer system facilitates forecasting and inventory management.
- The company gains important advantages in opening new stores through its warehouse distribution system which is strategically located. Moreover, a just-in-time distribution system is maintained with some manufacturers.

As the 21st century emerges Toys "R" Us has lost market share to new niche retailers and discounters. Therefore, new strategies have appeared, such as:

- The development of a learning and discovery center.
- The carrying of various types of children's apparel.
- The stocking of pre-teen electronic items.

- The development of online marketing to combat the competition of eToys and other firms that are selling toys on the Internet.
- An aggressive policy of increasing the number of proprietary items sold only by Toys "R" Us.
- The building of a store shopping environment that will delight customers. This strategy has been deliberately set in place to offset focus group results that indicate that the store, like a supermarket, is difficult to navigate.

Charles Lazarus, founder of Toys "R" Us, originally sold children's furniture from his father's bicycle shop in Washington, D.C. Toys were added in response to customer requests, and by 1957 toys and furniture were sold by Lazarus from his own store. In 1966, Lazarus sold Toys "R" U, but poor management and overexpansion created financial difficulties. Lazarus returned to the organization, and since the late 1970s the firm's overall philosophy has remained essentially the same: each store offers about 18,000 toys in convenient locations at low prices. By the end of the 1980s Toys "R" Us had driven its two biggest competitors, Child World and Lionel, into bankruptcy. Emphasis is on the control of expenses and systemic labor scheduling to allocate workers properly. Great care is taken to ascertain that each item is in stock—the term stock-out is not acceptable. The physical organization of the stores in the past has resembled supermarkets and customers use shopping carts. Prices on the average are set about a third below department stores for comparable merchandise but not as low as Wal-Mart, Kmart, or Target. The firm in the past has not offered any special price promotions. Toys "R" Us gained a foothold in the toy business by serving mostly suburban families with children who desire popular, nationally advertised toys. This strategy has begun to change in recent years and more proprietary items have been added. Moreover, Toys "R" Us has always stressed a great depth and breadth of merchandise assortment to satisfy all customers.

A single focus has remained constant throughout the fifty-year history of Toys "R" Us and that has been a concentration on satisfying the target market namely, children. Originally started as a store selling juvenile furniture, the company has expanded its target market to embrace all facets of the children's market. Toys "R" Us became a public company in 1978, and the first Kids "R" Us store opened in 1983 offering kid's fashions. The first Babies "R" Us opened in 1996, and Toys "R" Us merged with Baby Superstore. Kids World Superstore also opened in 1996. Kids World combined advantages from Toys "R" Us, Kids "R" Us, and Babies "R" Us, plus other innovations such as Kids Foot Lockers, Focus Pocus (a photo studio), Cartoon Cuts (a hair salon), Jeeper Junior (a restaurant) , Fuzzig's Candy Factory, plus arcade games and rides. Toys "R" Us has expanded beyond the United States and has established more than 400 stores in twenty-six countries around the world. Franchise operations were established in such places as Italy, Saudi Arabia, South Africa, and Turkey.

In 1996, Concept 2000 was developed in thirteen stores. Since customers in the past had complained about narrow aisles and crowded conditions, Concept 2000 featured friendly store designs. Wider aisles and color-coded merchandise displays added shopping convenience, and sales assistants were present in various categories to explain important product features and answer questions. Specialty areas were added for video games and popular toys to entertain and motivate children and parents as they shop. Toys "R" Us has approximately 38 million customers in its database and this should help in Internet and catalogue selling.

Unlike many other retailers, Toys "R" Us has found a partnership with toy manufacturers in product development. The company recognizes that product differentiation is critical for its long-term success. Product development will also include private label development, branded exclusives produced by prominent toy manufacturers, and exclusive licenses. Toys "R" Us anticipates that this new role in product development will lead to greater profitability and promote customer loyalty. This new thrust is supported by the addition of personnel with experience in toy manufacturing.

Toys "R" Us has not ignored the area of public relations. McDonald's is well known for its "Make A Wish" and Ronald McDonald Foundation. Toys "R" Us established the Children's Benefit Fund to provide support for programs and health initiatives that benefit children. Approximately $15 million has been contributed by the Children's Benefit Fund to hospitals and children's charities. Toys "R" Us has also been instrumental in helping disabled children and has produced a Toy Guide designed to assist consumers in making informal decisions about toy selection for children with special needs.

Store units in the past have generally been situated as freestanding units or in strip centers. Where feasible, preference on location is given to highway visibility. Toys "R" Us has avoided crowded malls since it did not desire customers to be encumbered with lots of packages. Toys "R" Us originally located its stores in the suburbs but expansion has also included the central city. Another facet of store location strategy has been to situate outlets near retailers that draw store traffic such as Circuit City or Home Depot.

The competitive advantage that Toys "R" Us has enjoyed through the years is not necessarily because it offers the lowest prices. Stores originally carried diapers and baby formula and sold these items at low prices, a strategy that continues. These items were placed in the rear of the store thereby forcing customers to pass by more than twenty aisles stocked with games and toys convenient to reach. Impulse buying led to increased purchasing.

CHALLENGES CONFRONTING TOYS "R" US IN THE 21ST CENTURY

Toys "R" Us was founded on the philosophy of offering everyday low prices throughout the year in a supermarket environment. This original philosophy is questionable in the current retailing environment. First of all, distributors such as Wal-Mart, Target, and Kmart are able to offer lower prices. Second, the independent toy stores are able to provide better service in a more pleasant environment. Third, warehouse clubs like Sam's Club and Costco have moved into the toy business, further exacerbating the problem. Fourth, Zany Brainy has also moved into the toy end of the market with splendid customer service. And fifth, the Internet is attracting the shop-at-home market that finds it more convenient to buy toys without having children running up and down the aisles.

The merchandise selection at Wal-Mart, for example, is smaller, but prices are much lower. Toys "R" Us, in efforts to compete, has lowered its operating margin from 12 to 8 percent in recent years. Moreover, the company averages less than four inventory turns a year, compared to seven or eight at Wal-Mart and Target. Not only profitability is eroding, so is market share.

Concept 2000 was an effort to remodel the toy stores with an emphasis on less clutter and cleaner and more cheerful appearing outlets. Shelves were to be lower and more customer accessible and customer service improved. Separate departments were designated for books, video games, Barbie dolls, and Legos. Concept 2000 has not worked out according to expectations. To date, their modeled stores have not provided either the increase in sales revenue or the return on investment that was expected. Kids World has been criticized as too large and will not produce its needed volume. In response, Toys "R" Us is adding candy, fast food, sneakers, videos—just about everything—in efforts to accentuate scrambled merchandising and satisfy customer wants.

In 1999, the company acquired Imaginarium Toy Centers, Inc. which operates forty-one stores in thirteen states to tap into a higher-priced specialty-toy customer. The specialty-toy market represents almost 8 percent of the $23 billion toy-retail industry, with learning toys having a higher profit margin than traditional toys.

In an effort to streamline the organization there has been a consolidation of Toys "R" Us with Kids "R' Us stores. As of 1998, sixty-five successful combination stores, where Kids "R" Us shared approximately 6,000 square feet within Toys "R" Us stores were operating. Hopefully, these combination stores will utilize available space wisely and will be able to offer much more than the discount stores. An important feature of these combination stores is providing a more friendly shopping atmosphere than a supermarket environment. This strategy, too, will hopefully make inroads into the discounters share of the toy market. As the 21st century emerges Toys "R" Us is endeavoring not only to counter competition from Wal-Mart, Kmart, and Target but also to marginalize the impact of a niche toy retailer such as Zany Brainy.

BLUNDERS: CHILD WORLD

Child World, which operated some stores under the Children's Palace name, was the number-two competitor to Toys "R" Us in 1989 and numbered more than 170 outlets. After a roller coaster restructuring effort, the Child World chain (now consisting of about 125 units), filled for bankruptcy protection in 1992. The end of the number-two toy chain was in sight as the company was hopelessly in debt.

The economic downturn, a softening of the video-game market and poor business management contributed to the downfall of Child World. An aspect of poor business management was the Child World price war with Toys "R" Us. The price war led to prices below regular prices and eventually below merchandise costs to attract consumers away from Toys "R" Us. This price war meant low profits and, over time, losses for Child World. Moreover, Child World could not make purchases in such large quantities as Toys "R" Us and therefore could not arrange favorable purchasing terms. Child World tied its performance in 1989 to the sale of Ninetendo and the video game market, but unfortunately the Nintendo Entertainment System experienced fierce declines in a saturated market.

The economic downturn also aggravated the situation for Child World Stores. But Toys "R" Us survived and so did some other toy retailers. The development of a distribution mission needs to be reconciled with the purpose of the retail outlet. A market-oriented definition of the retail outlet's primary purpose would be an appropriate guide for business planning and strategy and, although limited, would serve a good beginning. Child World desired to develop strategies aimed at increasing both child and adult awareness of its stores differently than from the competition. While this is a broad mission, it does not identify the main problem. Consumers were aware of the Child World chain. That was not the problem. The problem was to differentiate from Toys "R" Us, and this was the failure of Child World. A corporate mission needs to be clear and specific and above all to identify the direction and not a symptom of the problem.

BLUNDERS: LIONEL

Lionel operated toy supermarket formats under the names of Lionel Playworld, Lionel Kiddie City, and Lionel Toy Warehouse. Company strategy was to expand in major metropolitan markets. As of 1990, at the height of its strength, Lionel operated more than one hundred stores. However, in 1991, Lionel filed for protection from creditors under Chapter 11 of the Bankruptcy Code.

Lionel utilized a toy supermarket concept much like that of Toys "R" Us. The firm made purchases early in the year and provided its customers with a broad assortment of toys and related products at competitive prices throughout the year. Much like Toys "R" Us, Lionel offered about 18,000 products and attracted customers with bargain prices on diapers, formula, and other infant care products. Unlike Toys "R" Us, Lionel promoted special sales of popular items periodically. Toys "R" Us in contrast, maintained low prices throughout the year and refrained from special sales or promotions. This strategy probably accentuated the competition between Lionel and discounters such as Wal-Mart and Target. On the other hand, Toys "R" Us tried to avoid direct competition. Moreover, Lionel lacked the strength with manufacturers to insist on a great many exclusives and a partnership system of product development. Lionel's database system for customer names and computer system for purposes of inventory control was no match for the systems of Toys "R" Us.

Lionel suffered from strong intra- and inter-type competition. Poor positioning, foggy target marketing—or both—gave Lionel an image of a "me too" operation that did not do things as well as Toys "R" Us, Wal-Mart, Kmart, or Target. The lack of genuine innovation in merchandising strategies gave Lionel an image of a nonprogressive store and a relic of the past. Lionel was not the classic case of a retailer failing by declining sales and profits for some years. An important reason for the company demise was that Lionel had been sidetracked by expanding too rapidly and growing by acquisition instead of by an organized plan. There did not seem to be any uniformity to the stores or logic in their development. Poor credit was an additional symptom of the pending disaster, but poor management played a much more important part in this story.

KB TOYS: EFFECTIVE LOCATIONS

KB Toys was acquired by Consolidated Stores from the Melville Corporation in 1996 and has 1,322 outlets consisting of three divisions. KB Toys are mall-based stores that average 3,500 square feet and have about 1,000 units. KB Toy Works are neighborhood toy stores usually situated in strip shopping malls with 6,000 to 12,000 square feet. Management desires that these stores be perceived by consumers as destination stores. KB Toy Outlets and KB Toy Liquidators are located in major outlet malls and specialize in selling toys that are closeouts. The purchase by Consolidated Stores in 1996, and its name change from Kay-Bee Toys to KB Toys contributed to its success. One of the company's biggest problems in the early 1990s was shrinkage. Executives did not realize its vulnerability for

NOODLE KIDOODLE AND ZANY BRAINY: NICHE RETAILERS

Zany Brainy and Noodle Kidoodle were the retail innovators of the 1990s. Zany Brainy established its first store in 1991 and Noodle Kidoodle in 1993. The chains compete directly with one another: both are niche retailers targeting the educational toy market. Educationally oriented products include creative and nonviolent children's products, such as toys, books, games, video and audiotapes, computer software, crafts, and other learning products. Instrumental to the success of each organization has been the selection of site locations. Zany Brainy located in southern New Jersey, suburban Philadelphia, and Washington, D.C., while Noodle Kidoodle concentrated in northern New Jersey, Long Island, Connecticut, Texas,s Oklahoma, and Florida and the Boston, Chicago, and Detroit metropolitan areas.

Zany Brainy and Noodle Kidoodle are organizations that feature interactive toys, generally of a safe, nonviolent, and gender-neutral nature. Each promotes learning as entertainment and enhances creativity. Zany Brainy was the winner of the 1998 National Retail Federation Independent Retailers of the Year Award for its focus on providing children with an interactive environment that was conducive to viewing computer-based education materials as well as concentrating on the selling of traditional learning toys. Playthings also in 1998 gave an award to Zany Brainy for innovative promotional campaigns.

Although niche stores provides a unique selling message, niche strategy presents special challenges. Both toy chains feature toys that help to develop intelligence and promote creativity such as building toys and puzzles. Zany Brainy and Noodle Kidoodle do not compete with Toys "R" Us on the basis of price. For the most part, efforts are made not to carry toys that compete with discounters. For Zany Brainy to succeed, there must be customer relationship building and service. This relationship building is a key strategy and a staff of former teachers and learning specialists is trained to provide insights on product selection. The stores provide superior customer service while providing an entertaining shopping environment through interactive play areas and frequent in-store events.

The use of educational consultants reflects the culture of these toy niche retailers. Zany Brainy tries to remain close to the needs and wants of its customers and to develop strategies to reflect customer preferences. Zany Brainy depends on events marketing. A constant offering of readings, crafts, workshops, and fund-raising events are provided as family fun destinations. The key to success is location.

The educational toy market is large enough for both Zany Brainy and Noodle Kidoodle. However, Toys "R" Us has changed the format of many of its stores and is much more competitive in the areas of educational toys. eToys and Internet selling by Toys "R" Us is bound to take away sales from Zany Brainy. Unfortunately for these niche toy retailers, merchandise offerings can be duplicated by Toys "R" Us and *e*Toys. Even Wal-Mart and Amazon.com have begun to make inroads into the educational market. What would be difficult to duplicate is the advice of educational consultants employed by Zany Brainy. Customers could neutralize that strength by receiving the advice of these educational consultants and then actually making their purchases at lower prices elsewhere. This actually happened many years ago in the appliance market as customers obtained information from traditional retailers and then made purchases in the discount stores.

*E*TOYS: INTERNET SELLING AND CANNIBALISM

*e*Toys.com and Toys.com joined forces in 1998 to combine resources and offer a selection of about 15,000 toys on the Internet. In 1997, *e*Toys initially offered no more than 1,000 toys. Amazon.com had also entered the cyber toy business using its 1.7 million customers as a potential market. It has been estimated that online toy sales will hit $1.5 billion by 2003.

Toys "R" Us, FAO Schwarz, KB Toys, and other toy retailers have also entered the world of Internet selling. Like Barnes & Noble and Gap, toy retailers were initially reluctant to join Internet selling because it required them to cannibalize their own offerings. That is the challenge that confronts toy and other specialty retailers as they contemplate an online entry. Potential customers are reached faster, but for many it may mean directly competing with themselves.

Purchasing toys from the Internet is accelerating because many parents have an aversion to taking children to toy stores where they might be pressured to buy toys that they might prefer not to purchase. Moreover, battling the holiday crowds in search of a gift that might not even be in stock is an unsettling experience. A significant number of shoppers are opting for the more quiet environment of their own homes, in front of a computer while the children are asleep, to do their shopping. Internet shopping for many is still preferable to in-store purchasing.

*e*Toys would seem to be the first place to browse in cyberspace when shopping for more popular toys. The company carries everything from Hot Wheels to Barbie to Thomas Trains. Video games, music, books, and software have been recently added to their selection. *e*Toys plans to become the dominant retailer of merchandise for children up to age twelve. *e*Toys has developed a kid-safe site where children cannot come across R-rated toys, and software and where parents can talk to experts over the telephone or through e-mail. *e*Toys has the ability to put personalized "to-from" tags on each gift so that multiple gifts to different recipients can be sent to the same address instead of in separate boxes. In an attempt to make customers more loyal, eToys is planning to set up a parent pass-word-protected gift registry, and spare parts and repair services for toys. FAO Schwarz and Toys "R" Us make only a portion of their in-store inventories available online. There are other Internet firms such as Holt Educational Outlet, a well-known educational supplier retailer, but it is too early to predict which companies will survive the competition. Online retailing is still in its infancy with the Toys "R" Us Website difficult to navigate and the FAO Schwarz catalogue more comprehensive than its Website selection.

MANAGING CHANGE

One of the most significant changes confronting toy retailers and manu-facturers is age compression. Age compression is a term that means chil-dren are growing up more quickly than they did a generation or even a decade ago. The tweens are defined between the ages of nine and thirteen and are an important target market for toy retailers. Although the number of tweens in this age category has declined since the mid-1970s, increased discretionary income and a shift in family purchase decision making has increased the importance of this target market.

The tweens congregate at the shopping mall. These kids are not neces-sarily spoiled or wealthy. They may have earned their own money or saved their allowances to purchase brand names that are meaningful to them and their peer group. The malls have become the center of their fashion and music, and tweens are not only interested in toys but also in household items such as high-tech electronics. Some authorities believe that in these days of divorced parents and extended families, brand name items make up the emotional support that once were provided by the family unit. Tween closets contain such brands as Benetton, Esprit, and Polo. Tweens look to California rather than Europe for fashion standards. Girls as young as nine can select from their own brands of lipstick and cosmetics, and children of both genders have high brand awareness.

Sales of traditional toys have fallen dramatically for tweens. Replacing Barbie and Lincoln Logs are computer games and clothes. Children no longer have to play dress-up since they can wear miniature versions of their parents' clothes from stores like the Gap.

The tweens were brought up in a different cultural environment than their 1960s-nurtured parents. The 1960s tweens dreamed of driving VW's. The 1990s tweens dream of driving BMWs. The 21st century will find the current generation of children as the first to grow up surrounded by computers and the Internet. Zany Brainy has established computer kiosks in its stores so that children and their parents can test software. Zany Brainy sells most of its toys to children under the age of eight, and 10 percent of its revenue is derived from computer programs. The sales of computer games will be a more attractive area in the future. Technology has been woven into the future and into the fabric of tween lives.

Age compression has meant shorter and shorter life cycles. Therefore, toy retailers manufacturers need to accelerate their response to the market. Toys "R" Us is proceeding in the right direction by helping manufacturers to design toys. A proactive strategy with manufacturers that might even result in partnership marketing should be favorably viewed.

Licensing remains a driving force in the toy industry. Batman, Crayola, Winnie the Pooh, Harley-Davidson, and Star Wars are all popular names that are licensed for use with products sold by retailers. Licensing is an agreement that allows the licensee to make and sell products with the sponsor's identification, in return paying royalties to the licensor. Licensed products have increased in popularity, and movies such as *The Lion King* and *Star Wars* have benefited the toy industry. Another factor in the success of toy licensing has been age compression that has resulted in more mature branding programs such as professional wrestling. The automotive industry has had the greatest impact on the toy industry. Chrysler, General Motors, Ford, Harley Davidson, Caterpillar, and John Deere are licensers where brands have had a significant impact on toy retailers. Replica vehicles, from ride-on to remote control to die-cast, have become important in recent years. Classic brands such as Betty Crocker and Kodak have also been successfully licensed on a broad range of toys. In addition, toys using interactive technology play an important part in the future of the toy industry.

Niche retailers in the toy industry have acknowledged that many time-honored ways of doing things are rapidly becoming obsolete. An operating reality for niche retailers has been the departure from past strategies that has been made possible by new technologies. Many formulas that were successful in the past have led to failure. Toys "R" Us is endeavoring to change in a volatile environment.

10

Automotive Stores: Multidimensional Buyer Behavior

Successful Automotive Store Strategies

- Private branding of products
- Understanding market segmentation
- Use of Internet selling
- Customer friendly consultative selling
- Product availability
- Use of customer and market intelligence information
- Strong distribution and information systems infrastructure based on technology
- Store location
- Stepping up of sales to commercial customers

Automotive Store Mistakes

- Rapid expansion into new market areas
- Failure to recognize changes in buying behavior
- Poor store layout
- Lack of inventory management
- No strategy for lagging do-it-yourself market
- No service installation

General Motors, Ford, and Chrysler have devoted little attention to the power of their distribution channels as full-service automotive stores and have lost market share for their automotive replacement parts and accessories business to retailers like AutoZone, NAPA, Western Auto, Pep Boys, Midas, Firestone, and others. They have resisted making needed changes in their dealer franchise networks. The dealers have objected to the assignment of new car sales quotas without dealer consultation, the insistence that dealers accept a "minimum" supply of parts and accessories, and the pressure to contribute specified amounts of dollars for promotion purposes. The extension of new warranties by the manufacturers places more responsibility on the dealers and creates a lower profit margin on parts. However, the extension warranties can stimulate additional repair business and make possible higher earnings if the dealers know how to market these services.

In the automobile industry, the manufacturer endeavors to maximize sales at retail levels while the franchiser or the dealer endeavors to maximize profits—hence intra-organizational conflict. This conflict within the automotive industry has allowed firms outside the traditional distribution system to seize a sizable share of the market.

The $170 billion automotive aftermarket, composed of such firms as AutoZone, Pep Boys, NAPA, and Western Auto, uses a distribution system that begins with the auto parts manufacturers, moves to warehouse distributors, from there to jobbers and to retail stores, and finally to consumers. Some manufacturers sell directly to large retail store chains and warehouse clubs. The retailers' customers include the do-it-yourself market, commercial fleets such as Avis and Hertz, used car dealers, and automotive repair shops.

The current state of the automotive aftermarket indicates a steady but slow growth rate over the years. During periods of uncertainty, when new car sales decline, consumers are more likely to maintain older automobiles than to purchase new cars. Moreover, there are many more two- and three-car families possessing both new and older cars. There is an increasing number of self-service gas stations and a decreasing number of gas stations that perform automobile services. And there is a growing trend for consumers to perform their own maintenance. This situation, in turn, has helped the growth of such chains as AutoZone and Pep Boys. Manufacturers aware of this changing environment have aggressively marketed their products directly to retail chains and have advertised directly to consumers and specifically to women. Women are often uneasy when shopping for automotive products because of their general lack of knowledge about automotive parts. When women enter an automotive store, they tend to shop initially on price. Therefore, salespeople need to be attentive and prepared to provide information when dealing with women.

Consumers spend an average of $653 a year on vehicle maintenance and buy automobile replacement parts and accessories such as oil, air filters, and batteries in supermarkets, drug stores, discount department stores, Kmart and Wal-Mart, other automotive stores, and over the Internet. The existence of brand name auto parts by manufacturers is common. Technology improvement has increased the product life span of many products and has created new competitive pressures in the automotive aftermarket industry.

Retail chains have varied their inventory stocking policies as they relate to automotive products. Some sellers of automobile replacement parts carry a full range of products, while others have found their niche by selling only the most common and fastest moving parts. The number of automobile parts has proliferated as a result of government mandated safety and emission control equipment and more American and foreign automobile models. Retailers have been confronted with larger investment requirements, which increases overhead and reduces profitability. Manufacturers have helped ease the situation by utilizing standardized products. For example, standardized parts are the fastest moving items and should be stocked by all sellers. Nonstandardized parts may not be as popular but need also to be stocked by all levels of the traditional aftermarket industry, particularly for national automobile store chains. Other parts should by stocked with caution depending upon local conditions.

Franchising was first introduced by General Motors in 1893 and is an example of a manufacturer-retailer franchise system that is common in the automotive industry and for gasoline service stations. Individual owners who are franchised directly by manufacturers operate the retail outlets. Western Auto was franchised in 1909 as the first in the automotive aftermarket industry. Genuine Parts operates over 750 retail units and franchises more than 5,000 stores, known as NAPA independents.

The United States automobile industry is a differentiated oligopoly with few manufacturing firms existing in the industry. Manufacturers of automobiles have been confronting difficult environmental factors that have played a significant role in new car production. To a large degree, the government has taken over the design of automobiles because of noise, safety, emission, and fuel standards. In distribution, automobile manufacturers market their products through franchised dealers who sell to consumers. The manufacturer-dealer network operates effectively as an integrated system with the manufacturer assuming the role of channel captain directing the activities of the members of the distribution system. The complexity of administering this distribution system is awesome when the number of franchised dealers selling new automobiles is considered. These dealers are bound by a contractual franchise agreement, but they are still relatively independent in making decisions involving inventory levels, pricing, promotion, sales-force management, and servicing. To succeed, dealers must be adequately financed and strategically located with satisfactory service facilities.

According to Alfred P. Sloan, Jr., in the 1920s there were 13,700 dealers in the United States, and it was company policy to take a major interest in the franchise relationship.[1] Today, the National Automobile Dealers Association is made up of 19,600 members, a number that includes 7,700 General Motors' U.S. dealers. The manufacturer typically administers an educational program that improves dealer competency in sales, service, and general management. The dealer accepts the assistance, training, and guidance for his organization. Conflict can erupt when auto dealers object to practices of the manufacturers. The most frequent disagreements between manufacturers and dealers are over parts availability, product quality, warranty work, and vehicle ordering systems. Even though conflicts exist in the distribution system, dealer satisfaction is probably high, based on all considerations, since the franchise has great resale value. However, the traditional franchise system of manufacturer and dealer did not realize the potential of the do-it-yourself market and the new developing commercial market for automobile parts and accessories. This change in purchase-demand patterns was induced by the rising number of motor vehicles sold to consumers and commercial users. Organizations such as Western Auto, and subsequently the newer retail chains such as AutoZone and Pep Boys, grew in response to new consumer purchasing patterns.

Growth in specialty store retailing has in the past evolved from a definite structure. Drugstores, clothing stores, furniture stores, and other specialty retailers developed through an orderly and well-planned framework. In contrast, automotive stores have come about because dealers spent most of their effort selling vehicles. Environmental forces have been such that consumer buyer behavior was left unsatisfied and automotive stores took the necessary step to close the gap.

None of the retail auto chains have developed noteworthy strategies for market segmentation. Pep Boys has developed an image in the industry as being an innovator. AutoZone is known for its distribution centers and information systems. Discount Auto Parts has assumed a leadership role in the pricing of its products.

An approach using the variables of market segmentation, image, innovation, physical store decor, and effective human resources could improve the marketing efforts of automotive retailers. Specialty automotive chains could expand their market and modify their image by becoming more user friendly to women. Home Depot and Lowe's, in the home improvement sector, have successfully accomplished this objective and increased profitability. Best Buy, in the retail electronic sector, has found that sales presentations that educate consumers are welcome. Another dimension that deserves further exploration is location. Zany Brainy, in the retail toy sector, has successfully located its stores on sites near a consumer market interested in purchasing educational toys. Automotive chains could locate in areas where trade schools give courses in automotive repair for consumers. Automotive stores might even form an alliance with the schools by supplying the instructors or providing guest lecturers.

BUYER BEHAVIOR

The number of multiple-car families has grown in the past two decades. Automobile repairs are typically shopping goods that involve some search effort in comparing price, location, and quality. Some retailers in the automobile aftermarket industry have developed their own private label brands to take advantage of pricing and promotion opportunities and to build customer loyalty. More consumers in the past two decades have begun to perform their own maintenance or repair jobs on their cars. There is a combination of reasons for consumer involvement in these activities:

- An increasing number of self-service stations,
- A decreasing number of gas stations that perform service on automobiles,
- An increase in labor costs for automobile maintenance and repairs,
- Ease in purchasing such parts as batteries, oil, and air filters from a growing number of retailers selling these products.

Buyer purchase behavior varies in different parts of the United States. For example, do-it-yourself work is easier in warm climates. Demographics operate against the growth of auto parts chains in an area where the population is older. Chains that do not offer service to this market segment will not succeed in this market. Instead, many retail chains might be adopting short-term objectives by eliminating their service bays rather than by observing long-term trends.

Another dimension of buyer behavior is the phenomenal growth of the multiple-car family. Brand loyalty may not exist. The family might own a new Volvo, a three- or four-year-old light pickup truck, a seven-year-old Ford for one child to drive while at college, and an eight-or nine-year-old Toyota for a child who is in high school to drive. Depending upon the ages and number of children, a sports utility van with greater seating capacity might also be considered. There might be a tendency for the family to do its own repair and maintenance work on older vehicles but have service performed by automobile dealers while warranties are in effect.

There is also an opportunity for niche retailers based upon buyer behavior patterns. Niche retailers would do well to segment the market
for appearance products such as waxes, polishers, and cleaners. Special
interest vehicle owners tend to take pride in the appearance of their
automobiles. These consumers spend a considerable amount of money
on restoring and dressing up their vehicles. Expenditures are made on
high performance parts and chrome-plated bumpers as well as wheels
and valve covers, paint, refinishing services, and products to enhance
and protect their vehicles' finishes.

The market segmentation of car enthusiasts and owners of special interest vehicles would seem appropriate for retail chains and manufacturers.
A partnership relationship between manufacturers and retailers might be
forged for mutual profitability. These car buffs tend to gather at clubs
and social events. Therefore, these car shows provide a group that might
respond to appropriate marketing appeals. Car buffs tend to share information on services for hard-to-find replacement parts, paints, and restoration procedures.

Consumer shoppers in retail automotive stores are noted for their multidimensional buyer behavior. The do-it-yourself market as cited in the
home improvement store chapter has flourished in recent years by appealing to buyers who are motivated to save money and who take personal pride in building something themselves. In understanding the
automotive aftermarket, much can be learned from the home improvement market. These motives, combined with others, are referred to as
multidimensional buyer behavior. This type of motivation is common
with organizational buyers but can operate as well as in the automotive
aftermarket. Motivational concepts can be applied to buyer behavior patterns in efforts to determine product benefits and problems. Many of the
items purchased in automotive stores are seen as emanating from the
salient benefits the products offer consumers or the problems they solve.
Multidimensional techniques such as multidimensional scaling can be
used to determine the degree to which product benefits are desired by
the consumer and the extent to which these benefits are received.

An analysis of product benefits that could provide a basis for market
segmentation is known as benefit segmentation. Benefit segmentation
divides the market into groups according to the different benefits that
consumers seek from the product. Benefit segmentation is closely allied
to psychographic and product usage bases. A consumer's attitude, value,
lifestyle, and past purchasing habits have a great impact on the benefits
sought in specific purchasing situations. Cause and effect relationships
are emphasized. Benefit segmentation techniques have not been used that
widely in the automotive aftermarket. If the industry is to mature with
some structure, manufacturers and retailers would do well to join in a

partnership to provide the industry with additional insights into consumer behavior situations. A core of attitudes and values can be used as the foundation for a meaningful framework for attracting potential purchasers.

The automotive retailers may have already saturated the do-it-yourself market and as a result there has been a major consolidation in this retail segment. Chief Auto Parts and APS have found themselves heavily in debt. Western Auto has been purchased by Sears. Retailers such as Auto-Zone are adding more stores to preserve their sales and earnings growth. Even with consolidation, since 1995 the big ten automotive retailers have grown in sales by 83 percent as a result of an additional 4,400 stores they control. Seven retailing companies have emerged as the leaders—Auto-Zone, Advance, CSK (Checker, Schucter, Kragen), Genuine Parts, Pep Boys, Western Auto, and Discount Auto. Yet, regional chains like O'Reilly Automotive Inc., have succeeded because they sell to do-it-yourself customers, professional mechanics, and service technicians. High-performance parts sold to automobile enthusiasts are one of O'Reilly's niches. Founded in 1957 by the O'Reilly family, the company operates stores in Missouri, Arkansas, Texas, Oklahoma, Nebraska, and Iowa. Today, O'Reilly is a publicly traded company with more than 500 stores.

MARKET STRUCTURE

Consumers maintain their cars an estimated 8.5 years compared to 6.5 years in 1980. Trucks in use show the same dramatic increase, and together the vehicle fleet in use is the highest in thirty years. There has been a growing popularity for the purchase of light trucks or pickup trucks on the part of consumers. Multiple car ownership by families has soared in the past thirty years. Therefore, families own vehicles that are in use for a number of years with some of these vehicles being passed down to children of driving age.

The cost of automobile maintenance has more than doubled since 1980. The cost of new vehicles is often over $20,000. A typical new car is under warranty for about three years. Once the warranty ends the dealer sees less of his customers. Customers then go to aftermarket providers, such as specialty oil-change shops and full service facilities such as Wal-Mart or Pep Boys. The defection from dealerships is also a result of customer dissatisfaction with dealership service during the warranty period. This unhappiness is due to the amount of time required to service the vehicle, the need to return to the dealership because of unsatisfactory work, and the price charged for the service. A vehicle that is over five years old is the target market of auto-parts retailers.

The do-it-yourself market will purchase parts that include starters, alternators and radiators. Those consumers who are not so serious do-it-yourselfers will buy oil, brake pads, filters, and fluids. Those concerned with cosmetic appearance will purchase wax, washing compounds, and accessories such as floor mats and seat covers. Those consumers who can be described as medium do-it-yourselfers will replace wiper blades, change oil, and even install mufflers. The do-it-yourself market segment constitutes about 15 percent of old-car owners.

A part of this consumer market is comprised of women. Another part of this market that is quite sizable is made up of automobile repair shops. There are millions of old-car owners who do not patronize auto-parts stores but rely on professional mechanics. Gasoline stations still do a sizable portion of repairs. Auto-parts stores have not endeavored to cultivate the market as the home improvement stores have in the past. Classes are not held for do-it-yourselfers, and the female market is largely ignored. There are indeed few auto parts stores that have encouraged their personnel to educate consumers in the style of either Home Depot or Lowe's.

Western Auto originally started as a wholesaler-sponsored voluntary chain that developed a contractual relationship with small, independent retailers to standardize and coordinate purchasing procedures and merchandising programs and to take advantage of economies of scale and volume discounts. In 1988, Sears added Western Auto to its specialty group of retailers. Sears operates 1,415 Western Auto and Parts America stores to serve do-it-yourself auto enthusiasts. Auto bays will be removed from stores that Sears owns, but independents will retain their bays. This is part of an effort to change the way the company does business. Parts America stores will focus exclusively on the do-it-yourself market, and therefore Western Auto stores owned by Sears will be converted and the name will be changed.

AutoZone is the leader in this industry, with Pep Boys acknowledged as the innovator and a major threat to its leadership. AutoZone has made it easy for commercial auto repair shops to buy parts in its more than 2,650 stores situated in thirty-two states. Auto Zone has created a partnership relationship with its suppliers.

Pep Boys offers three different formats that include the traditional parts and service, parts only, and now service-only retail units. In contrast to Western Auto which is dropping auto service, Pep Boys plans to open stores with more service bays through store expansion. Pep Boys has 638 stores in thirty-three states. Pep Boys has agreements with more than thirty service contract administrators such as CarMax and Auto Nation USA. Pep Boys was founded in 1921 in Philadelphia and managed not only to survive the depression of the 1930s but grew during this period.

Genuine Parts (NAPA) wholesales auto parts to National Auto Parts Association dealers throughout the United States. NAPA retail units are the major suppliers of parts to gas station, independent auto-repair shops, and do-it-yourselfers. The Genuine Parts Company was founded in 1928

Table 10.1
An Overview of Automotive Chains

	Number of Units 1998
AutoZone	2657
Advance Auto	1700
General Parts Inc.	1500
Western Auto/Parts America	1415
CSK Auto	926
NAPA (Genuine Parts Co.)	775
Pep Boys/Parts USA	638
Discount Auto	565

and serves approximately 5,600 NAPA Auto Parts stores throughout the country. The company has more than sixty distribution centers, 755 company-owned stores, and access to more than 200,000 items. NAPA has an image much like an independent operation and therefore is vulnerable to chains such as AutoZone and Pep Boys.

Advance Auto Parts, Chief Auto Parts, CSK Auto, and General Parts are all retail establishments having varying degrees of difficulty. Advance Auto Parts had expanded aggressively and is short of cash for expansion and consequently may be a candidate for acquisition. In 1998 AutoZone acquired Chief Auto Parts. Chief Auto Parts tried to segment the market by servicing consumers with foreign replacement parts. Chief Auto Parts was heavily in debt. General Parts/CARQUEST owns more than 1,500 stores and supplies more than 1,000 independents. General Parts has merged with Genuine Parts. Both companies developed as wholesalers. The merged should give each company added competitive strength.

Discount Auto Parts has been the target of a recently settled civil suit charging the retailer with problems relating to Freon and is on the rebound. The firm has developed a training program for its managers and sales personnel and recognizes the importance of the deployment of human resources. Discount Auto Parts stands out for employee training in an industry that gives only little attention to employee development. Discount Auto Parts was founded in 1971 and has earned a reputation as an innovator in the industry.

APS, a warehouse distributor, filed for Chapter 11 of the Bankruptcy Code. The company, which owns twenty distribution centers and 300 stores, still remains in business, a victim of uncontrolled growth. APS operates under severe financial constraints in the short-term, while long-term growth is uncertain. A good management team may make this feasible.

Table 10.1 reflects the dominance of such chains as AutoZone, Genuine Parts, and Pep Boys. The industry is gradually reaching maturity, and a shakeout is likely in the future. It is anticipated that AutoZone, Genuine

Parts (NAPA), Western Auto, and Pep Boys will survive the shakeout. This market is sizable, but longer lasting parts might be responsible for a future contraction in the industry.

STRATEGIES IN A CHANGING MARKET

The retail life cycle is considered a natural, evolutionary institutional process. This theory maintains that retail institutions, like goods and services, pass through an identifiable cycle in four stages: innovation, accelerated development, maturity, and decline. The evolutionary process in the past moved very slowly. However, in the 1980s and 1990s the time period from introduction and innovation to maturity has grown short and appears likely to grow even shorter in the future.

The time sequence of the retail life cycle is indefinite. It is quite possible that an institution could remain in a specific stage of the institutional life cycle for some years. Innovation and early growth, the first stage of retail development, generally reflect a significant departure from accepted practices in product assortment, shopping convenience, location, or promotional methods. Auto retailers have varied the merchandise assortment by developing a particular niche, either stocking a full range of products or selling the most popular and fastest moving parts. Manufacturers have developed a product code designating A, B, C, D, and E, then allowing retailers to segment the market by product categories based upon multidimensional buyer behavior. During the second stage, known as accelerated development, profits and market share experience rapid rates of growth. New firms that were not original innovators enter the field. Conventional store outlets usually try to retaliate during this stage. More complex internal systems, larger staffs, and higher costs characterize the end of the accelerated development stage. The maturity stage shows a reduction in profits. Stores generally suffer from overcapacity and increased competition. Typically, a shakeout results in an increased number of consolidations. The final stage in the retail life cycle is decline. During this stage, many firms change the institutional format, and newer formats attract consumers previously committed to that retailer type. Pep Boys, by offering different store formats, is endeavoring to avoid decline by repositioning the company.

Automotive retailers have not taken full advantage of the do-it-yourself trend. Instruction in maintenance and repair for customers would be appropriate. More women are interested in performing simple repairs, a market that has been neglected by automobile retailers. The home improvement retailers were able to expand their market by aiming special marketing programs to women. However, automotive retailers suffer from myopia in this area.

Niche retailers in the toy industry have used geographic cluster segmentation strategies advantageously. There are geographic areas based on climate and demographics that are more responsive than others to the do-it-yourself market. Climate plays a significant role in the buying of certain automotive parts. More research is needed to learn about buyer behavior habits in these markets.

The development of human resources and, in particular, the training of personnel need to be intensified. Discount Auto Parts has assumed a leadership role in this area. The home improvement industry has benefited tremendously from this approach, and it is a strategy that should be followed by automotive retailers.

ENVIRONMENTAL CHANGE RESPONSES

Internet selling has become an important strategy in specialty store retailing. Bookstores, clothing stores, and other specialty retailers, while sometimes slow to use Internet selling, have found it necessary today to compete with all the E-commerce companies. Toy stores such as Toys "R" Us, electronic stores such as Circuit City, and even furniture stores such as La-Z-Boy are selling over the Internet. Automotive retailers are slowly realizing the need for Websites. Automotive retailers may find that competitors in areas such as drugstores, supermarkets, home improvement centers, and others have already established a strong foothold in the sale of automotive products. Kmart and warehouse clubs sell auto supplies.

Monitoring the environment could lead to success for automotive retailers. Consumer demographic patterns, values, attitudes, and lifestyles have changed and present opportunities for firms in the automobile aftermarket. These changing consumer forces are especially important in retailing because of the retailers' direct contact with the customer. The willingness of consumers to participate in the do-it-yourself market has given encouragement to the growth of automotive retailers. The escalating cost of automobile repair has motivated many consumers to try their own maintenance and repair work. Buyer behavior is no longer focused in this market but is multidimensional. The same household might own a Lincoln, a Ford and a Honda. This family might do simple maintenance such as oil changes on the Ford and more extensive repairs on the Honda. The Lincoln, under manufacturer warranty, would be serviced at the dealer. For repairs that this family could not do, automobiles might be serviced either at gasoline service stations or independent repair shops. Many attitudes, motives, and values might be reflected in the same household owning different aged products.

Competitive actions have created market opportunities for automotive retailers. The consolidations have led to stronger bargaining positions with manufacturers and more private branding opportunities. At the same time, chains like AutoZone have pushed the local automotive retailer out of the market since the local retailer cannot compete on the basis of price, promotion, and product assortment with large national chains. Another factor affecting automotive stores is weather conditions. Weather drives consumer demand for many auto aftermarket products, and knowledge of future weather can provide a competitive advantage. Most of the retail chains such as Pep Boys, Kmart, Sears, and Wal-Mart subscribe to weather information services to factor weather into markdowns and promotion for weather sensitive products. JC Penney and other large retailers have exited the automotive repair business. Gasoline service stations have become self-service and have also withdrawn from the repair business.

AUTOZONE: SEGMENTING THE PRICE-SENSITIVE MARKET

The inflation of the late 1970s and the deep recession that followed in the early 1980s had the impact of reducing real income for consumers. A recession led to reductions in discretionary income, and this situation lowered consumers confidence in their ability to maintain current standards of living. As a result, consumers became more price sensitive in purchasing automobiles and automotive products. Buyer behavior for automotive parts and accessories manifested itself in the purchase of store-owned brands. Consumers searched for price specials and bargains.

The 1980s and 1990s accentuated an increase in double-income families and the desire for families to own more than one automobile. Labor repair costs soared, and families were trying to economize even while elevating their standard of living. Thus, the numbers of price-sensitive consumers increased, and AutoZone segmented this market with private branding and other merchandising strategies to get consumers into its stores. AutoZone brought discounting to the automotive aftermarket.

AutoZone serves the do-it-yourself market and also targets commercial accounts. AutoZone's strategy has always been to provide do-it-yourselfers with the lowest available price and to offer good service. Company philosophy maintains that customers perform their own repairs out of economic necessity. The company pushes its own private brands rather than national brands. AutoZone buys directly from manufacturers and manufacturer's representatives and ships to its stores through regional distribution centers.

AutoZone has instilled in its employees a culture of thrift that is transferred to customers. Customers want inexpensive and durable products that fit the parameters of AutoZone's merchandising philosophy. The company is targeting smaller communities by opening new stores in these locations. AutoZone has developed a partnership relationship with its suppliers by working closely in areas such as product development, distribution, and marketing. AutoZone was founded in the late 1970s and is the largest auto parts retailer in the United States with 2,657 stores. Its goal is to be regarded as a neighborhood auto parts store with a friendly shopping environment. The chain looks at each store and "tailors the store mix based on the vehicles that live around it." A flexigram system of planogramming allows each store to be merchandised based on Polk vehicle registrations. Store stocking units range from 17,000 to 21,000 items. In addition, 55,000 more stocking units are available for both retail and commercial customers through overnight delivery. In 1999, AutoZone made substantial investments in technology, including a satellite-based communications system to all outlets and a large data warehouse. An electronic parts catalog, maintained in-house, allows the store to find the right part for its customers fast. AutoZone is planning to open stores at a rate of one day in the year 2000. This growth is the result of a company-wide focus on customer service and new technologies that allows the company to operate more profitably and effectively.

WHOLESALING IN THE AUTOMOBILE AFTERMARKET

The wholesale management role performed by Western Auto and NAPA has been greatly reduced from what it was in the past. Chains such as AutoZone and Pep Boys are serving the dual markets of do-it-yourself consumers and the traditional auto repair shops and gasoline service stations. Although automobile manufacturers dominated a certain part of the market with their own franchised dealers, they made no effort to serve do-it-yourselfers, independent repair shops, or gasoline service stations.

The voluntary chain has been successful for strengthening firms in serving the automobile aftermarket. Notably, Western Auto and NAPA have performed a wholesaling function. AutoZone and Pep Boys are now carrying out these activities for the professional user market.

Another method used by wholesalers in the automobile aftermarket has been to develop private label brands. Since auto replacement parts are largely undifferentiated, this strategy has been successful. However, retailers are also developing their own store brands. The wholesaling function in the automobile aftermarket is losing market share, but wholesaling still has a dominant position in serving the automobile aftermarket. One of the most productive wholesaling groups has been in motor vehicles and automobile equipment. Voluntary wholesale chains help retailers with purchasing, inventory management, promotion, and a host of other merchandising activities.

WESTERN AUTO: A NEIGHBORHOOD CHAIN

In 1988 Sears acquired Western Auto. At that time, the goal of Sears was to become the second largest auto specialty retailer in the United States. Western Auto was a wholesale-sponsored voluntary chain that developed contractual relationships with small, independent retailers to coordinate the buying, merchandising, and inventory management of automotive parts and accessories. Since buying power would be concentrated, Western Auto would be able to make purchases at prices that would help it to compete with AutoZone and others.

Western Auto offered services to member retailers, including store identification material such as signs and decals, model stock plans, seasonal merchandising programs, complete store operation manuals, accounting and management information services, and the use of a centralized computer system.

Sears then converted its Western Auto business into Parts America and closed more than 100 Western Auto stores in nonstrategic markets. Sears owns 1,375 Parts America stores and about forty Western Auto stores. Sears also operates over 300 National Tire and Battery stores and continues to upgrade Sears Auto Centers and partners with Jiffy Lube. Its is the leading retailer of tires and batteries in the United States. With the development and extension of Parts America, Western Auto is not prominent in the future plans of Sears.

GENUINE PARTS (NAPA): SUCCESSFUL SEGMENTATION OF GASOLINE STATIONS

With its blue-and-yellow signs, Genuine Parts (NAPA) is a familiar company to consumers. More than two-thirds of the NAPA target market consists of gasoline service stations. Genuine Parts was founded in 1928 and has historically performed a wholesaler function to independent gasoline service stations. The company's sales have declined as a result of competition from AutoZone and Pep Boys and the number of gasoline service stations that no longer perform repair and maintenance services. NAPA has not responded well to these changes, although efforts have been made to increase its do-it-yourself consumer business.

Genuine Parts owns 775 NAPA Auto Parts stores and operates more than sixty distribution centers. The company distributes automotive replacement parts to 5,600 independently owned stores. The NAPA marketing program provides independent repair facilities with national advertising and promotional programs. NAPA provides a variety of services to its customers, including the Tele-diagnostic Service which gives independent repair shops access to experts who are able to provide solutions for customer's repair problems.

The upgrade of facilities has been an important strategy. NAPA, The Parts Store (TPS), and Pipeline Plus stores have been redesigned to attract retail customers and make it easier for them to find merchandise. More than 2,000 independent retail stores have upgraded their facilities to TPS Pipeline Plus. Although NAPA has addressed part of the challenge of the automotive aftermarket, competition from such firms as AutoZone, and Pep Boys has not been fully addressed in areas such as merchandising, pricing, and new product introductions. Yet it is encouraging to observe that the strength of the NAPA system is its combination of national buying power and training resources in conjunction with local ownership and commitment. NAPA has also developed Auto Care Centers, which are locally owned repair facilities.

PEP BOYS: THE INNOVATOR

Pep Boys operates 638 stores in thirty-seven states and was the first aftermarket retail and service chain in the United States capable of reaching the do-it-yourself market, the repair service market, the commercial market, and tires. Supercenters total 18,200 square feet and include twelve service bays. The express stores total 8,100 square feet and target the do-it-yourself and commercial markets. Repair service centers are open seven days a week, including evenings. In the past decade, Pep Boys has more than tripled its retail store outlets and service bays. In 1998, Pep Boys began going after the growing do-it-for-me segment of the automotive aftermarket with the opening of service-only stores. These stores have eleven service bays including two dedicated to tire mounting and front-end alignment and one dedicated to quick lube.

Pep Boys was founded in 1921, a time when automobile ownership was not common. Pep Boys started with stores in Philadelphia and California. During World War II much of the merchandise was in the nonautomotive category. Pep Boys went public in 1946. By the 1980s nonautomotive merchandise such as bicycles were removed from the merchandising mix. National brand holdings were expanded with the intent of providing category dominance. A special effort was made to hire knowledgeable salespeople and certified service center technicians. The merchandise assortment of automotive parts was increased from 13,000 to 18,000 items.

Pep Boys started to change its store image by redesigning its signature in a contemporary motif, adding a gray and red striped color scheme and unifying the interior and exterior of its new stores. The color red, designated as the corporate color, was reinforced by red banners. The seventy-year-old caricature of Manny, Moe, and Jack was updated. The new store layouts emphasized cross-selling of products and services. The wall decor changed from old earth tones to color-coded department identification banners.

In the 1990s the computer department was expanded from five employees to more than 100. Computer operations and training of store management personnel is interwoven. While managerial training does exist, it is not at the level of Home Dept or Lowe's where salespeople became solution providers to customers.

Pep Boys, as an innovator in serving the automotive aftermarket, has emphasized special amenities. For example, a shuttle van will take customers to nearby corporate offices, and beepers notify customers when their cars are ready. In addition, Pep Boys is the only retailer that serves all market segments of the automobile aftermarket. Pep Boys is still the only nonfranchised, comprehensive diagnostic and repair chain in the United States. Pep Boys' marketing program focuses on private brand development, and in many instances its private brands are as known as the national brands they sell.

DISCOUNT AUTO PARTS: A TEAM SYSTEM

Discount Auto Parts was founded in 1971 and its 565 stores are located mostly in Florida, Georgia, Alabama, South Carolina, and Mississippi. The company was founded on a philosophy that human resources are essential for operating a successful organization, and therefore a team effort will lead to successful retailers. Second, knowledge of the customer's needs and wants are vital. Third, ideas that involve better ways of conducting business are fundamental to success. Consequently, the "T-C-I" concept—team, customer, and ideas—is paramount to Discount Auto Parts.

The mission of Discount Auto Parts is similar to Home Depot and Toys "R" Us: establish large stores with stacked merchandise and offer everyday low prices. This mission has worked well. To achieve these objectives, the company will need to develop more private label brands. Also, distribution center efficiencies have enabled Discount Auto Parts to maintain low prices. Moreover, a quality information system enables the company to link store inventories with the distribution center's logistics program. Since, because of differences in location, Discount Auto Parts does not compete with either AutoZone or Pep Boys, the organization has been virtually untested.

Discount Auto Parts has an effective human resource program but needs to establish its image more firmly and build a stronger market segmentation strategy.

RETAILING BLUNDERS: CHIEF AUTO PARTS, APS INC., AND CSK

The most frequent cause of financial difficulties in the automotive store sector is over-expansion. Also, retailers establish store units without adequate management know-how. Site selection is often not considered carefully. Information systems monitoring inventory levels and reserves are not in place, and costs of operating are underestimated. These factors have caused a number of automotive store chains to seek protection under the Bankruptcy Act including Chief Auto Parts, APS Inc., and CSK.

AutoZone acquired Chief Auto Parts with more than 500 stores in 1998. In an effort to reposition Chief Auto Parts, various store units were expanded and/or remodeled. Carrying larger inventories was the proposed solution, but this strategy failed. In 1978, Southland Corporation, the parent company of 7-11 stores, purchased Chief Auto Parts, which owned the Chief until 1988, when a leveraged buyout by the Trust Company of the West took place.

APS is primarily a warehouse distributor and was the sixth largest automotive distributor in 1998 at the time of its filing for Chapter 11 bankruptcy. The biggest problems for APS were uncontrolled growth, units with too much autonomy and a store delivery system that created problems on the ordering cycle.

Advance Auto was to be sold in 1997 to Western Auto, but negotiations broke down. While negotiating the sale, Advance Auto opened twenty new stores. A family operation, Advance Auto added toys, furniture, and sporting goods to its inventory during the shortage of auto parts during World War II. By the middle of the 1970s, 70 percent of its sales was derived from automotive products. It wasn't until the 1980s that Advance Auto redefined its image as an automotive store and began to carry more automotive products. Advance Auto stands out in the auto chain industry for its information systems, target marketing, and distribution know-how.

MANAGING CHANGE

Although there are few certainties for retailers, one is that business conditions will change at an accelerated rate. Automotive retail store chains recognize that business decisions have grown more complex as a result of the changing environment. The only way to ensure profitability and survival is to provide an organizational structure that not only can develop long-range planning but also respond to changing consumer purchasing patterns. Another way to survive is to consolidate—namely, buy or merge with other automotive retailers. The consolidations address saturation issues in particular geographic markets, allowing the automotive retailer to expand into new markets and cut costs. Large supercenter-type automotive stores are expanding nationally with the help of technology, buying power, and distribution expertise.

The advantages and disadvantages of particular distribution policies from a specialty retailer's perspective may differ radically from those of manufacturers who are the suppliers. Small retailers may not be as growth-oriented as the large manufacturers whose products they sell. Automotive retailers originally started as single-store independents, and it has only been in the 1980s that some of these retailers have developed into larger corporate chains. Unlike many specialty store chains, automotive retailers seem to have grown without strategic planning, often competing on opposite sides of the street. Growth for many chains has been by chance not choice.

The home improvement center market has been successfully penetrated by Home Depot and Lowe's. Their successes might serve as a model for automotive retail chains to follow. Short-range strategies might include developing more private brands to increase independence from manufacturers and offering lower prices to the do-it-yourself market. Pep Boys has a strategy that includes experimental innovations that can be viewed positively by the industry. Serving all the facets of the automobile aftermarket, including service, should be carefully examined. Long-range planning should include repair instructions for consumers and educational materials for the do-it-yourself market. Concentration of the large retail chains such as AutoZone should be on the development of proactive sales and marketing strategies rather than reaction to changing environmental conditions. The do-it-yourself market, the opening of more self-service gasoline stations, and the trend for families to own more than one automobile are changing market conditions. Likely further change in the automotive aftermarket will cause automotive chains to revisit their location decisions, store layout patterns, introduction of Internet selling, and the ways they merchandise their products and services. The automotive store chains that will survive are those that put their customers first and use technology to keep their stores adequately filled with merchandise without overstocking. These stores will also compete with Wal-Mart, Kmart, and Home Depot for customers as these chains begin to carry more of the most-used automotive products. Like the automotive stores, these chains are receptive to new automotive products and merchandising such as new packaging and cross promotion. Scrambled merchandising in other retail sectors may make the future of automotive retailers more risky.

Epilogue

The 21st century will focus on market segmentation strategies as a key ingredient to specialty store retailing success. Three types of retail structures will exist. The first will be specialty superstores such as bookstores, home improvement centers, electronic stores, and toy stores. The second will be the differentiation within retail categories such as children's bookstores and educational toy stores. And the third will be shopping online. The challenge to retailers will be to select among these categories or use a combination of them to differentiate themselves from their competitors. For each type of retail structure, the objective will be to attract a consumer segment of the market and to serve those consumers profitably. Specialized retail stores such as history or science fiction bookstores may also develop but will be difficult to operate profitably. Niche retailers will seize market share from superstores. And the Web may become the shopper's paradise. When market segmentation strategies are considered, company resources, customer variation, the feasibility of grouping customers, and competition become key variables.

Specialty store retailers in some instances have used scrambled merchandising as a strategy. Drug, book, and home improvement stores have used a scrambled merchandising strategy to their advantage by carrying other products that complement their core products. However, this has not been true with apparel, electronic, furniture, shoe, toy, and automotive stores. Therefore, merchandise lines become an important determinant of strategy development.

Discount pricing has been used advantageously by book, electronic, and automotive stores. A few specialty-clothing organizations have used discount pricing strategy, but many have not. Many prominent shoe, toy, and drug store chains are not discounters. Consequently, competition, consumer approach to buying the product, and the retailing environment may dictate discount-pricing strategy.

Store size and the scope of geographical operations may be other variables that have a bearing on strategy formulation. National, regional, and local specialty stores in some merchandise lines may carry higher-than-average quality lines of merchandise. In contrast, some regional and local specialty stores may carry lesser quality lines. Turnover ratios are generally low and debt loads may be high because of the need to finance inventories that reflect a depth and breadth of assortment. Strategy development will also be influenced by turnover ratios and gross margins. It is entirely possible, for example, that chains operating different size establishments in diverse locations, such as drug chains in large cities versus medium cities, would develop their strategies differently relating to scrambled merchandising and/or pricing.

Physical resources include site election, distribution center locations, and inventory management information systems. Walgreens has done a superb job by developing freestanding stores and drive-through pharmacies. IKEA has left its mark by offering ready-to-assemble furniture., Home Depot has used physical environmental resources to effectively create its image as a low-price store. It displays its merchandise on the selling floor in cut cases, on floor-to-ceiling open shelving, or staked on pallets.

Home Depot has also used manpower resources effectively. Initiative is encouraged, bureaucracy is avoided, and each employee is trained to treat customers well. In selling educational toys, Zany Brainy employs former schoolteachers and personnel with educational backgrounds to explain the benefits of specific products.

Some specialty retailers grow and prosper while others perform poorly. Success often depends upon broadening the product lines, segmenting geographical markets and establishing pricing strategies for a carefully defined target market. Fundamental to success has been the use of key variables such as innovation, target market segmentation, image, and physical and human resources. Some of these variables may be more important than others depending on environmental conditions.

EFFECTIVE SPECIALTY STORE STRATEGIES

The concept of store image may be envisioned as a composite attitude that consumers in a particular market segment have about a retail store as it relates to their set of expectations. The perceived personality of the retail store is the development of the perceptions, emotions, and attitudes of consumers toward the various characteristics of the store. Market position is the sum of images that consumers have about the retailer's merchandise assortment, ambience, personal communication, and internal and external nonpersonal communications. These factors must be coordinated to create a favorable store image that will attract the patronage of consumers in defined target-market segments and create a competitive differential.

Especially pertinent to specialty store strategy is store positioning, namely, that retailers should determine where their opportunities are present in the market rather than determining core competencies. For example, IKEA determined that its target market had not been effectively served and therefore introduced a whole new self-service approach to selling products such as furniture to homeowners. Positioning establishes consumer loyalty and protects the retailer from other retailers. To further illustrate this theory of market segmentation, the Limited offers trendy clothes for fashion-conscious women aged twenty to forty. The Limited Express offers trendy clothing for women fifteen to twenty-five years of age, and Lerner's sells budget apparel for young women.

One of the most important aspects of modern markets is their heterogeneity. While some women customers want designer original clothes, others may desire clothes from designer collections, while others may desire ready-to-wear clothes with a recognized brand name, and still others may want inexpensive ready-to-wear clothes regardless of brand names. In some instances, an assortment of these types of clothes is desired for the wardrobe. It is difficult for retailers to satisfy the needs and wants of all customers; therefore, retail specialty stores identify a specific market and concentrate their efforts on serving it well. This retail segmentation reduces waste of resources and marketing efforts and stimulates consumers to buy.

Specialty store retailing in the 21st century will endeavor to target more fragmented markets. For example, apparel retailers may endeavor to target the tween market instead of the entire teen market segment. Individual bookstores may serve only business book readers instead of all book readers. If specialty retailers select target markets more precisely, the results should be more profitable than attempting to please all customers. In this way, a retail organization can offer a greater variety of stock in a specialized merchandise line and better service to target customers who are likely to be satisfied and loyal.

Another aspect of retail market segmentation is consumer patronage motives. The most important patronage motives are store prices and values, merchandise selection, purchasing convenience, store services, merchandise quality, customer treatment by store personnel, and store reputation and status. Consumers patronize some retail stores because of their proximity and in-store shopping convenience. Other stores are selected because of the depth and breadth of their merchandise assortment. A consumer's in-store shopping behavior is affected by such factors as sales personnel and displays.

Consumers engage in a decision process approach for store choice as well as for product and branch choices. These decisions may be complex or routine. Demographic and lifestyle characteristics and other purchaser characteristics, such as perceptions of store attributes, lead to general opinions and activities related to shopping and search behavior. The growth of shoe retailers selling exclusively athletic shoes is a reflection of market segmentation strategies and changing lifestyle characteristics.

Internet selling as a marketing strategy is not underestimated as consumer buying behavior changes. Amazon.com has revolutionized the way books are sold. The Gap has also done well over the Web, while other specialty stores may find that Internet selling will not live up to expectations. There has been a rush on the part of toy stores, drugstores, and even furniture and electronic stores to establish Websites. A caveat should be mentioned in the form of comparison. The decision to enter the field of television home shopping was indeed a controversial area for retailers. JC Penney encountered many obstacles and withdrew. Meanwhile, other retailers have been successful. The dangers of Internet selling are cannibalism, high costs, and poor service. Firms using the Internet may experience a shakeout, making it difficult to identify the long-term winners or losers.

QUALITATIVE VERSUS QUANTITATIVE DIMENSIONS

It is not possible to choose one measure that will define operational success. Performance operating ratios, such as gross margin, inventory turnover, sales per store, a comparison of current sales with past sales, store-to-store sales over time, sales per square foot, return on investment, and other measures, may all be useful and valuable for avoiding potential blunders. However, performance ratios will vary depending upon such factors as store size, merchandises lines, and pricing strategies—among them, discount or regular price line, regional and local location, and national geographical coverage. Quantitative measures are an aid in developing effective strategies that will lead to a successful operation.

Qualitative guidelines are also needed to develop successful long-term strategies. Used with quantitative measures the employment of certain fundamental approaches can lead to retailing triumphs. Many strategists maintain that a firm is similar to a biological organism and can grow only if the firm is adaptable to environmental changes. A strategic plan that considers long-range planning would enable a company to respond to changes involving customer preferences, technology, competition, population, age patterns, income fluctuations, and legislation. Business decisions have grown more complex as a result of a changing retailing environment. And the only way to ensure profitability and survival is to promote proactive strategies rather than reactive strategies.

How specialty retailers make use of key variables, such as innovation, target market segmentation, image, physical store decor, and the effective use of human resources, determine the success of their operations. Not all variables need to be used concurrently; some may be more important than others depending upon competitive conditions, and the effective use of one variable may cancel the ineffectiveness of another.

Many specialty retailers successfully anticipate change, while others have simply become part of retailing history. The point is this, specialty retailers live in a world of change. Adjustment to this world, by understanding the customer and competition, is vital for specialty retailers if they are to operate profitably in a dynamic marketplace challenged by the Internet and other forms of technology.

Notes

CHAPTER 1

1. Stanley C. Hollander, "Notes on the Retail Accordion," *Journal of Retailing* 42 (Summer, 1966), 29–40, 54.

2. Fred M. Jones, "Retail Stores in the United States," *Journal of Marketing* (October, 1936, 134–142).

3. Malcolm P. McNair, "Significant Trends and Developments in the Postwar Period," A. B. Smith (ed.), *Competitive Distribution in a Free, High Level Economy and Its Implications for the University* (Pittsburgh: University of Pittsburgh Press, 1958), 1–25.

4. Stanley C. Hollander, "The Wheel of Retailing," *Journal of Marketing* 25, July 1960, 37–42.

5. Stanley C. Hollander, "Notes on the Retail Accordion," *Journal of Retailing* 42 (Summer, 1966), 29–40, 54.

6. A.C.R. Dreesman, "Patterns of Evolution in Retailing," *Journal of Retailing* 44 (Spring, 1968), 64–81.

7. Joseph Guiltenan, "Planned and Evolutionary Changes in Distribution Channels," *Journal of Retailing* 50 (Summer, 1974), 90.

8. William R. Davidson, Albert D. Bates, and Stephen J. Bass, "The Retail Life Cycle," *Harvard Business Review* 54 (November–December 1976), 89–96.

CHAPTER 2

1. David M. Schwartz, "Life Was Sweeter, and More Innocent in Our Soda Days," *Smithsonian* 17 (July 1986), 114–119.

CHAPTER 3

1. F. P. Reynolds, W. R. Darden, and W. S. Martin. "Developing an Image of the Store-Loyal Customer," *Journal of Retailing* 50 (Winter, 1974–75), 73–84.

CHAPTER 4

1. Michael E. Porter, *Competitive Advantage: Creating and Sustaining Superior Performance* (New York: The Free Press, 1985), 36.
2. Louis P. Bucklin, "Postponement, Speculation, and the Structure of Distribution Channels," *Journal of Marketing Research* 2 (February 1965), 26–31.

CHAPTER 5

1. Adapted from Louis Kreisberg, "Occupational Controls Among Steel Distributors," *American Journal of Sociology* 61 (November 1955), 203–212.

CHAPTER 7

1. Philip Kotler, "Atmospsherics as a Marketing Tool," *Journal of Retailing* 49 (Winter, 1973–1974), 48–64.
2. See Michael E. Porter, *Competitive Advantage* (New York: The Free Press, 1985), 17, 123, 515.
3. Melvin T. Copeland, "Relation of Consumers' Buying Habits to Marketing Methods," *Harvard Business Review* 1 (April 1923), 282–289.
4. Louis P. Bucklin, "Retail Strategy and the Classification of Consumer Goods," *Journal of Marketing* (January 1963), 50–55.

CHAPTER 8

1. Everett M. Rogers, *Diffusion of Innovation's*, 3rd ed. (New York: The Free Press, 1962, 1971, 1983).
2. Michael E. Porter, *Competitive Advantage* (New York: The Free Press, 1985), 57.
3. Michael E. Porter, "How Competitive Forces Shape Strategy," *Harvard Business Review* 57 (March–April 1979), 137–145.

CHAPTER 10

1. Alfred P. Sloan, Jr., *My Years with General Motors* (New York: Doubleday and Company, 1964), 279–301.

Selected Bibliography

BOOKS

Amerman, John W. *The Story of Mattel, Inc.: Fifty Years of Innovation.* New York: Newcomen Society of the United States, 1995.

Emmet, Boris, B., and John E. Jeuck. *Catalogues and Counters: A History of Sears, Roebuck and Company.* Chicago: University of Chicago Press, 1950.

Gorman, Leon A. *L. L. Bean Inc.: Outdoor Specialties By Mail From Maine.* New York: Newcomen Society, 1981.

Kantowicz, Edward R. *True Value: John Cotter 70 Years of Hardware.* Chicago: Regnery Books, 1986.

Katz, Donald R. *The Big Store: Inside the Crisis and Revolution at Sears.* New York: Viking, 1987.

Marcus, Stanley. *His and Hers: The Fantasy World of the Neiman-Marcus Catalogue.* New York: Viking Press, 1982.

Martindale, Wight. *We Do It Every Day: The Story Behind the Success of Levitz Furniture.* New York, Fairchild Publications, 1972.

Miller, G. Wayne. *Toy Wars: The Epic Struggle Between G. I. Joe, Barbie, and the Companies That Make Them.* New York: Times Books, 1998.

Montgomery, M. R. (Drawings by Mary F. Rhinelander). *In Search of L. L. Bean.* Boston: Little, Brown, 1984.

Moschis, George P. *Marketing Strategies for the Mature Market.* Westport, Conn.: Quorum Books, 1994.

Myers, James H. *Segmentation and Positioning for Strategic Marketing Decisions.* Chicago: American Marketing Association, 1996.

Ortega, Bob. *In Sam We Trust: The Untold Story of Sam Walton and How Wal-Mart Is Devouring America.* New York: Times Business, 1998, 1st ed.

Peppers, Don, and Martha Rogers. *The One to One Future: Building Relationships One Customer at a Time*. New York: Currency Doubleday, 1993, 1st ed.

Ries, Al, and Jack Trout. *Positioning: The Battle for Your Mind*. New York: McGraw-Hill, 1981.

Schiffman, L. G., and Leslie Kanuk. *Consumer Behavior*. New York: Prentice Hall, 1996.

Smalley, Orange A., and Frederick D. Sturdivant. *The Credit Merchants: A History of Spiegel, Inc.* Carbondale: Southern Illinois University Press, 1973.

Smith, Harry A., and Stephen Joel Coons, Editors. *Marketing Pharmaceutical Services: Patron Loyalty, Satisfaction, and Preferences*. New York: Pharmaceutical Products Press, 1992.

Solomon, Michael R. *Understanding Consumer Behavior*. New York: Prentice Hall, 1999.

Stern, Sydney, and Ted Schoenhaus. *Toyland: The High-Stakes Game of the Toy Industry*. Chicago: Contemporary Books, 1990.

Treacy, Michael, and Fred Wiersman. *The Discipline of Market Leaders: Choose Your Customers, Narrow Your Focus, Dominate Your Market*. Reading, Mass.: Addison-Wesley, 1995.

Trimble, Vance H. *Sam Walton: The Inside Story of America's Richest Man*. New York: Penguin, 1990.

Vance, Sandra S., and Roy V. Scott. *Wal-Mart: A History of Sam Walton's Retail Phenomenon*. New York: Maxwell Macmillan International, 1994.

Vanderbilt, Tom. *The Sneaker Book: Anatomy of an Industry and an Icon*. New York: New Press, 1998.

Walton, Sam, with John Huey. *Sam Walton, Made in America: My Story*. New York: Doubleday, 1992, 1st ed.

Wedel, Michel, and Wagner A. Kamakura. *Market Segmentation: Conceptual and Methodological Foundations*. Boston: Kluwer Academic, 1998.

Wilber, Philip I. *Drug Emporium, Inc.: Taking Care of Customer's Needs*. New York: Newcomen Society of the United States, 1990.

PERIODICAL ARTICLES

Aaker, David A. "Measuring Brand Equity Across Products and Markets." *California Management Review*, September–October 1997, 135.

Aaker, Jennifer. "Dimensions of Brand Personality." *Journal of Marketing Research*, August 1996, 347.

Aelwadi, Kusum, L., Norm Borin, and Paul W. Farris. "Market Power and Performance: A Cross-Industry: Analysis of Manufacturers and Retailers." *Journal of Retailing* 71, no. 3 (1995): 203.

Allegrezza, Ray. "Tool Time: Home Center Builds Bottom Line With Furniture." *HFN—The Weekly Newspaper for the Home Furnishings Network*, May 26, 1997, 1.

"Amazon, Netscape Ink New Deal." *Publishers Weekly*, October 27, 1997, 14.

Amirani, Shahrzad, and Julie Baker. "Quality Cues and Retail Target Marketing Strategy: A Conjoint-Based Application." *International Journal of Retail & Distribution Management* 23, no. 5 (May 1995): 22.

Ammeen, Jim. "Making A Niche A Perfect Fit." *Fortune*, February 19, 1999, 8.

"Analysts Call Home Depot No. 1 Based on 8 Performance Criteria." *HFN The Weekly Newspaper for the Home Furnishings Network*, October 9, 1995, 11.

Andaleeb, Syed Saad. "An Experimental Investigation of Satisfaction and Commitment in Marketing Channels: The Role of Trust in Dependence Relationships." *Journal of Retailing* 72 no. 1 (1997): 4.

Andel, Tom. "Learning: The Only Sustainable Competitive Advantage." *Transportation & Distribution*, December 1994, 82.

Andreoli, Teresa. "Taking a Casual Step: Florsheim Prototype Emphasizes Contemporary Styles." *Stores*, July 1993, 73.

Angehrn, Albert, and Jean-Louis Barsoux. "Catching Customers in the Web." *Financial Times*, January 20, 1997, FTS6.

Angelo, Jean Marie. "New B. Dalton Policy: More Pain Than Gain?" *Folio: The Magazine for Magazine Management*, May 1989, 25.

Anschuetz, Ned. "Building Brand Popularity: The Myth of Segmenting to Brand Success." *Journal of Advertising Research*, January–February 1997, 63.

Anthes, Gary H. "Online Booksellers Are On the Right Page." *Computerworld*, May 12, 1997, 61.

Arnold, Ted. "Customers—Nuisance or Lifeblood?" *Automotive Marketing*, August 1994, 2.

BarnesandNoble.com Expects 1998 Sales to Exceed $100 Million; Affiliate Network Adds High-Profile partners to Broaden Consumers Reach." *PR Newswire*, January 15, 1998, 115.

"Barnes & Noble Sounds Call." *Chain Store Age Executive with Shopping Center Age*, September 1996, 3A.

Barr, Vilma. "Zany Brainy." *Stores*, January 1998, 108.

Bauman, Ruth. "Drugstore profits Soar with Private-Label Brands." *Drug Topics*, October 23, 1995, 60.

Beatty, Gerry, and Sharyn Bernard. "Best Buy Building Its Mix; More White Goods and Housewares." *HFN The Weekly Newspaper for the Home Furnishings Network*, February 19, 1996, 1.

Beatty, Sharon E., Morris Mayer, James E. Coleman, and Kristy Ellis Reynolds. "Customer-Sales Associate Retail Relationships." *Journal of Retailing*, no. 3 72, (1996): 215.

Belsky, Gary. "Get It Quick—And Pay Less—By Shopping on the Web." *Money*, September 1997, 174.

Bendapudi, Neeli, and Leonard L. Berry. "Customers' Motivations for Maintaining Relationships with Service Providers." *Journal of Retailing* 73 No. 1 (1997): 7.

Bernstein, Elizabeth. "B&N Will Launch Online Bookstore on AOL." *Publishers Weekly* February 3, 1997, 12.

Berry, Leonard L., and A. Parasuraman. "Building a New Academic Field—The Case for Services Marketing." *Journal of Retailing* 69, no. 1 (1993): 3.

Berst, Jesse. "Prescription for Success: The Smart Way to Shop for Drugs Online." *ZDNET Anchor Desk* February 25, 1999, 27.

"Best Buy, Circuit City Downsize." *Television Digest*, September 23, 1996, 1.

"Best Buy Readies New Departments." *Television Digest*, June 30, 1997, 16.

Bettencourt, Lance A. "Customer Voluntary Performance: Customers as Partners in Service Delivery." *Journal of Retailing* no. 3 (1997): 307.

Bianco, Anthony. "Virtual Bookstores Start to Get Real." *Busines Week,* October 27, 1997, 146.

Blischok, Thomas J. "Welcome to the Grand Store (Virtual Malls and Other Electronic Shopping Technologies." *Chain Store Age Executive with Shopping Center Age,* March 1996, 26.

Bloch, Peter H., Nancy M. Ridgway, and Scott A. Dawson. "The Shopping Mall as Consumer Habitat." *Journal of Retailing* 70, no. 1 (1994): 44.

Bobinski, George S., Jr., Dena Cox, and Anthony Cox. "Retail Sale" Advertising, Store Credibility, and Price Rationales." *Journal of Retailing* 72, no. 3 (1996): 218.

Boehning, Julie C. "Accessorizing the Brand." *Footwear News,* May 26, 1997, 31.

Bombay's New Inclusiveness: Systems Development Binds Organization." *Chain Store Age Executive with Shopping Center Age,* June 1995, 50.

Brown, Paul B. "Marketing As Theater." *Inc.,* September 1998, 123.

Brumback, Nancy. "Home Depot Pushing Its Own Brands." *HFN—The Weekly Newspaper for the Home Furnishings Network,* March 6, 1995, 11.

Byrne, Harlan S. "Wickes Lumber: Rebuilt and Revived." *Barron's,* August 1, 1994, 20.

——— "Wait 'Til Next year." *Barron's,* January 5, 1998, 48.

Cahill, Dennis J. "Target Marketing and Segmentation: Valid and Useful Tools for Marketing." *Management Decisions,* January–February 1997, 10.

"Capitalizing on Life Styles." *Discount Store News,* March 4, 1991, S10.

Champion, J. "The Radio Shack House." *Compute!,* April 14, 1998, 36.

Charry, Tamar. "Marketers From Ford to La-Z Boy Are Hit By a Computer-Aided Outbreak of Anthropomorphism." The *New York Times,* April 24, 1997, D7.

Christman, Ed. "Best Buy, Circuit City a Potent Combo.; 2 Chains Change Entertainment Retailing." *Billboard,* June 17, 1995, 1.

Clepper, Irene. "Price, Convenience Put True Value in Front: Customer Service and Buying Clout Combine For Winning Formula.' *Playthings,* July 1993, 36.

"Closing It All Down: Negotiations Start When a Chain Folds." *Chain Store Age Executive with Shopping Center Age,* May 1995, 84.

Cory, James M. "Depot's Big Problem: Success." *Home Improvement Market,* February 1997, 10.

Creno, Glen. "Earnings Club As Ethan Allen Expands Its Product Lines."*Knight-Ridder/Tribune Business News,* November 2, 1996, 110.

Crispens, Jonna. "Cataloguing Customers: Mail-Order Merchants Bring Furniture to Broader Clientele." *HHFN—The Weekly Newspaper for the Home Furnishings Network,* April 14, 1991, 21.

"Crown Books Turns Over a New Leaf in IS." *Chain Store Age Executive with Shopping Center Age,* November 1996, 17A.

Cuneo, Alice Z. "Private-Label Lessons—Back To School: Top Retailers Showcase Store-Brand Clothing For Fall As Sales In Segment Keep Surging." *Advertising Age,* July 27, 1998, 1.

Curan, Catherine, Miles Socha, Don Kaplan, Stan Gellers, and Rachel Spevack. "Barneys Vendors Love Firm, Hate Politics." *Daily News Record*, January 12, 1996, 8.

Darrow, William P., Raymond D. Smith, and Ross A. Fabricant. "Home Depot and the Home Center Industry: Competitive Strategies & Mobility Barriers." *Mid-Atlantic Journal of Business*, December 1994, 227.

Day, Courtney, "The Elderly: Pharmacy's Best Repeat Customer." *Drug Store News*, June 7, 1999, 96.

De Chernatony, Leslie, and Kevin Daniels. "Developing a More Effective Brand Positioning." *Journal of Brand Mangement*, 1994, 373–379.

De Chernatony, Leslie, and Gil McWilliam. "The Strategic Implications of Clarifying How Marketers Interpret 'Brands.'" *Journal of Marketing Management*, 1989, 153–171.

Dinley, Brigg. "The Top 100 Furniture Stores." *HFD—The Weekly Home Furnishings Newspaper*, September 7, 1992, 17.

"Discounters Drive Home Fashion Sales." *Discount Store News*, August 7, 1995, H4.

Donner, JoAnne. "Bernard Marcus Talks About Corporate Culture." *Georgia Trend*, July 1994, 14.

Doyle, P. "Building Successful Brands: The Strategic Points." *Journal of Marketing*, 1989, 77–95.

"Drugstore Dominance (Walgreens)." *International Journal of Retail & Distribution Management* 22, no. 4 July–August 1994.

Duagan, I. Jeanne. "The Baron of Books." *Business Week*, June 29, 1998, 109.

Easton, Thomas. "Let Your Modem Do the Walking." *Forbes*, November 17, 1997, 170.

Edelson, Sharon, and Valerie Seckler. "Bendel's Said Near Closing Stores or Sale." *WWD*, February 9, 1998, 2.

"Edison Bros. Reinvents Itself." *Chain Store Age Executive with Shopping Center Age.* November 1997, 10B.

"Emerging Trends in Distribution." *Building Supply Home Centers*, February 1995, 48.

Fahey, Alison. "Ikea Building a Loyal Following With Style." *Advertising Age,*January 28, 1991, 23.

Fallon, James. "Nine West Launches Lifestyle Shop." *WWD,*April 20, 1998, 1.

"Fanfare for the Consumer (Lowe's Companies Inc's Merchandising Strategy)." *HFD—The Weekly Home Furnishings Newspaper*, October 4, 1993, S16.

Faught, Leslie. "At Eddie Bauer You Can Work and Have a Life." *Workforce*, April 1997, 83.

Feder, Barnaby J. "In Hardware War, Cooperation May Mean Survival." *New York Times*, June 11, 1997, D1.

"Feet Lead Way In Specialty Stores." *Chain Store Age—General Merchandise Edition*, May 1984, p. 28.

Feldman, Amy. "But Who Is Minding the Store?" *Forbes*, November 22, 1993, 47.

Fitzgerald, Kate. "Drugstores: Price Proves Right in Drugstore Wars." *Advertising Age*, September 17, 1990, 58.

Fleming, Harris, Jr. "Medicine Shoppe Int'l, Marches to Different Beat." *Drug Topics*, April 20, 1998, 33.

Forger, Gary. "Eddie Bauer and Spiegel: Two Catalogues, One High Efficiency Warehouse." *Modern Materials Handling*, December 1995, 24.

"Future Shop: Selling on the Web Offers a Potentially Huge Market. Some Hotshots Are Taking the Leap, While Others Only Talk About It. Here's a List of the Winners, Losers, and Trailblazers." *Forbes ASAP*, April 6, 1998, 37.

Gaffney, Andrew. "FootAction." *Sporting Goods Business*, October 1993, 28.

Ganesan, Shankar, and Barton A. Weitz. "The Impact of Staffing Policies on Retail Buyer Job Attitudes and Behaviors." *Journal of Retailing*, no. 1 (1997): 2.

Garau, Rebecca. "Energetic La-Z-Boy: Vigorous Campaign Promotes Company's Full Line of 'Real' Furniture." *HFN—The Weekly Newspaper for the Home Furnishings Network*. December 8, 1997, 11.

Garfield, Bob. "Crown Books Shows It Has the Write Stuff." *Advertising Age*, October 13, 1997, 53.

Gibson, Campbell. "The Four Baby Boomers." *American Demographics*, November 1993, 36.

Gilbert, Les. "Heilig-Meyers Poses for Growth." *HFD—The Weekly Home Furnishings Newspaper*, December 16, 1991, 20.

Goddard, Connie. "Kroch's and Brentano's to Close Half Its Stores." *Publishers Weekly*, July 12, 1993, 9.

Goldbogen, Jessica. "Retailers: Vive La Difference; Panelists Agree: Stores Must Compete On Product, Not Price." *HFN—The Weekly Newspaper for the Home Furnishings Network*, March 23, 1998, 32.

Goldgaber, Arthur. "Tandy: Out of Juice." *Financial World*, June 17, 1997, 26.

Goldman, Abigail. "Moving In On Southland's Home Improvement Market. *Los Angeles Times*, Julay 18, 1999, C1.

Greco, JoAnn. "Retailing's Rule Breakers." *Journal of Business Strategy* 18, no. 2 (March—April 1997): 28.

Halverson, Richard. "AutoZone Places Patrons 1st, Aims For Value, Low Prices." *Discount Store News*, December 6, 1993, 109.

Hamilton, William L. "Recline (But Not Fall) of the Baby Bom Empire.' *New York Times*, April 13, 1998, A22.

Hammond, Teena. "Banana Republic Eyes New Formats and Revived Catalog." *WWD*, April 21, 1997, 1.

Hammond, Teena, and Kristi Ellis. "High Tech and High Design: Gap, Banana Republic." *WWD*, November 26, 1997, 104.

Hartnett, Michael. "Barnes & Noble Reshapes Book Market With Superstore Success." *Stores*, April 1996, 40.

Hazel, Debra. "What's Next for Retail Mergers?" *Chain Store Age Executive With Shopping Center Age*, August 1997, 35.

Heneman, Robert L., and Andrea L. Thomas. "The Limited, Inc.: Using Strategic Performance Management to Drive Brand Leadership." *Compensation and Benefits Review*, November–December 1997, 33.

"He's Baaack! Group Buys Crazy Eddie Trademark." *Discount Store News*, January 29, 1990, 27.

Hill, Dawn. "Selling Points: IKEA Increases Housewares Assortment as Part of Plan to Offer One-Stop Shopping." *HFN—The Weekly Newspaper for the Home Furnishings Network*, September 22, 1997, 73.

Himelstein, Linda. "The World According to Gap." *Business Week,* January 27, 1997, 72.

Hisey, Pete. "Best Buy: Customer-Friendly Computing." *Discount Store News,* January 3, 1994, S8.

Hof, Robert D. "The 'Click Here' Economy." *Business Week,* June 22, 1998, 123.

Hoke, Kathy. "Abercrombie Could Provide Pattern; Could Parent Firm Limited Learn Lesson From 'Branding'?" *Business First-Columbus,* June 13, 1997, 1

Hollreiser, Eric. "Zany Brainy Storming Ahead to Keep Its Edge." *Philadelphia Business Journal,* December 8, 1995, 1.

"Home Centers Still Have Room to Build." *Chain Store Age Executive with Shopping Center Age,* August 1997, 37A.

"HP Grants Circuit PC Exclusive." *HFN The Weekly Newspaper for the Home Furnishings Network,* March 27, 1995, 61.

Hyde, Linda. "Cross Competition Escalates Battle for Market Share." *Chain Store Age Executive with Shopping Center Age,* August 1993, 11A.

"Incredible Universe Crashes to Earth; Computer City Pulls Plug on 19 Units." *Discount Store News,* January 20, 1997, 3.

"Is Edison Seeing the Light at the End of the Tunnel?" *Chain Store Age Executive with Shopping Center Age,* January 1997, 60.

Jeffrey, Don. "Borders Branches Out in Asia: Retailer Plans Singapore Store, Buys 22-Outlet Chain." *Billboard,* October 11, 1997, 12.

Jensen, Christopher A., Walter E. Johnson, and Scott H. Wright. "What's the Next Hot Format?" *Do-It-Yourself Retailing,* August 1997, 248.

Joachim, David. "Making the Business Case for E-Commerce." *Internet Week,* March 30, 1998, 34.

Johnson, John R. "Competition Floods the Channel (Ace Hardware's Move Into the Industrial Market)." *Industrial Distribution,* February 1997, 15.

Johnson, Walter E. "Competing in the Toughest Markets; Retailers Share Their Survival Secrets." *Do-It-Yourself Retailing,* August 1993, 225.

" 'Just-In-Time' Methods Help Fuel IKEA Growth; Success of Furniture Chain is Based On More Than Marketing Savvy." *Chain Store Age Executive,* July 1991, 49.

Kalb, Peggy Edersheim. "Lifestyles of the Rich—and House Poor." *The Wall Street Journal,* Decembere 19, 1997, B16.

Kaplan, Don. "Reinventing Edison Bros." *Daily News Record,* November 25, 1996, 4.

Katcher, Paul. "Searching for New Markets (Auto Aftermarket)." *Automotive Marketing,* January 1997, 9.

Kehoe, Ann-Margaret. "Team Spirit: Unity of Vision Gives Power Retailer Its Edge." *HFN—The Weekly Newspaper For the Home Furnishings Netework,* April 28, 1997, 1.

Kelley, Scott, W., K. Douglas Hoffman, and Mark A. Davis. "A Typology of Retail Failures and Recoveries." *Journal of Retailing* 69, no. 4 (1993): 369.

Kelly, Jason. "Radio Shack Will Market Wireless Phone Service." *Atlanta Business Chronicle,* September 26, 1997, 20A.

Kim, Junu Bryan. "Generation X Gets Comfortable With Furnishings, Housewares." *Advertising Age,* January 10, 1991, 52.

King, Stephen. "Brand-Building in the 1990s." *Journal of Marketing Management,* 1991, 3–13.

King, Suzanne. "Sprint Opens Up Shop In 6,000 Radio Shack Stores." *Kansas City Business Journal,* September 26, 1997, 4.

Kinsella, Bridget. "Kroch's & Brentano's: What Went Wrong?" *Publishers Weekly,* September 14, 1995, 21.

Klebnikov, Paul. "Trouble in Toyland." *Forbes,* June 1, 1998, 56.

Knecht, G. Bruce. "Book Superstores Bring Hollywood-Like Risks to Publishing Business." *Wall Street Journal,* May 29, 1997, A5.

Lagnado, Ike. "Circuit City, Best Buy Deal." *HFN—The Weekly Newspaper for the Home Furnishings Network,* December 23, 1996, 10.

LaMonica, Paul R. "List In Space (Rite Aid Drugstores)." *Financial World,* November 21, 1995, 46.

Laskoski, Gregg. "Sleeping With the Enemy Entry of Drug Store Chains Into the Mail-Order Business." *American Druggist,* December 1993, 25.

Lee, Carrie. "The Wal-Mart Way: Furniture Retailer Heilig-Meyers Has a Great Strategy. But Can It Handle the Volume?" *Financial World,* November 7, 1995, 52.

Lee, Louise. "Bombay, Amid Falling Sales, Aims to Refinish Strategy." *Wall Street Journal,* May 13, 1997, 34.

Lewis, Jeff. "It's Insane'—Crazy Eddie Opens Again." *HFN—The Weekly Newspaper for the Home Furnishing Network,* March 30, 1998, 56.

Liebeck, Laura. "Babies 'R' Us Rides Baby Boom and Corners Growing Market." *Discount Store News,* September 15, 1997, 25.

Linafelt, Tom. "Growth Guru: He's Souping Up Retail at Western Auto." *Kansas City Business Journal,* December 20, 1996, 3.

"Lionel Closing 27 Stores In Struggle for Survival." *Discount Store News,* February 1, 1993, 6.

"Longs Drug Stores' Systems Prescription" *Chain Store Age Executive with Shopping Center Age,* December 1996, 126.

Lisanti, Tony. "The 'Crazy' Tale of Second-Chance Eddie." *Discount Store News,* January 26, 1998, 13.

Lubove, Seth. "A Chain's Weak Links (Building Supply Retailers: Lowe's Cos. And Home Depot)." *Forbes,* January 21, 1991, 76.

MacDonald, Laurie. "Malling It Over: The Athlete's Foot & Foot Action Stand Their Ground." *Footwear News,* January 23, 1995, 18.

Malone, Scott, and Greg Melville. "Nike, Nine West Results Dismal: Lean Times Ahead." *Footwear News,* March 23, 1998, 1.

"Manifest System Streamlines Distribution; Williams-Sonoma Cuts Shipping Costs, Mail Order Backlog." *Chain Store Age Executive with Shopping Center Age,* November 1989, 199.

Marcial, Gene G. "Fresh Looks and New Fans For Ethan Allen." *Business Week,* August 2, 1993, 78.

Martin, Michael H. "The Next Big Thing: A Bookstore?" *Fortune,* December 9, 1996, 168.

Martinez, Barbara. "Nine West, Footwear Firm, to Step Into Other Goods; Accords with Stores to Sell New Products Are Termed Risky By Some." *Wall Street Journal,* February 3, 1998, B4.

McLaughlin, John. "Books: Reading Is More Than Just Fundamental at New-Age Cafes—It's Also a Great Way to Bring In Business." *Restaurant Business,* May 1, 1996, 111

McLoughlind, Bill. "Eyes On the Horizon: Department Stores Dig In to Retain Home Goods Share." *HFN—The Weekly Newspaper for the Home Furnishings Network,* November 24, 1997, 1.

McNally, Pamela. "Florsheim Moves Ahead With Revitalized Outlook." *Footwear News,* June 27, 1994, 2.

Meeks, Fleming. "Preserving the Magic: At a Time When Many Catalog Merchants Are Flagging, Williams-Sonoma Is Going Strong. What Does It Do That's Different?" *Forbes,* February 18, 1991, 60.

Mildenberg, David. "Tooth and Nails (Competition Between Lowe's Companies Inc. and Home Depot Inc.)." *Business North Carolina,* January 1993, 16.

Mitchell, Russell, "A Humbler Neighborhood for The Gap." *Business Week,* August 16, 1994, 29.

Moin, David. "Barney's Future: A Work in Progress." *WWD,* October 18, 1996, 12.

Moin, David, and Bobbi Queen. "Henri Bendel: Do the Goods Measure Up?" *WWD,* May 7, 1998, 1.

Moschis, George P. "Life Stage of the Mature Market." *American Demographics,* September 1996, 44.

Moschis, George P., Lee Euhun, and Anil Mathur. "Targeting the Mature Market: Opportunities and Challenges." *Journal of Consumer Marketing* 14 no. 4–5 (Fall–Winter 1997): 282.

Mottley, Robert. "How The Gap Fills Its Gaps in Logistics." *American Shipper,* January 1997, 36.

Mutter, John, and Elizabeth Bernstein. "Books Wherever You Look: The Mall As Market Microcosm." *Publishers Weekly,* September 16, 1996, 22.

Negley, Jennifer. "Tandy Opens Reformatted Stores." *Discount Store News,* September 2, 1996, 1.

Niemira, Michael P. "The 16-Month Apparel Cycle: The Up-Phase of the Cycle Has Arrived." *Chain Store Age Executive with Shopping Center Age,* August 1996, 35.

Nourse, Robert. "Growing a Company." *Business Quarterly,* Autumn 1994, 32.

O'Brien, Maureen. "A Labor of Love at Barnes & Noble." *Publishers Weekly,* July 26, 1991, 214.

O'Donnell, Thomas. "Levization." *Forbes,* August 13, 1984, 42.

Olenick, Doug. "Mass Merchant Electronics Sales Up." *HFD—The Weekly Home Furnishings Newspaper,* September 19, 1994, 102.

"The Once and Future Mall: Internet Shopping." *The Economist,* November 1, 1997, 64.

Overman, Stephanie. "Ethan Allen's Secret Weapon." *HRMagazine,* May 1994, 61.

Paley, Norton. "Stepping Up Sales: How Market Segmentation Increases Sales Opportunities." *Sales & Marketing,* September 1996, 34.

Palmieri, Jean E. "The Closing of the Men's Wear Mecca at 7th Avenue and 17th Street." *Daily News Record,* June 18, 1997, 2.

Parr, Karen. "Edison Bros. On Growth Path." *WWD,* June 5, 1997, 10.

"The Payless Bankruptcy: How It Came Together—Where It's Headed." *Ingram's,* September 1997, 41.

"Pep Boys: More Than an Industry Leader, an Institution." *Aftermarket Business,* December 1, 1991, 19.

"Pep Boys Tests Service-Only Units; Acknowledges Slow Growth in Parts Division." *Discount Store News,* January 26, 1998, 6.

"Pier 1's Classic Direct Mail Strategy Targets New Movers." *Direct Marketing.* November 1995, 18.

"Pier 1 Imports Company Cards That Work: Program Targets Present Customers and Expanded Credit Sales." *Chain Store Age Executive with Shopping Center Age,* February 1992, 77.

Postman, Lore. "Lowe's To Go West into Tough Market." *The Charlotte Observer,* April 26, 1998, 1D.

"Pottery Barn's Unique Alchemy Turns Red Ink Into Gold." *HFN The Weekly Newspaper for the Home Furnishings Network,* April 13, 1998, 4.

Pressler, Margaret Webb. "The High End Gets Higher; Home Depot's Luxury Stores Ride a Trend of Rising Expectations—and Spending." *Washington Post,* July 11, 199, H01.

Purpura, Linda. "Lowe's Draws Women, Grows." *HFN—The Weekly Newspaper for the Home Furnishings Nertwork,* June 17, 1996, 40.

"Radio Shack's New Image." *Television Digest,* August 14, 1995, 13.

Ramirez, Anthony, and Andrew Evan Serwer. "Can Anyone Compete With Toys "R" Us?" *Fortune,* October 28, 1985, 71.

Rawsthorn, Alice. "US Bookseller Seeks Online Growth." *The Financial Times,* February 3, 1998, 8.

"Retail Do-It-Yourself Market Profile." *Do-It-Yourself Retailing,* November 1997, 61.

Ritzer, Julie. "New Life for Troubled Chains: Abercrombie & Fitch, FAO. Schwarz Target New Customers." *Chain Store Age Executive with Shopping Center Age,* September 1986, 21.

Robaton, Anna. "Electronics Retailers Dig In for Mkt. Share Fight." *Billboard,* August 7, 1993, 42A.

Roberts, Len. "Radio Shack's Service Hallmark." *HFN—The Weekly Newspaper for the Home Furnishings Network,* November 6, 1995, 60.

Roed, Beth. "The Best Cyberstores." *Computerworld,* December 15, 1997, 80.

Rossi, William A. "Going Nowhere: Is Footwear Retailing Stuck In a No-Growth Rut?" *Footwear News,* December 18, 1995, 12.

Ryan, Ken. "Amid Red Ink, Heilig-Meyers Forecasts Blue Skies Ahead." *HFN—The Weekly Newspaper for the Home Furnishings Network,* March 30, 1998, 1.

Schindler, Robert M., and Thomas M. Kibarian. "Increased Consumer Sales Response Through Use of 99-Ending Prices." *Journal of Retailing* 72, no. 2 (1996): 114.

Schneider-Levy, Barbara. "Recrafting Makes Pricey Shoes Bargain." *Footwear News,* February 8, 1993, 87.

Schulman, Milt. "Toy Retailing in Turmoil." *Playthings,* March 1996, 36.

Schulz, David P. "Ace Expands Through Beefed-Up Retail Support." *Stores,* September 1996, 83.

Schwartz, David M. "Life Was Sweeter. And More Innocent, In Our Soda Days." *Smithsonian,* July 1986, 114.

Schwartz, Vira Mamchur, and Rich Westerfield. "Who's Making Money With Electronic Commerce?" *Information Week* (Special Supplement), April 27–29, 1998, 1.

Seideman, Tony. "Barnes & Noble Jumping to Multimedia at 60 Stores." *Publishers Weekly*, November 7, 1994, 8.

Sender, Isabelle. "Blueprints for Success." *Footwear News*, February 12, 1996, 18.

Sharma, Arun, and Michael Levy. "Categorization of Customers By Retail Salespeople." *Journal of Retailing* 71, no. 1 (1995): 4.

Shaw, Jan. "Williams-Sonoma Cooks Up Growth." *San Francisco Business Times*, November 28, 1998, 1.

Shuster, Laurie. "Do-It-Yourselfers: The X Generation." *Chilton's Hardware Age*, November 1995, 56.

Silberg, Lurie. "Analysts Saw the End For Incredible Universe." *HFN—The Weekly Newspaper for the Home Furnishings Network*, January 6, 1997, 4.

Silverman, Dick. " '94 Offers Cornucopia of Opportunity." *Footwear News*, December 20, 1993, 14.

Silvers, Cary. "Smashing Old Stereotypes of 50-Plus America." *Journal of Consumer Marketing* 14, no. 4–5 (Fall-Winter 1997): 303.

Slezak, Michael. "Mail-Order Changes Its Colors." *American Druggist*, December 1995, 22.

Sparks, Debra. "Circuit City: : Short Circuit." *Financial World*, March 18, 1997, 26.

Spector, Robert. "Bauer's Winning Ways." *WWD*, October 6, 1993, 20.

Stambaugh, Sandie. "The AutoZone Story." *Aftermarket Business*, December 1994, 8.

Steinhauer, Jennifer. "Getting the Chance to Do It Himself: Out of the Shadows to Run Home Depot. *New York Times*, May 13, 1998, 3.

Stross, Randall, E. "Why Barnes & Noble Crush Amazon." *Fortune*, September 29, 1997, 248.

"Superstore Sales Soar at Crown." *Publishers Weekly*, February 21, 1994, 12.

Sutton, Rodney K. "Growth at Depot Shows No Limit." *Building Supply Home Centers*, February 1995, 22.

Switzer, Liz. "Heilig-Meyers CEO Issues Big Challenge." *HFN—The Weekly Newspaper for the Home Furnishings Network*, March 9, 1998, 19.

"Tandy Corporation: First and Foremost, We're a Retailer." *Inc.*, December 1992, 64.

Taylor, Cathy. "Toy Claims Learn to Play a New Game; Discount Stores Pose Tough Competition in an Industry Driven By Price." *ADWEEK Eastern Edition*, December 16, 1991, 9.

"This Toy War Is No Game." *Business Week*, August 9, 1999, 86.

Thomson, Kevin. "Oodles of Opportunity." *Sales & Marketing Management*, August 1995, 20.

"Top Home Décor Chains Just Keep Getting Bigger." *Discount Store News*, July 5, 1993, 80.

Tosh, Mark. "Off-Pricers: Ready to Rebound." *WWD*, December 27, 1995, 5.

Tucker, Michael Jay. "The Wiz That Was." *Datamation*, October 1997, 11.

Ukens, Carol. "Is Mail Order Bombing? (Mail Order Pharmacy)." *Drug Topics*, July 20, 1992, 56.

Walser, Clarke L. "It's the Customer, Stupid." *Electronic Business*, March 1998, 19.

Warner, Bernhard. "How Big Is Too Big?" *Brandweek,* December 2, 1996, 38.

Warner, Melanie. "Drug Test." *Fortune,* July 19, 1999, 88.

Weimer, De'Ann. "The Houdini of Consumer Electronics." *Business Week,* June 22, 1998, 88.

Weiss, Lisa Casey, and Marie Griffin. "Williams-Sonoma Outlet Debuts: Center Selling Closeout, End-Of-Season, Overstocked Items From All 5 of Its Concepts." *HFD—The Weekly Home Furnishings Newspaper,* July 22, 1991, 44.

Weisz, Pam. "Trying to Move From the Wardrobe to the Bathroom." *Brandweek,* April 24, 1995, 36.

Wells, Edward O. "The Fall of Bombay." *Inc.,* January 1996, 48.

Werner, Holly M. "Pottery Barn Caters to Harried Home Decorators." *HFN—The Weekly Newspaper For the Home Furnishing Network,* March 23, 1998, 8.

Whelan, Carolyn. "Blending Cable, Retailing." *Electronic News,* February 16, 1998, 43.

Williams,Stan. "Netting the Net: Using the Web as a Marketing Tool." *Daily News Record,* May 13, 1996, 4.

"Williams-Sonoma Tries New Design Concept; Larger Flagship Store Enhances Original Merchandising Concept." *Chain Store Age Executive,* February 1989, 32.

Wilson, Marianne. "Brand Name, High-profile Stores Create a Splash." *Chain Store Age Executive with Shopping Center Age,* February 1994, 22.

Winkler, Connie. "How Longs Got Centralized." *American Druggist,* February 1995, 37.

Wirebach, John. "Advance Auto to Sell Stores; Will Western Auto Buy?" *Automotive Marketing,* March 1997, 14.

"Wired Ventures Links Up With Barnes & Noble for National Online and In-Store Marketing Partnership." *PR Newswire,* March 25, 1998, 3.

"WIZ Near Liquidation, Crazy Eddie Seeks Comeback." *Television Digest,* January 19, 1998, 13.

Wray, Kimberly. "Ethan Allen: Not Just Traditional; New Logo Reflects Broadening of Contemporary and Eclectic Furnishings." *HFD—The Weekly Home Furnishings Newspaper,* December 2, 1991, 20.

ANNUAL REPORTS (1998)

Ace Hardware Corp.

Amazon.com

American Stores Company

Ann Taylor

AutoZone, Inc.

Barnes & Noble

The Best Buy Co., Inc.

The Bombay Company

Books-A-Million

Borders Group, Inc.

Cardinal Health, Inc.

Circuit City Stores, Inc.
CompUSA
Consolidated Stores
Crown Books
CVS Corporation
Dayton Hudson
Discount Auto Parts
Drug Emporium
Edison Brothers Stores Incorporated
Ethan Allen
Florshiem Group, Inc.
Footstar Inc.
The Gap, Inc.
General Parts
Genesco Inc.
Genuine Parts Company
Haverty's Furniture Companies Inc.
Hechinger
Heilig-Meyers Company
The Home Depot
JC Penney
K-Mart Corporation
La-Z-Boy
Levitz
The Limited, Inc.
Longs Drug Stores Corp.
Lowe's
Marks & Spencer
Nike Inc.
Nine West Group, Inc.
Noodle Kidoodle
Payless Cashways
Payless ShoeSource
Pep Boys
Pier 1 Imports
Reebok International Ltd.
Rex Stores Corp.
Rite Aid
Sears Roebuck & Co.
Sherwin-Williams
The Spiegel Group
Talbots
Tandy Corp.
TJX Companies, Inc.
Toys "R" Us
Venator Group Inc.
Walgreens Co.
Wal-Mart

Walt Disney Company
Wickes Inc.
Williams Sonoma, Inc.
Woolworth Corporation

WEBSITES

Etoys: http: / / www.etoys.com
FAO Schwarz: http: / / www.faoschwarz.com
Genevese: http: / / www.genovese.com
IKEA: http: / / www.ikea.com
Imaginarium: http: / / www.imaginarium.com
JC Penney: http: / / www.jcpenney.com
Lionel: http: / / www.lionel.com
Longs Drug Store: http: / / www.longs.com
National Automotive Parts Association (NAPA): http: / / www.napaonline.com
Toy Manufacturers of America: http: / / www.toy-tma.com
Western Auto: http: / / www.westernauto.com

Index

About the Authors

RONALD D. MICHMAN is Professor Emeritus of Marketing, Shippensburg University. He is widely published in professional journals, a member of several editorial boards and an editor of two bibliographies. He has also served as chairman and discussant at various national and regional conferences in his field. He is coauthor of two Quorum books, *Retailing Triumphs and Blunders* (1995) and *The Food Wars* (1998), and two published by Praeger Publishers, *Lifestyle Market Segmentation* (1991), and *Marketing to Changing Consumer Markets* (1983).

EDWARD M. MAZZE is Dean of the College of Business Administration and holder of the Alfred J. Verrecchia-Hasbro Inc. Leadership Chair in Business at the University of Rhode Island. He is author, coauthor, or editor of ten books and more than 150 articles in numerous journals of his field. Dr. Mazze also serves on the editorial boards of two periodicals and as a member of the Board of Directors of various corporations. Among his publications is one book with Dr. Michman: *The Food Industry Wars* (1998).